The Palestine Papers

The Palestine Papers

The End of the Road?

Clayton E. Swisher

Introduction by Dr Ghada Karmi

HESPERUS

First published by Hesperus Press Limited 2011
Foreword and Analysis © copyright Clayton E. Swisher 2011
Introduction © copyright Ghada Karmi 2011
Publisher's note © copyright Karl Sabbagh

Designed and typeset by Bookcraft Ltd, Stroud
Printed and bound in the UK by CPI Mackays, Chatham ME5 8TD

ISBN 978 1 84391 353 5

Contents

Publisher's Note

Peace talks usually take place to end wars, but the last real war between Israel and the Arabs took place thirty-five years ago, and in any case the peace talks described in the Palestine Papers are not between Israel and the Arabs, but between Israel and the Palestinians, a people who lived for hundreds of years in the land that Jews now claim as their own, and were expelled as part of the process by which Israel sought to establish a purely Jewish state.

It has been said that 'diplomacy is war by other means', but that could be said equally of these 'negotiations', which are revealed as nothing less than an attempt by Israel, with America as its enforcer, to achieve many of its past war aims – expansion of territory, preventing the return of Palestinians to their land, continued control over the West Bank and Gaza – by refusing to acknowledge any of the rights claimed by the people it has dispossessed and occupied.

It is easy to look at the negotiations from the outside and say 'Surely, both sides must compromise?' What many people don't realise is that in all recent negotiations with Israel, the Palestinians have arrived at the table having made the largest compromise any displaced people has ever made – by revoking claims to 78% of the land that used to be Palestine, and seeking to cling on to the 22% that remains. But among the many things the Palestine Papers reveal is the extent to which Israel has taken for granted the major 'gift' of 78% of Palestinian land, and now insists on 'compromise' over what remains.

Clayton Swisher's Foreword and Analysis takes us through some of the key revelations in the papers, picking choice quotes from the participants who were expressing views that they never thought would be publicly revealed. But while individual quotes can throw a shaft of light on a moment during the discussions, it is the hour after hour of grinding detail that repays the reader's attention too. Someone who imagines that negotiations like these consist of an organised step by step analysis of a situation, the cut and thrust of well-resourced argument, the acceptance by one side of evidence offered by the other, the refutation of 'facts' with contradictory data, is going to be surprised. Instead, we get bickering and outright denial of attested facts, and in the case of Israel to the Palestinians, a kind of 'arms folded' smugness that says 'say what you like, we are only interested in what is good for the Jews.' The US role as the so-called 'honest broker' is revealed as a sham time after time in the papers, as American officials object to Palestinian claims on the basis that 'Israel wouldn't accept it.' We don't have similarly leaked Israel papers, but I would be very surprised if at any point in private discussions with Israel negotiators, the Americans said "You can't say that – the Palestinians would never accept."

Another thing that is surprising in these papers is the systematic way in which the Israelis deny basic facts which are easy to prove. One example is the constant refusal, supported up to the hilt by the US, to accept responsibility for the Palestinian refugee problem. Such a refusal might have been understandable 20 or 30 years ago, but today, when a succession of Israeli historians have probed Israel's military archives, there is no longer any doubt that what the Palestinians have been saying for decades is true – the refugees left as a result of a planned and systematic campaign to rid the country of as many Arabs as possible before the state of Israel declared its independence.

The Papers published here are a selection of the most recent material, presented in full. The earlier papers, which can all be read on the Al Jazeera website[1], involved people who are no longer playing a part in Israel-Palestinian relations and are therefore of more historic interest. But the later meetings were against a background of issues and events which are still continuing – settlement building, house demolitions, the strangling of Gaza – involving people who are still in power or who have only recently left it.

They are presented as they were written, with misprints, misspellings, and occasional hiatuses, and there is a brief glossary on page 74, covering some of the frequently used terms and acronyms.

After reading these accounts no one should be in any doubt that the only valid 'peace negotiations' – if there are to be any more – should be between representatives of *all* Palestinians, not just one faction, and an Israel which is forced to go it alone rather than rely on the automatic financial and political support of an America in thrall to its lobbies.

Karl Sabbagh, Managing Director, Hesperus Press, March 2011

---

1   http://transparency.aljazeera.net

Introduction
Dr Ghada Karmi

Reading through the Palestine Papers' records of the negotiating process between Israel and the Palestinians, it would be tempting to walk away with the impression that their principal value lies in what they reveal about a pathetic, inept and weak Palestinian team, unable to handle the negotiations and hopelessly outclassed by their Israeli counterparts. It was always going to be easy to pick on the Palestinian side as the main culprit for the failure to reach an accommodation with Israel as shown by the leaked papers, despite having betrayed the core principles on which the Palestine case rests, and the subservience it showed towards Israel and the US. Indeed it is the same failure that started with the Oslo Accords of 1993. The more the Palestinians conceded to Israel, the less they got in return, but it only led to further concessions until they had hit rock bottom, as now. In complex situations such as this, where knowledge of the underlying political and historical context is essential for understanding them, attacking the weaker party instead is the lazier and more usual reaction.

There is no doubt that the display of Palestinian subservience that emerges so clearly from the Papers is deeply embarrassing. As the peace talks went on over the period covered by the revelations, from 1999 to 2010, without result the picture on the Palestinian side is one of hopeless gamblers, trying frantically to win, if even a little, until they eventually stake everything they have but still gain nothing. In this agonised bargaining, they succumbed to making what they believed would be offers irresistible to the Israelis. The most spectacular of these were over the most important issues for Palestinians: Jerusalem and the right of refugee return.

The Israeli colonisation and the increasingly fundamentalist Jewish threats to take over or damage the Muslim holy places on the Haram al-Sharif (Temple Mount) had made Jerusalem a rallying point for Palestinians, Arabs and Muslims worldwide. Palestinians also hoped to make Jerusalem their capital in a two-state solution, and the cessation of settlement building in Jerusalem had become a major Palestinian demand. On 20 October 2010, the PA issued an unequivocal statement to Wafa, the Palestinian news agency that all types of Israeli settlement on Palestinian land were illegal. Yet, in May 2008 Palestinian negotiators were secretly offering Israel all except one of the Jewish settlements built in East Jerusalem[1]. They excepted Har Homa (Arabic, Jabal Abu Ghneim) a large settlement on the road to Bethlehem, but they entertained ceding Sheikh Jarrah to Israeli settlers, and made the huge ring of settlements surrounding Jerusalem legitimate (though not legal under international law).

In making this generous offer to Tzipi Livni, the Israeli foreign minister Saeb Erekat joked archly, "It is no secret that we are offering you the biggest Yerushalayim in history (Jerusalem's Hebrew name)". By 2009 the Palestinians had proposed a committee to take over arrangements for the Haram al-Sharif., but they offered Israel parts of the Armenian Quarter which Arafat had refused to cede. Erekat spoke of the "creativity" of people like him to find a solution for the holy places. Ingratiatingly, Ahmed Qurei', a senior Palestinian negotiator, told Livni, who was preparing for the Kadima party elections in June 2008, "I would vote for you!" This cringing compliment did nothing, however, to soften her heart. Despite all their concessions, when the Palestinians refused to cede Har Homa or Maale Adumim, the huge settlement which links East Jerusalem almost to the Jordan Valley, or Ariel, the settlement by Nablus in the heart of the West Bank, Livni rejected all Palestinian offers. In July 2008, Condoleezza Rice, the secretary of state to George Bush, reiterated the same message. She told them that if they insisted on Israel not keeping Maale Adumim and Ariel, then "you won't have a state".

The most striking concession, however, concerned the right of return, an issue all Palestinians considered fundamental to their case. Enshrined in international law and historical precedent, it had acquired an almost sacred quality for Palestinians. UNGA resolution 194, which required Israel to repatriate the Palestinian refugees, was passed in 1948, and has been affirmed at the UN countless times since then. The 1948 Universal Declaration of Human Rights states that anyone can leave his home for whatever reason and return to it. International precedents of refugees returned to their original place, for example, Kosovo in 1999, exist to shore up this Palestinian right. For generations, the Palestinian refugees, estimated by UNRWA in 2006, at 6.3 million, dispersed in the camps of Jordan, Syria, Lebanon, and the

---

1   http://www.ajtransparency.com/en/document/2648

occupied territories, have been reared on the expectation of returning to the homeland.

Israel's power and its determined rejection of a refugee return had convinced many Palestinian leaders that they would have to compromise on this basic right. But the right of return remained the official Palestinian position. After the 1993 Oslo Accords which deferred discussion of the right of return to the final stages, this right started to be toyed with as a possible bargaining chip. In fact, the acceptance of a two-state solution was in itself an argument against the right of return. If the Palestinian side accepted Israel as a Jewish state, then how could that be reconciled with an influx of non-Jews (the refugees) which would destroy that state's Jewishness? The matter was left ambiguous, and the public assurances on the right of return remained the same. The 2002 Saudi-sponsored Arab peace plan spoke of a just settlement for the refugee issue according to international law, without detailing what that meant. Since the late 1990s, various European and American plans for settlement of the refugees outside Israel had been proposed, but the refugees themselves were never consulted or informed. They still looked for deliverance and a return to the homeland.

Undeterred, the Palestinian negotiators were recorded in the Palestine Papers as giving in on the right of return. In talks with Tzipi Livni and Ehud Olmert between 2007 and 2008, and with George Mitchell, the US Middle East envoy, in 2009 the Palestinians agreed that just 10,000 refugees and their families could return as part of an overall peace settlement. Saeb Erekat ruled out holding a referendum on the agreement amongst the refugees. In February 2009, he told Mitchell that, "on refugees, the deal is there". In the next month, Abbas was recorded as arguing that Israel could not be asked to accept a return of even one million refugees, since it would mean the end of Israel. This, despite the fact that he himself was a 1948 refugee from Safad. In December 2010, Tzipi Livni said she was against any refugee return and had said so to the Palestinians.

The surrender on the right of return was part of the Palestinian negotiators' acceptance of Israel as a Jewish state. Between 2007 and 2008, the Papers show that the Israeli negotiators continually stressed Israel's Jewish character, even suggesting that Arab citizens of Israel could be moved into a Palestinian state. This went unchallenged by the Palestinian side. In fact in November 2007, Erekat was recorded as telling Tzipi Livni that if Israel wanted to define itself as a Jewish state it could do so. He said later, in June 2009, that Israel's Jewishness was a "non-issue." In this atmosphere, it is no wonder that Condoleeza Rice proposed in June 2008 that Palestinian refugees could be moved to Chile and Argentina.[2] It was left to Palestinian community leaders in Chile and Argentina to point out that such immigration would be a violation of the refugees' internationally recognised rights to return.

The Palestine Papers revealed many more betrayals of Palestinian rights and entitlements. But simple condemnation of this abject surrender by the Palestinian negotiators, deplorable as it is, will not throw light on how and why it happened. Behind the unseemly behaviour of Abbas and his negotiators lies a larger issue. What was the political and historical context in which the surrender of basic Palestinian rights was exacted, and who was ultimately responsible for the sorry picture that emerged? It is in answers to these questions that the full significance of what the Palestine Papers tell us can be seen.

The core of the problem is encapsulated in the exchanges between various members of the US administration and the PA that took place at different times from 2007 to 2009. From these it becomes clear that after 2006 when the Hamas government was elected in the occupied territories and subsequently boycotted by the west, the Fateh dominated PA was the only leadership that Washington would allow. In November 2008, David Welsh, the US assistant secretary of state, told the Palestinian prime minister, Salam Fayyad, that the Obama administration wanted to see "the same Palestinian faces" in office if it was to continue funding the PA. When in November 2009, Mahmoud Abbas announced he would not run for re-election, Hilary Clinton, the US secretary of state, declared that "was not an option" for him, and no elections too place. Before that, in March 2007, when a national unity government between Fateh and Hamas with Ismail Haniyeh[3] as prime minister had been agreed, the US pressured Abbas into disrupting it through a clumsy Fateh coup executed against Hamas in Gaza three months later. In the same year, the US security coordinator in charge of training PA militias on the West Bank, General Keith Dayton, warned against Fateh elements trying to undermine Salam Fayyad. The Pales-

---

2   http://www.ajtransparency.com/en/document/2797
3   The Hamas prime minister elected in 2006.

tinian prime minister is regarded as the lynchpin of US schemes for a settlement and so, indispensable.

These American interventions, which also reflected Israeli priorities, had no regard for the questions of legitimacy and representation so crucial to the validity of the agreements that were being discussed in the name of the Palestinian people. The issue of representation had angered many Palestinians. As Al-Quds's editorial of 25 January pointed out, and in numerous interviews on the Aljazeera channel subsequently, no one had deputed this group of individuals (the PA officials) to negotiate on behalf of the 10 million Palestinians throughout the world. But as we have seen, the issue of representation was continually side-stepped by the negotiators themselves, by Israel and the US sponsor of the peace negotiations, and by the rest of the Quartet comprising the UN, Russia, and the European Union.

Had America's public stance − that the Palestinians were free to choose their own leaders − been matched by its private one, the whole PA would have been declared null and void.

The Palestinian president's term of office expired in January 2009, and without new elections Mahmoud Abbas's presidency was invalid after that date. The same applied to his prime minister, Salam Fayyad, except that his appointment had never been valid. According to the Palestine Basic Law, he would have needed the agreement of the Palestine Legislative Council (PLC) to be appointed. But this itself, last elected in 2006, was up for re-election and had no legal mandate. Neither did the PLO executive committee which could no longer act in the name of the Palestinian people, a point of relevance for any future resumption of peace talks. Most of the period which the Palestine Papers covers, however, relates to an earlier time, from 1999 to 2010, but that in itself does not resolve the problem.

For, even if there had been valid representation from the electoral point of view, the PA's remit concerned only the 3.5 million people on the West Bank, that is, one third of the Palestinian population worldwide, estimated at 10-11 million. The split between Fateh in the West Bank and Hamas in Gaza, which had started in 2007, meant that Gaza was excluded from PA rule, and the division was nowhere near being resolved. This problem could be mitigated by the fact that Abbas and the negotiators participated in the peace talks on the basis of their affiliation to the PLO, of which the Palestinian president was chairman and which had been originally set up to represent the whole Palestinian people. This was encouraged by Israel and the US, but it provided a spurious legitimacy.

Ever since the Oslo Accords and the return of the PLO leadership to the Palestinian territories in 1994, the PLO had become effectively defunct, its committees and branches inactive. The Palestine National Council (PNC), the Palestinian government-in-exile and PLO supreme body, had not met since 1998 in Gaza. Its members were admitted by Israel at the time on condition they voted to revoke parts of the Palestine National Charter considered hostile to Israel. The PNC was reconvened in 2009 in Ramallah in order to replace six deceased members of the PLO executive committee without whom the committee was illegitimate. However, the PNC meeting itself was illegitimate since it lacked a quorum, and its regular meetings as required to preserve its legitimacy had not taken place for years. Though supposed to include all Palestinian factions and sectors, the PNC had neither Hamas nor Islamic Jihad members. There was no escaping the fact that PLO titles and positions in such circumstances were meaningless.

But even if the negotiators had been legitimate, they still had no popular mandate, either through consultation or by referendum, to negotiate away issues of such critical importance to all Palestinians. No refugees, whose future featured prominently in the negotiations as revealed by the Papers, were asked for their views, and no Jerusalem Palestinians were consulted about the Jewish settlements to remain in their neighbourhoods. In these circumstance, had Israel responded positively and a deal been drawn up on the lines presented in the Palestine Papers, did anyone amongst the negotiators or the American and western sponsors of the peace process really imagine that such a deal would have held for long? The Camp David talks in 2000 between the then Israeli prime minister, Ehud Barak, and Yasser Arafat broke down precisely because Arafat knew he could not sell the poor deal over Jerusalem and the right of return of refugees he was offered to the Palestinian people. With all his popularity and status, Arafat could not go beyond certain limits. So how would a man like Abbas, with little public support, and a coterie of widely criticised, even reviled negotiators stand a chance of selling an even worse deal to the Palestinian people?

The answer must be that no one, aside from the Palestinians, cared. Had it been otherwise, the "peace process" as it has been to date would have been abandoned long ago as a failure. The faces and assumptions, far from remaining frozen sine die as the US wished, would have been changed. It is difficult to escape the conclusion that the end of the peace process is not a settlement, but precisely what we have been witnessing: a long-term prevarication by Israel and its western backers, punctuated by periodic bouts of criticism of Israeli policy and exhortations to both parties to make compromises. The spat over the Jewish settlement building freeze required by the PA and the US in September 2010 and largely ignored by Israel is a case in point.

Had Israel been remotely interested in a peace deal with the Palestinians, it had ample opportunity in these last negotiations, and certainly long before. Even with such far reaching Palestinian concessions, Tzipi Livni could still tell Ahmed Qurei in November 2007 that, with regard to settlement building, "Israeli policy is to take more and more land day after day and that at the end of the day we'll say that it is impossible, we already have the land and we cannot create the [Palestinian] state," adding in case of doubt that it had been her government's policy "for a really long time"[4]. These views are supported by various Israeli sources. Commenting on Israel's insistence that the Palestinians recognise the Jewishness of the state ahead of any deal, the Israeli daily, Yediot Ahoronot, ("This is the whole story", 16 September 2010) noted that the only reason for this demand, not imposed on any state in the world, was to create further delays to a peaceful settlement. Another article in Haaretz ("Israel is not interested in peace", 16 December 2010), reviewed Israel's rejection of all Arab peace offers to date and also concluded that Israel, neither government nor people, was genuinely interested in peace.

Nor, it would seem is the US. A meeting between Saeb Erekat and General James Jones, National Security Advisor to the U.S. President, on 21 October 2009[5] set out the US position eloquently. Responding to a despairing plea from Erekat that Israel's prime minister, Binyamin Netanyahu, was making no contact with the Palestinians, despite all their climb downs, Jones fobs him off with a series of soothing platitudes to the effect that President Obama was committed to a two-state solution, but that the "real problem is finding a path to get there". Dennis Ross, the former US Middle East peace envoy and ardent

4   http://www.ajtransparency.com/en/document/2003
5   http://www.ajtransparency.com/en/document/4902

Zionist, present at the same meeting, follows that with assurances of honesty and "speaking from the heart". What is clear is that there was no substance to the US utterances and no action to pressure Israel in any way. When the UN Security Council voted on 19 February 2011 to condemn Israel's' settlement as illegal, the US was the only member state to vote against.

The European Union, despite its massive funding of the PA and official postures, was basically no different. The story of the Israeli-Palestinian peace process since 1993 has been one of persistent dishonesty on the part of the US and its European allies. They let the Palestinians believe that statehood was just around the corner, with "state building" enterprises and preparations for independence, while in reality doing nothing to curb Israel's hold on Jerusalem or the West Bank, supposed to form the territory of the putative Palestinian state. In consequence, the Palestinian leaders, impotent and unwise, put their faith in the west, and especially the US. As Israel rebuffed every peace overture, the Palestinian leadership was led into lowering its demands even more, with the starting point for new talks set at the last low level. By 2007, the Palestine Papers show that it was no big step to yet more concessions for Palestinian negotiators with this history behind them.

The blame for this state of affairs falls on the inept and unprincipled Palestinian leadership of course, but far more so on the context in which they had been forced to operate: where the major world powers chose to line up with the stronger party against the weaker one. The Palestinian capitulation and desperation that followed were inevitable in such a situation. However, the massive wind of change sweeping through the Arab world in 2011 is unlikely to leave the Israeli-Palestinian situation untouched. The issue for the rebellious Arabs was one of dignity and self-respect. The Palestine Papers' exposure of Palestinian humiliation, indignity and lack of respect, may yet lead to unexpected consequences.

Foreword
Clayton E. Swisher

From January 23–26, 2011, Al Jazeera Network began releasing the Palestine Papers, the largest disclosure of confidential negotiation documents in the history of the Israeli–Palestinian conflict. The network's Arabic and English channels aired the most essential extracts, while articles exploring the failure of the Middle East peace process appeared on both its websites. The raw documents were published on Al Jazeera's Transparency Unit website (www.transparency.aljazeera.net). Those documents—more than 1,600 files spanning the period from 1999 to 2010—included minutes of high-level meetings between US, European, Israeli, and Palestinian Authority officials. The centre-left Israeli newspaper *Haaretz* declared the Papers "much more important than the documents released by WikiLeaks." Indeed, the meeting minutes in the Papers reflect the unvarnished candour one would find in top-secret wiretaps rather than formal diplomatic dispatches.

The publication of the Palestine Papers, in which Al Jazeera was joined by the UK-based *Guardian* newspaper, dominated the global news agenda for four days. Headlines from the Papers appeared in nearly every major US, European, and Middle Eastern newspaper, followed by international news outlets CNN, BBC, and Al-Arabiyya. Commentary in the blogosphere exploded on the topic, as social media sites Twitter and Facebook brought secret discussions into the daylight. Private conversations from the Papers were also beamed across digital platforms and on cell phone displays around the world.

By fate, epic events were taking place in the Middle East as the Papers were published. In Sudan, a referendum from January 9–15 paved the way for South Sudan's independence, and weeks of protests in Tunisia led on January 14th to the ousting and exile of Tunisian President Zine El-Abidine Ben Ali. As the joint Al Jazeera-*Guardian* coverage came to a close, the Tunisian example was spreading all over the Arab world. It rose to a fever pitch in Egypt, where thousands began to protest their own dictatorship and demand not only the removal of Hosni Mubarak but an end to the three-decade state of emergency, a new Constitution, free elections and other democratic reforms. A critical mass began to form in Cairo's Tahrir Square, and demonstrators persevered for eighteen days, leading to Mubarak's resignation on February 11.

As the Palestinian Authority was still reeling from embarrassment caused by the Papers, the exit of its longtime Egyptian ally only served to weaken the organization. PA President Mahmoud Abbas declared his public support for Mubarak until the very end, despite overwhelming public demands in Egypt for his removal. The US-trained PA security forces in the West Bank physically assaulted protesters as they gathered to support the Egyptian people's demonstrations against the dictator. As evidenced by the Papers, Mubarak's regime had become a crutch for the PA, its dominant Fateh party, and President Abbas. Indeed, the Papers reveal the collaborative effort by the United States and Egypt to support Israel's siege of the Gaza Strip, a collective punishment intended to weaken Fateh's political rival Hamas. (A franchise of the Muslim Brotherhood movement, Hamas had won the January 2006 democratic elections in Palestine. However, the PA, along with Israel and the United States, refused to recognize the results and did everything possible to undermine Hamas's authority. With Egyptian and US help, the PA prepared a coup against Hamas in 2007, which Hamas crushed that June. Ever since, Hamas has ruled Gaza while the PA has ruled the West Bank.)

Even as the Arab world's revolutionary winds blew elsewhere, aftershocks of the Palestine Papers continued as many thousands downloaded their contents, allowing for both private study and public debate. Many Palestinians were stunned by the scale of concessions offered by the PA in their name. A common sentiment was expressed on January 24 by a young Palestinian named Tarik Kishawi, speaking to Al Jazeera English live from a refugee camp in Lebanon. Kishawi charged Nabil Shaath, a former PLO foreign minister, with belonging to a "puppet regime for the Israeli occupation." Sitting on Al Jazeera's set in Doha, Shaath smiled and replied in a patronizing manner, "I will forgive him," fueling the perception of an out-of-touch PA leadership. The outrage extended elsewhere in the Palestinian Diaspora. Former PLO representative-turned-Oxford academic Karma Nabulsi declared in the *Guardian* that "this seemingly endless and ugly game of the peace process is now finally over. The peace process is a sham. Palestinians must reject their officials and rebuild their movement."

On January 27th, students and intellectuals went so far as to stage a sit-in at the PLO's London offices, protesting their disapproval of the PA's conduct.

The resignation on February 12 of Dr. Saeb Erekat, for years the PLO's chief negotiator, proved to be only a marginal event. On various programs, Erekat claimed that the disclosures were part of a CIA plot to overthrow the Palestinian Authority, while PLO Executive Committee member Yasser Abed Rabbo launched personal attacks against the Emir of Qatar, who owns and finances Al Jazeera. The Papers showed the PA's animus not only against the Emir but against other Arab leaders. The charges became so personal following Al Jazeera's broadcast—including the burning of effigies—that Abbas took the step of issuing a presidential decree on February 13 ordering all PLO officials to cease and desist in the name of preserving good relations with other Arab countries. As the controversy boiled, Erekat, Abed Rabbo, and Abbas refused to address the substance of the Papers, preferring instead to label them as forgeries, even as other Fateh officials, including Shaath and other former PA negotiators, gave interviews confirming the Papers' authenticity.

After Mubarak left office, the PA announced a cabinet reshuffle and expressed its desire to hold municipal, parliamentary, and presidential elections by September 2011. However, its constitutional authority to do so is open to question, as Abbas continues to serve as President without any legal mandate, his term having expired in January 2009. And calls for an election in the absence of national unity are questionable; as long as the West Bank is dominated by PA security forces and the Gaza Strip by those of Hamas, there is little chance of free and fair elections. The Papers indicate that reconciliation talks were far too often a public relations exercise, with Fateh moving behind the scenes to defeat Hamas, supported by Israel and the US.

More substantive than the hot PA rhetoric attacking the release of the Papers was its dissolution of the Negotiation Support Unit, an organization of lawyers and policy experts who authored many of the documents. The dismissal of these young legal minds is akin to the US State Department firing its own legal advisors over the embarrassing WikiLeaks disclosures rather than addressing the causes of the leaks or the misguided policies exposed by them.

Reacting poorly in the wake of political embarrassment, the public outcry in the PA-controlled West Bank grew louder. Abbas dismissed the Papers as "soap opera" theatrics, while his supporters attacked and vandalized Al Jazeera's Ramallah bureau. Among those leading the charge, according to the *New York Times*, were plainclothes officers of Abbas's Preventive Security. Threats and intimidation against Al Jazeera journalists continued, as the PA-controlled media accused Jazeera of every conspiracy imaginable. On Facebook, Fateh supporters circulated pictures of an Israeli flag emblazoned with the Al Jazeera logo. As PA officials began to recant the charges of forgery, one after another, they shifted to a familiar refrain in the age of WikiLeaks: that there was "nothing new" in the Papers. By that time, the officials' reputation as negotiators had sustained severe damage, nearly all of it self-inflicted, as an opportunity to explain their political strategy was lost in the desire for revenge.

Unsurprisingly, condemnation of the PA was immediate in the Hamas-controlled Gaza Strip. There was little shock expressed by Hamas officials, who argued that the PA records were inescapable proof of the depth of the Authority's collusion with Israel. Indeed, the Papers show the extent to which the PA had come to regard Hamas and resistance-oriented Palestinians as an enemy comparable to the Israeli occupation itself.

Amid Israel's entrenched culture of irredentist stonewalling on negotiations, the release of the Papers actually helped the political careers of those, like former Foreign Minister Tzipi Livni, who had generally been depicted in the media as interested in peace and willing to bargain in good faith. In fact, the Papers show that Israel conceded next to nothing—a badge of honor in the country's current domestic political environment. So impressed by the new evidence of Livni's willingness to transfer Arab villages to the future state of Palestine, Israeli hardliner and Foreign Minister Avigdor Lieberman went so far as to invite Livni to a coalition meeting. Other Israelis, along with many foreign observers, declared that the Papers showed there really was a Palestinian partner, a notion Israelis had been taught was untrue following the collapse of peace talks at Camp David in 2000. To the Israeli right wing, of course, the extensive PA concessions were dismissed as not going far enough.

Editorial pages around the world gave enormous coverage to the Papers, and many carried harsh attacks—especially from supporters of the "peace process"—on Al Jazeera for publishing the documents.

Thomas Friedman of the *New York Times* condemned Al Jazeera for its "nasty job" in releasing the Papers, while former AIPAC official and US Ambassador to Israel Martin Indyk scolded Al Jazeera for not congratulating the PA for being so pliable.

Similar criticism came from the so-called Quartet (the United States, Russia, the EU and the UN). Its Middle East envoy, former British Prime Minister Tony Blair, said Al Jazeera's intention was to "destabilize." Blair conveniently evaded the bigger question of whether his own efforts, revealed in the Papers, had perhaps been destabilizing. Take, for instance a plan tabled by MI6, the British foreign intelligence service, during his tenure as Prime Minister in 2004 that proposed the "temporary internment of leading Hamas and PIJ (Palestinian Islamic Jihad) figures, making sure they are well-treated, with EU funding." In the era of extraordinary renditions, it was just one of several plots hatched in US and European capitals to weaken Hamas and strengthen Fateh, the West's preferred negotiating partner.

As journalists at one of the world's most influential news channels, Al Jazeera staff are used to being praised by people and condemned by governments. As an American reporter who has spent the past four years working there, I have learned to live with this background noise. If anything, I consider it a testament to our professionalism and editorial boldness rather than a source of embarrassment.

I should note here that my involvement as a writer and journalist covering the Israel-Palestine conflict precedes the release of the Palestine Papers; my book on the Oslo process, *The Truth About Camp David*, was published in 2004. Based on eyewitness testimony from top negotiators on the US, Israeli and Palestinian sides at those talks, that book demonstrated, among other things, that the joint US-Israeli strategy of blaming the Palestinians for the failure of those 2000 talks was based on lies.

The Truth About Camp David elicited considerable interest, especially among the Israeli left and among US-based foreign policy realists. That led to many invitations to travel, speak and work at think tanks, and ultimately landed me a job in television. My journey has been rich in irony. Indeed, the same PA officials who attacked me for my involvement in Al Jazeera's release of the Palestine Papers had frequently praised me for my book in earlier years, commending me for exposing the truth behind the distorted charges that had once turned the world against them. What those officials failed to realize was that then, as now, a journalist's obligation is to get the story right, a mission I have tried to pursue since my earliest days as a writer and reporter.

I spent hundreds of hours conducting interviews and reviewing official records and transcripts to complete *The Truth About Camp David*. Yet nothing could have prepared me for the shock I experienced, nearly seven years later, when I began reviewing the Palestine Papers. I knew the material was much too important to be buried in a book, and that its scope would require the analysis and presentation of far more than a single individual. As I had learned through hard experience, nothing short of total publication of the documents would satisfy the many interested stakeholders and critics who would understandably demand to see the evidence. To that end, others at Al Jazeera also quickly realized that monopolizing the Papers would have harmed rather than helped public understanding of the subject.

Fortunately, Al Jazeera had the resources to ensure its full presentation would be possible. For several months I was part of a team of journalists at the network who experienced many fascinating but agonizing discoveries. Authenticating the documents was our first priority. Working in the WikiLeaks era of massive document disclosures, our mission was to give the Papers context, nuance, and fair treatment, so that our audiences could become more informed. It was an altogether different challenge turning papers into television, setting up a website to display the Papers, and translating relevant documents, as some of the files were written in Arabic even though negotiations are conducted almost exclusively in English.

Fearing the possibility of viewer fatigue and diminishing returns, we decided, together with our *Guardian* partners, to focus our coverage around four distinct themes: Jerusalem/Borders, 1948 Arab Villages and Refugees, Security Collaboration, and the Gaza/Goldstone cover-up. There is much, much more in the Papers, since they span the period from 1999 to 2010, but the recent era, particularly the Annapolis process from 2007 to 2009 and the years of the Obama administration, have far greater relevance in today's political environment.

At the time of the Annapolis Conference, in November 2007, I wrote an analysis on the Al Jazeera English website in which I naively predicted that conference would become a "footnote in history." I realize now that I could not have been more incorrect. The more than 280 private meetings under the Annapolis umbrella, intended to resolve the core issues under the caveat "nothing agreed until everything is agreed," extended far beyond any previous discussions, including those at Camp David in 2000. In particular, the PA's presentation of maps on May 4, 2008 suggested it was willing to concede valuable Palestinian land—areas beyond anything the late Palestinian President Yasser Arafat had contemplated. There were proposals that many, if not most, Palestinians would oppose, made without the consent of landowners and families who risked becoming victims of land theft for a second time, this time with the acquiescence of their own leaders.

In my estimation, the central message of the Papers is not the story of the United States proving yet again that it is not an honest broker, although that current runs through nearly every meeting. No, the main story is the futile and pathetic attempts by the Palestinian Authority to do almost anything to show that it is an acceptable negotiating partner after Camp David and against the tide of 9/11 stereotypes and biases of the West and Israel. The documents show that PA officials failed to understand that neither Israel nor the West much cares about Palestinian statehood, and that no concessions short of a total Palestinian surrender would satisfy them.

In the fall of 2010, I traveled the world meeting with US, Israeli, and Palestinian Authority officials who had no idea that I held in my possession the secret records of their negotiations. Some gave general interviews on background; others, including Saeb Erekat, agreed to reflect on the talks while on camera. Those discussions, along with the meticulous guidance provided by sources, allowed me to understand the Papers more clearly. I hope that in reading this book, people of goodwill will undergo a similar process, and that it will increase the understanding of those who want to end an injustice that continues to stoke tensions throughout the world.

What follows is a summary of my own findings after studying the Papers over several months. It is a first, rough draft of history, bound to include mistakes, which I alone am responsible for. They are intended to orient the reader for the core of the book: the presentation in the later section of the book of selected documents and meeting minutes. It should be emphasized that this presentation is by no means comprehensive; indeed, it only begins to scratch the surface of the many stories contained in the Papers. My purpose is to encourage others—from universities to refugee camps to government offices and think tanks—to investigate and debate this historic set of documents.

Given what is happening in 2011 in Tunisia, Egypt and Libya—indeed, what is happening all over the Arab world—it is my hope that the public will not see these pages as simply an indictment of some governments, although it is certainly true that governments have failed and are worthy of criticism. It is far more important, in the wake of the Middle East revolutions, that the Papers be viewed as testament to the *inevitability* of failure when governments are not answerable to their people, and when people do not take control of their own destiny, without foreign meddling.

That, I believe, is the surest path to justice, if there ever is to be any in Palestine.

Analysis of the Palestine Papers
Clayton E. Swisher

1. East Jerusalem's Holy Sites

Focusing on that part of the Palestine Papers covering the Annapolis period, 2007–2009, it is clear the Palestinian Authority were prepared to make unprecedented concessions to the Israeli government, agreeing to relinquish parts of Occupied East Jerusalem and other West Bank lands. In return, the Israeli government pocketed those concessions while acknowledging that it had a project to confiscate more land and erect Jewish-only colonies. This was clearly admitted on May 29, 2008, by Udi Dekel, the head of Prime Minister Ehud Olmert's negotiating team.

> **Dekel:** Since 2000, something happened in those 8 years so we are not at the same starting point. You started a terror war on us <u>and we created facts on the ground.</u>[1] This is the reality that we live in today, so we can't go back to Camp David. Circumstances changed considerably since then.[2]

The Papers reveal that the most controversial of the PA's suggested concessions dealt with East Jerusalem and its holy sites. It had been several years since either had been discussed in any formal setting.

The Camp David 2000 talks marked the first time leaders from both sides bargained directly over the status of Occupied East Jerusalem and in particular its holy sites. International law and the 1967 lines clearly show that the Haram al-Sharif/Temple Mount is within the Occupied Palestinian Territories. But in 2000, Israeli prime minister Ehud Barak and Palestinian president Yasser Arafat were nonetheless willing to negotiate over them, and their willingness was no small controversy. Many participants in the talks attest that the failure to resolve the status of the Old City's holy sites was the chief reason the overall talks failed (rather than, as was frequently alleged by outsiders, the question of Palestinian refugees).

---

1 All underlinings in quotes from the Palestine Papers are the author's, for emphasis
2 http://www.ajtransparency.com/en/document/2681

In spite of President Bill Clinton's various proposals for dividing sovereignty, Arafat proudly defended the PLO's unwillingness to compromise on the sovereignty of the Haram, which is home to Al Aqsa Mosque, Islam's third-holiest site. It was a principled position that earned him scorn among Israelis and Americans—but universal support at home, and throughout the broader Islamic world.

Nearly a decade later, the Papers make clear that PLO Executive Committee member Saeb Erekat was willing to show flexibility on the Haram's final status.

It is unclear whether he made the statements below to gain the admiration of his American counterparts (as privately confided to me by his peers) or merely to break the deadlock created by the hard-line Netanyahu government. But this much is certain: any tinkering with the legal status of the Haram al-Sharif is dangerous and unprecedented.

Seemingly aware of the risks, Erekat nonetheless offered this exchange on Wednesday, October 21, 2009, during his meetings at the US State Department in Washington, DC.

Saeb Erekat to Deputy U.S. Envoy David Hale and US State Department Legal Advisor Jonathon Schwartz

Erekat: Even the Old City can be worked out [discusses breakdown of sovereignty over Old City] except for the Haram and what they call Temple Mount. There you need the creativity of people like me ... [George Mitchell rejoins the meeting] **Erekat**: I want to point out I am answering in my personal capacity on these questions ...   ... **Schwartz**: Discuss Jerusalem with the borders or separate? **Erekat:** It's solved. You have the Clinton Parameters formula. For the Old City sovereignty for Palestine, except the Jewish quarter and part of the Armenian quarter ... the Haram can be left to be discussed – there are creative ways, having a body or a committee, having undertakings for example not to dig. The only thing I cannot do is convert to Zionism. **Schwartz**: To confirm to Senator Mitchell, your private idea ... **Erekat**: This conversation is in my private capacity. **Schwartz**: We've heard the idea from others. So you're not the first to raise it. **Erekat:** Others are not the chief negotiator of the PLO. **Schwartz**: I meant this gives you cover – that it's not you who raised it. So you would separate Jerusalem from the border? **Erekat**: No. But we use Clinton Parameters – except for the Haram [separate from border]. **Hale**: So you're not talking about the border only. You're talking about Jerusalem, security

... **Erekat**: Yes. Once we define these, we can move to bilaterals. **Hale**: So this is a way of moving from proximity talks to bilaterals. **Erekat**: I repeat my message: no bilateral negotiations without a settlement freeze. **Hale**: You succeeded in making the point.[3]

Months later, on January 15, 2010, in the presence of Senator Mitchell's staff, Erekat again reaffirmed unprecedented Palestinian offers—including on Jerusalem—made during the Annapolis process:

Erekat: Israelis want the two state solution but they don't trust. They want it more than you think, sometimes more than Palestinians. What is in that paper gives them the biggest Yerushalaim in Jewish history, symbolic number of refugees return, demilitarized state ... What more can I give?[4]

These statements are critical, because the Haram al-Sharif/Temple Mount had seldom been raised in more than 280 bilateral meetings during the Annapolis process.

The reason for this was domestic Israeli politics: Prime minister Olmert's coalition partners demanded that the status of Jerusalem's holy sites not be negotiated, with the religious right-wing Shas party threatening to leave the government if the issue was even discussed. Thus the Israeli delegation was not allowed to speak about it, as reiterated to the PA by Dekel on July 2, 2008:

Dekel: Why does your side keep mentioning Jerusalem in every meeting – isn't there an understanding on this between the leaders?[5]

The Israelis, in other words, freely admitted that they could not entertain any bargain on Jerusalem. Yet in various meetings the Palestinian Authority went ahead and presented its ideas—regardless of the tactical consequences, and despite years of experience in which Israel pocketed PA concessions to use as a new starting point in later talks. Here is what the PA's overtures sounded like in the Annapolis meeting of June 30, 2008:

Qurei: Jerusalem is part of the territory occupied in 67. We can discuss and agree on many issues relating to Jerusalem: religious

---

3   http://www.ajtransparency.com/files/4899.pdf
4   http://www.ajtransparency.com/files/5012.pdf
5   http://www.ajtransparency.com/files/2870.pdf

places, infrastructures, municipal function, economic issues, security, settlements. However, the municipal borders for us are 67. This is the basis, and this is where we can start. [Silence] **Livni:** Houston, we have a problem. **Qurei:** Silence is agreement ... **Erekat:** It is no secret that on our map we proposed we are offering you the biggest Yerushalayim in history. But we must talk about the concept of Al-Quds. **Livni:** Do you have a concept? **Erekat:** Yes. We have a detailed concept — but we will only discuss with a partner. And it's doable. **Livni:** No, I can't.[6]

By the end of the Annapolis negotiations, the PA began to accept that some internationalizing of the Haram al-Sharif might be required — regardless of the potential implications.

In an offer conveyed orally to Abbas in the late summer of 2008 and recounted in a document dated August 31, 2008, Olmert floated the idea of allowing the United States, along with Egypt, Jordan, and Saudi Arabia, to form a committee that would determine the fate of the Haram al-Sharif/Temple Mount. According to the Papers, that committee would *not* have had the ability to force either Israel or the weaker Palestinian party to accept an agreement.

Erekat's comments appear to confirm that the PLO—speaking on behalf of all Palestinians—would find such an arrangement acceptable. The implications are profound: the United States has no historic standing on the issue of holy sites (it is not even a self-described Christian nation) and considers itself Israel's closest ally. Moreover, the Israelis could hardly have thought a formulation would be wise without trusted leaders in Jordan, Saudi Arabia, and Egypt—particularly problematic now, given the 2011 revolution in Egypt that ousted President Hosni Mubarak.

What's more, the Papers reveal eagerness by Jordan and in particular Saudi Arabia to shape the Haram's final outcome, perhaps to shore up the respective monarchs' own religious credentials among restive populations at home. King Abdullah of Saudi Arabia, the Custodian of the Two Holy Mosques in Mecca and Medina, is described in the Papers as wanting a resolution of Islam's third-holiest site regardless of the costs. Erekat described it as follows to US Assistant Secretary Welch on December 2, 2008—just weeks before the Gaza war:

---

6   http://www.ajtransparency.com/files/2826.pdf

Erekat: Saudi's main concern is Jerusalem – not swaps and neighbourhoods. To them Jerusalem is the Haram.

Welch: So they want to know who will "own" it?

Erekat: The status. I told them: I cannot tell you. What defines this "holy basin," what it includes ... I don't know. [Reference to the difficulties on getting Jerusalem addressed, Shas, and the Annapolis statement on the core issues].[7]

2. Borders

June 15, 2008 Trilateral US–Israeli–Palestinian Meeting (Principals: Rice, Livni, Qurei)

Qurei: We proposed that the ratio of swap should not exceed 1.9% from the total area of the West Bank, including East Jerusalem and the Gaza Strip, and that swapped land should be located on 1967 borders.

– As for settlements, we proposed the following: Removal of some settlements, annexation of others, and keeping others under Palestinian sovereignty.

– This last proposition could help in the swap process. We proposed that Israel annexes all settlements in Jerusalem except Jabal Abu Ghneim (Har Homa). This is the first time in history that we make such a proposition; we refused to do so in Camp David.[8]

The Palestine Papers provide further evidence of how the Palestinian Authority agreed to Israeli annexation of illegal East Jerusalem settlements, including Ramat Shlomo, Pisgat Ze'ev, French Hill, Neve Yakov, and Gilo, during a seminal negotiation on May 4, 2008.

Developed on stolen Palestinian land, these settlements still make headlines. In February 2010, the Netanyahu government announced 1,600 new settlement tenders in East Jerusalem's Ramat Shlomo just as US Vice President Joe Biden was visiting Israel. The announcement prompted a harsh reaction from the United States and the Palestinian Authority. Reacting with a sense of disbelief, Prime Minister Netanyahu told the *Jerusalem Post* on March 14 that "Everyone – including the Palestinians – understood that neighborhoods like Gilo and Ramat Shlomo would remain part of Israel in any final agreement, and that

---

7   http://www.ajtransparency.com/files/3610.pdf
8   http://www.ajtransparency.com/files/2825.pdf

this has been the case in all the various plans drawn up over the years."[9] Apparently not fazed by that controversy, Israel announced 625 new tenders in Pisgat Ze'ev in December 2010, just as President Obama's Middle East envoy was in town to push for a three-month settlement freeze.

The full text of the May 4, 2008, meeting where these areas were conceded under the "nothing agreed until everything agreed" headline is included, along with relevant maps, on page 143–148 of this book.[10] What follows is a summary of the exchanges between Tzipi Livni, Ahmed Qurei, Saeb Erekat and Samih al-Abed – exposing the intent, and the key details, of the maps they tabled to legitimize Israel's acquisition of Palestinian property.

> **Samih:** We have done our best to include the largest number of settlers. **Livni:** I want to say that we do not like this suggestion because it does not meet our demands, and probably it was not easy for you to think about it but I really appreciate it. I think we have a reason to continue. **Abu Ala' [Ahmed Qurei]:** We understand how hard it was for you as well. **Erekat:** In Jerusalem it was hard for us but we decided to give you. **Livni:** Can we have the maps?

> **Erekat:** I want to say something. I am from the leadership headed by Abu Mazen [Mahmoud Abbas] and the leadership does not accept the facts on the ground. **Livni:** That is why I said what I have said. **Erekat:** This is not the Koran. Gabriel did not come down from heaven and revealed it to us. We have taken your interests and concerns into account, but not all. This is the first time in Palestinian–Israeli history in which such a suggestion is officially made. What we are doing no one will do for us, not the Americans or the Europeans. **Livni:** I know about this.

The PA representatives continued with specifics on which areas of Occupied East Jerusalem they would relinquish in the pursuit of Palestinian statehood. While they did not allow Israel the major "Greater Jerusalem" settlement blocs – Ma'ale Adumim and Gush Etzion – they nonetheless offered to give permanence to sizable Israeli settlements with proximity to the Old City. Less than two months later, on June 30, 2008, it proved a slippery slope, as the PA were even ready to consider flashpoint Palestinian Jerusalem neighborhoods like Sheikh Jarrah:

---

9   http://www.jpost.com/Israel/Article.aspx?id=170912
10   http://www.ajtransparency.com/files/2648.pdf

Becker: We did not mean to assess, but to evaluate where we stand in the committees, to look at what is happening in each committee and see if there is something else we can start drafting or working on.

Qurei: [Regarding swaps] so for an area in Sheikh Jarrah, I have to see [an] equivalent area.

Becker: This is about making progress on issues on the table ... [11]

It should also be noted that, in spite of the PA's insistence that any swaps be equal in value, land in East Jerusalem is extremely valuable – if not invaluable – both financially and culturally which means that no land that Israel would be willing to offer from the Israeli side of the 1967 border could balance land in East Jerusalem. Moreover, the May 4, 2008, presentation not only showed the Israelis what portions of East Jerusalem the PA was willing to concede, it also tipped the PA's hand as to which undeveloped areas might be used to help bring contiguity to Israeli settlements:

Erekat: We are building for you the largest Jerusalem in history. **Khaled:** This area was the most difficult to delineate. **Tal:** How can Pisgat Ze'ev settlement be connected with the French Hill? **Samih:** A bridge can be built to connect them.[12]

Even after conceding the Jewish Quarter of the Old City (Arafat entertained the idea of giving up the Jewish Quarter and a safe passageway through the Armenian Quarter at Camp David in 2000), the Palestinian Authority asks for just 0.37 km of land in return for 6.68 km, as shown in full at the top of page 144). It would use that small concession to build up the Palestinian village of Beit Safafa, which has far less proximity to the holy sites than other neighborhoods it was willing to relinquish.

Then there is the concession of the Israeli settlement of Gilo. In December 2010, the Palestinian Authority publicly stomped its feet in protest against Gilo's "natural growth." But – since it had known from May 4, 2008, that the PA would be willing to accept Gilo's annexation – the Israeli government could claim it had justification to continue building.

---

11   http://www.ajtransparency.com/en/document/2826
12   http://www.ajtransparency.com/files/2648.pdf

Livni: Doesn't Har Homa exist? **Khaled:** The interest is to reconnect Jerusalem and Bethlehem. Such reconnection has a social, religious, economic and tourist significance. It is even more important than the connection between Jerusalem and Ramallah. The area is also important for the expansion of Beit Safafa, which has become an isolated town between Gilo and Har Homa settlements. **Abu Ala':** To address natural growth. **Livni:** Now we are talking about natural growth?![13]

Amid the intensive 2008 exchanges under the Annapolis Process, the PA's own statistics presented stark evidence of ongoing Israeli bad faith. Indeed, while the PA diplomats were meeting their US and Israeli counterparts, the number of illegal Israeli settlement housing tenders was 17 times the number the previous year (2,300 v. 137). The Papers contain a December 2008 internal PLO report cataloguing how:

In East Jerusalem alone, Israeli authorities have advanced plans for nearly 10,000 housing units in Israeli settlements since Annapolis ... Israeli authorities demolished at least 338 Palestinian homes and other structures in the year since Annapolis, 99 of them in East Jerusalem.[14]

Motivated by a desire to prove themselves after Camp David 2000, as "Palestinians for peace," the PA leadership continued shopping the May 4 maps, presenting them to the incoming Obama administration as a sign of their good faith. President Abbas personally deposited the maps with President Obama during their first meeting in Washington in May 2009, initialing them to signal his willingness to continue using them as a basis for a final agreement.

The Obama Administration appeared no more moved by the Palestinian offer than the former governments of George W. Bush or Ehud Olmert. In a meeting with US Middle East envoy Mitchell on October 21, 2009, an exasperated Erekat in effect asks the Obama administration to decide unilaterally Palestine's borders—a request almost guaranteed to work to Palestinians' detriment, given America's longstanding bias in favor of Israel:

Erekat: All these issues I've negotiated. They need decisions. The same applies to the percentage. A decision on what percentage. We

13   http://www.ajtransparency.com/files/2648.pdf
14   http://www.ajtransparency.com/files/3637.pdf

offered 2%. They said no. So what's the percentage? You can go back to the document we gave president Obama in May.[15]

The Papers also make painfully clear the extent to which the United States has attempted to further the hostile takeover of Palestinian land. It reached unprecedented levels in April 2004, in a letter written by President George W. Bush to Prime Minister Ariel Sharon, the operative portions reading:

> As part of a final peace settlement, Israel must have secure and recognized borders, which should emerge from negotiations between the parties in accordance with UNSC Resolutions 242 and 338. In light of new realities on the ground, including already existing major Israeli populations centers, it is unrealistic to expect that the outcome of final status negotiations will be a full and complete return to the armistice lines of 1949, and all previous efforts to negotiate a two-state solution have reached the same conclusion. It is realistic to expect that any final status agreement will only be achieved on the basis of mutually agreed changes that reflect these realities."[16]

It is important when reading the Papers to understand the impact those fateful words had on the behavior of the American negotiators, as they moved between "judge" of Palestinian behavior to full-on "jury" of deciding final-status issues, including Jerusalem.

Using the 2003 Road Map, which was supposed to create a Palestinian State by 2005, the United States assigned itself the role of judging the "performance" of both parties. A revolving door of monitors, including several US generals, trickled through the West Bank – almost all of them focused exclusively on Palestinian security "performance," discussed in greater detail later.

Under America's watchful eyes, Israeli settlement growth, particularly in East Jerusalem, was largely ignored, save for when it was declared "unhelpful" or "an obstacle" by various US spokespersons. Even Tzipi Livni, in this pre-Annapolis discussion on November 13, 2007, seemed honest about the broad intent of the settlement projects with her Palestinian peers:

---

15   http://www.ajtransparency.com/files/4899.pdf
16   http://www.mfa.gov.il/MFA/Peace+Process/Reference+Documents/
Exchange+of+letters+Sharon-Bush+14-Apr-2004.htm

Livni: I'd like to say something to Abu Ala about the settlements. Just like you said you understand our security needs. I understand the sentiments of the Palestinians when they see the settlements being built. The meaning from the Palestinian perspective is that Israel takes more land, that the Palestinian state will be impossible, the Israel policy is to take more and more land day after day and that at the end of the day we'll say that it is impossible we already have the land and we cannot create the state [It was the policy of the government for a really long time. Now it is still the policy of some of the parties but not the government...][17]

The following series of quotes, many of them delivered after the Palestinian Authority's May 4, 2008, map presentation, reflect the work of the American "jury" on permanent-status issues. It shows an American push to "condition" the Palestinians on conceding specific settlements—and to go much farther. The argument here is that the Palestinians risk missing a "historic" opportunity based on a few stubborn percentage points; in American eyes, the Palestinian Authority is acting intransigent for trying to apply inconvenient principles of international law.

The Palestine Papers provide evidence for a more compelling narrative: namely, that the United States is willing to subordinate Palestinian statehood (a self-described core US national security priority) to the whims of thousands of Jewish settlers—a position first enunciated in President Bush's 2004 letter, which only snowballed in the midst of the Annapolis talks. Even worse for the Palestinians, it would turn out that the settlements in question included Ma'ale Adumim and Ariel: the former, which lies east of Jerusalem, splits the West Bank in half, while the latter is deep inside in the northern West Bank, nowhere near the 1967 border. Taken in the aggregate, a clear picture emerges:

Date: July 16, 2008, Meeting: US–Palestinian bilateral

Rice: I don't think that any Israeli leader is going to cede Ma'ale Adumim. **Qurei:** Or any Palestinian leader. **Rice:** Then you won't have a state!...Israel had to put away some of their aspirations – like taking all of Judea and Samaria.[18]

---

17   http://www.ajtransparency.com/files/2003.pdf
18   http://www.ajtransparency.com/files/2942.pdf

Date: July 29, 2008, Meeting: US-Palestinian bilateral

Rice: You terrify her [Livni] when you say two things – you want an army. Second when you say no Ma'ale Adumim and Ariel. No Israeli leader can accept without including them in an Israeli state.[19]

Date: March 31, 2008, Meeting: Condoleezza Rice, Saeb Erekat, David Welch

Welch: Do not interrupt the negotiations for other reasons, such as the announcement of constructing new residential units in settlements ... _Rice: I told Abu Mazen that we cannot give others the right of veto whenever there is a declaration of bids to build new residential units ... There will always be people in Israel who are against cease of settlement construction, but these activities should not stop you. You must find a way to continue.[20]

Date: July 29, 2008, Meeting: Condoleezza Rice, Ahmed Qurei, Saeb Erekat

Rice: Maybe the perfect answer is an open Jerusalem. I don't want Palestinians to wait forever for an answer that will not come ... 1967 as a baseline. But if we wait until you decide sovereignty over the Haram or the Temple Mount ... Your children's children will not have an agreement! When it comes to holy sites, no one will argue the sovereignty of the other – leave it unresolved, [i.e. both Palestine and Israel could simultaneously claim sovereignty over the Haram/ Temple Mount].[21]

Date: July 29, 2008, Meeting: David Welch, Ahmed Qurei

David Welch: You can't leave Jerusalem out, but how do you include it given the political realities? [...] It doesn't help anyone if their [the Israeli government's] coalition falls.[22]

Date: July 29, 2008, Meeting: Condoleezza Rice, Saeb Erekat

Rice: I spoke to [Olmert] and he doesn't think that he's changed anything. We've always known that Jerusalem is difficult. We've looked for ways to address issues. But in an agreement, there will have to be an agreement on Ma'ale Adumim ... On territory, if we take as the base, everything that is occupied in 1967 – you will find that their position on 7.3% is close. It may not be enough, but it is close. 7.3 – 5 = 2.3%. Plus the corridor. If the goal is that Palestine should not

19   http://www.ajtransparency.com/files/3048.pdf
20   http://www.ajtransparency.com/files/2436.pdf ·
21   http://www.ajtransparency.com/files/3048.pdf
22   http://www.ajtransparency.com/files/3048.pdf

lose territory, then you are a couple of percentage points away. [...] But I hope that you won't lose the chance at a Palestinian state by sticking to 1.9%.[23]

Those who believed that the Obama administration—on the heels of its Muslim world media blitz, launched with Obama's June 2009 speech in Cairo—would perform any better as an "honest broker" are bound to be deeply disappointed by the Papers. Rather than take a principled stand on settlements, Obama's team publicly backed away from its insistence on a freeze in October 2009, after being told "no" by the Israelis.

One month earlier, the PA learned it would be getting a less favorable deal, including language referencing Israel as a "Jewish state," a pledge to "maybe" mention core issues as a term of reference, and a notice that East Jerusalem would not be part of the US efforts at the time to gain an Israeli moratorium on settlements.

September 16, 2009, Meeting: David Hale, Rami Dajani, Saeb Erekat

Hale: There are some important issues that need to be discussed prior to the 22nd [of September 2009] but there are others that do not. ... The outcome is that the President will emerge from the meeting with the two leaders and he will make comments to the press ... He will also announce the intention to meet in Egypt towards the end of October. He will say a 'contiguous, viable democratic state of Palestine living side by side' – you know the formula – with the Jewish state of Israel. **Dajani:** You said 'Jewish'? **Hale:** Yes. **Erekat:** Will he mention the core issues? **Hale:** To compensate for less than 100% freeze, maybe he will mention the core issues ... **Erekat:** Have you asked Netanyahu about his seriousness and willingness to enter negotiations? Have you considered the lessons learned from Camp David – failure to prepare properly can lead to explosion? What about the rest of the Road Map phase I obligations? And ... **Hale:** Regarding Netanyahu's willingness to enter into negotiations, I'm not a mind reader, but he has told us he is willing to enter meetings for the "two state outcome.' On Camp David – you know there are positive and negative lessons from all previous rounds. This time it's different from Camp David. It is not a 'summit' and will not lead to collapsed expectations. Rather we are looking at launching a process. You asked about Road Map obligations: we've touched on all of them; they've been on the agenda with

---

23   http://www.ajtransparency.com/files/3048.pdf

Israel since April – based on our discussion with you back in April. East Jerusalem institutions are not part of the package. However, access and movement is part. On Gaza, the humanitarian situation needs to be addressed ... **Hale:** We do consider the credibility of the US. The Cairo speech shows that the President understands the consequences and the need to rebuild US image. This is the foundation of his approach. We need the help of friends like you. **Erekat:** I hope this so [sic]. His success is my survival.[24]

Some have defined insanity as repeating the same experiment over and over and expecting different results. To that end, it is puzzling throughout the Papers to see the Palestinian Authority dignify what has become a US-led charade. Time and again, successive US administrations, Republican and Democrat, have proven themselves unable or unwilling to play the role of honest broker. The PA repeated these experiments with varying Israeli governments (led by Labor, Likud, or Kadima), all of which have proved their unwillingness to allow a Palestinian state with territory coming anywhere close to satisfying minimal Palestinians aspirations—or international law.

Before releasing the Papers, I confronted Saeb Erekat on the matter in an interview on November 5, 2010. Here is the exchange:

Swisher: I've heard your statements here in Washington. You discussed your experience of negotiating with the Israelis for more than 17 years. Now in spite of those negotiations it has not stopped radical Jewish settlers from taking over parts of East Jerusalem, has not stopped the Wall, did not stop the Gaza war, it did not stop Israeli incursions into the West Bank, it did not stop the economic hardships and policies against the people, it did not stop the siege of Gaza, I could go on and on. Why continue in negotiations. And if I could add that, you've been in it for 17 years as a key player and you haven't been able to stop those things from happening for negotiations so why do you continue? **Erekat:** Number one, you may insinuate because you're angry or people who said these things are angry and they have the right to be angry, that it's because that negotiations Israel continues settlements, attacks, aggressions, state terrorism and so on. This is not the truth. There's nothing wrong with negotiation. Negotiation is not the objective. It's the civilized means of conflicting parties to achieve —

---

24   http://www.ajtransparency.com/files/4835.pdf

Swisher: But some would say a view that it has become an end, not a means, because these negotiations haven't stopped all these things [cross-talking] **Erekat**: Wait a minute. Yes. **Swisher**: You haven't even been able to influence them to stop these things. **Erekat**: There is much more than that ... .

Swisher: But if you take stock [cross-talking] and do a forensics of all the failures of the past 17 years ...

Erekat: If I look at the stocks, Clayton, in 17 years, we have had 18 months of negotiations only. Now, when Netanyahu chose settlements, we stopped negotiations. We stopped negotiations. Were we cheated? Yes, we were cheated. **Swisher**: What would you say to critics who say that you have become a serial negotiator? **Erekat**: Well, it's not a job. It's not a job, Clayton. This is not a job for me.

3. Palestinian Refugees

It has long been assumed by many observers of the conflict that the question of the right of return of Palestinian refugees, encompassing the 750,000 who were expelled or fled the violence in 1948-49 and their descendants, would be the most difficult of final-status issues. While UN General Assembly Resolution 194 of December 1948 stipulates that "refugees wishing to return to their homes and live at peace with their neighbours should be permitted to do so at the earliest practicable date, and that compensation should be paid for the property of those choosing not to return and for loss of or damage to property," the overwhelming majority of Israelis, and Israeli government officials, have steadfastly refused to entertain this right. At the same time, the right of return has been one of the bedrock principles of the Palestinian national movement. So it should have been no surprise that the negotiators at Camp David in 2000 didn't advance very far on this issue (though significant progress was made at follow-up talks in Taba, in January 2001).

In the Annapolis period, the Israelis introduced two new, potentially explosive elements that were intended not only to forestall the right of return but also to address what Israelis have increasingly come to call their "demographic problem"—the Palestinian citizens of Israel. Those two elements were the demand that the PA recognize Israel as "Jewish state," or as a "state of the Jewish people," and that they accept the principle of population transfer, i.e., transfer of Palestinian citizens of Israel into the new Palestinian state, thus ridding Israel of an unwanted minority.

Here is more of my November 5, 2010, discussion with Saeb Erekat:

> **Swisher**: Did the Israelis raise the possibility of transferring Arab land and population? **Erekat**: Never. **Swisher**: Never? Were they talking about the Jewish nature of the state of Israel as they are, say, today? **Erekat**: Before Annapolis, Madame Livni, there's this question with us for the first time and we told her, aside from the issue of refugees and Arabs living in Israel, are you asking us to join the Zionist movement because that's what she was all about. I cannot accept that. I will not accept that under any circumstance. **Swisher**: But yet there have been other Palestinians like Yasser Abed Rabbo who have shown some flexibility. **Erekat**: I don't think so. I saw Yasser's statements and I saw Yasser denials to all things that were attributed to it. This is a very clear concept to all Palestinians. We have recognized Israel's right to 1967 and we will never accept what Israel defines itself in terms of religious things.[25]

The Palestine Papers reveal that Erekat's responses to me were less than candid. In the days leading up to the November 2007 Annapolis conference, Tzipi Livni, then Israel's foreign minister, often described Israel as an exclusively Jewish state.

Behind closed doors, Erekat did not categorically reject her claims. Far from it: in a meeting on November 13, 2007 – in the presence of both senior Fateh and Israeli officials – the records show that Erekat was not opposed to Israel's efforts to insert its identity as a "Jewish state" in the negotiations.

> **Erekat**: ... We've never denied Israel's right to define itself. If you want to call yourself the Jewish state of Israel—you can call it what you want. [Notes the examples of Iran and Saudi Arabia].[26]

Yasser Abed Rabbo, a PLO negotiator, made a nearly identical statement in November 2010; his remarks generated controversy, condemnation, and official back-pedaling. But Abed Rabbo expressed the same position in a meeting with Foreign Minister Livni on November 12, 2007:

---

25   Interview Erekat-Swisher, November 5, 2010.
26   http://www.ajtransparency.com/files/2003.pdf

Abed Rabbo: We can't interfere with the nature of states. [Sovereign states are sovereign states and can do whatever they'd like with their states.] We are sovereign people and don't want to interfere with yours even if you let us! It's your decision—we recognize your state however you want [to define it yourselves].

Livni: You are referring to the last line as a Jewish state.

Abed Rabbo: No—until we solve the issue of refugees we don't want any sentence to complicate our life. We don't want our intellectuals to debate the true meaning of that sentence.[27]

One probable reason Abed Rabbo may have wanted to avoid having Palestinian intellectuals debate the rebranding of Israel as a Jewish state could be because of its deep implications for the country's Palestinian minority, which constitutes an estimated 20 percent of the population.

More importantly, it would also exclude, *a priori*, the right of return of more than five million Palestinian refugees in the context of a "two states for two peoples" solution. This phrase may sound innocuous to the outsider but it actually embodies two key preconditions the Israelis harp on whenever they have the opportunity – that Israel is for the whole Jewish people, leading to unlimited immigration to Israel of Jews from around the world, and that Palestine (i.e. the West Bank and Gaza) is for all the Palestinians, or to put it another way, Palestinians do not belong in Israel (when in fact most of the Palestinian refugees came from what is now Israel.)

As suggested in the next extract, one way of denying Palestinian refugees their right to return is by enlisting the PA's support for excluding them—if the PA were to recognize Israel as a Jewish state, then they would also presumably be acknowledging that the Jewish state would not be obliged to welcome anyone as residents other than Jews. In case the PA negotiators had any doubt, Livni further fleshed out the concept in the November 12 and 13 meetings:

November 12, 2007

Livni: If we can't say two states for two people then we have a problem. This is not a core issue. **Qurei:** There is two states or one state [i.e. there are only two solutions to the conflict]. **Livni:** There is also two states with one on the other side of the Jordan [River]. **Yasser**

---

27   http://www.ajtransparency.com/files/2002.pdf

Abed Rabbo: Or three states – Gaza. **Qurei:** The two-state solution is what we agreed. Since this means sovereignty – two states – we don't want to describe the two states! **Livni:** There is no two states if there is no [two states for] two people.

November 13, 2007

Tzipi Livni: Our idea is to refer to two states for two peoples. Or two nation states, Palestine and Israel living side by side in peace and security with each state constituting the homeland for its people and the fulfillment of their national aspirations and self-determination... **Akram Haniya:** This refers to the Israeli people? **Livni:** [Visibly angered.] I think that we can use another session – about what it means to be a Jew and that it is more than just a religion. But if you want to take us back to [UN Resolution] 194 —it won't help. Each state constituting the homeland for its people and the fulfillment of their national aspirations and <u>self-determination in their own territory</u> ... <u>Israel the state of the Jewish people -- and I would like to emphasize the meaning of "its people" is the Jewish people</u> -- with Jerusalem the united and undivided capital of Israel and of the Jewish people for 3007 years... [The Palestinian team protests.] **Livni:** You asked for it. **Ahmed Qurei:** We said East Jerusalem! **Livni:** ... and Palestine for the Palestinian people. We did not want to say that there is a "Palestinian people" but we've accepted your right to self-determination. Now I have to say, before we continue, in order to continue we have to put out Jerusalem from your statement and from our place. We have enough differences, without putting another one out there.

Left unanswered before Annapolis, the discussion of Israel as an exclusively Jewish state only expanded to include how to rid the country of its Arab population. Consider the context in which it later resurfaced, in a meeting on borders on April 8, 2008:

Livni: Let us be fair. You referred to 1967 line. We have not talked about Jerusalem yet. There are some Palestinian villages that are located on both sides of the 1967 line about which we need to have an answer, such as Beit Safafa, Barta'a, Baqa al-Sharqiyeh and Baqa al-Gharbi-yyeh. There are also some settlements that were built behind 1967 line but expanded inside 1967 line illegally, such as Uranit settlement south of Hebron.[28]

---

28 http://www.ajtransparency.com/files/2484.pdf

Livni was hinting that the PA should consider allowing the transfer of Israeli-Arab neighborhoods inside Israel – particularly those in the Haifa District—as a deposit in the future state of Palestine, a move that would erase citizenship for Israel's Palestinian citizens by drawing new borders around them. Both Livni and others in her delegation again floated the idea in a meeting two months later, on June 21, 2008:

> **Livni:** Two issues related to the borders. When you talk about the line of 1967, there were some Palestinian villages separated by 1967. I visited an Israeli Palestinian village on Friday – in Wadi Ara. **Qurei:** What were you doing there? Campaigning? **Livni:** There are 12,000 Palestinian members of Kadima. **Udi Dekel:** Israeli Arabs. [**Livni** defends using "Palestinians." She also notes that all they want are equal rights in Israel and "they deserve it."] **Livni:** I said from the beginning that it can be part of the swaps. **Qurei:** Absolutely not. **Livni:** We have this problem with Ghajar in Lebanon. Terje Larsen put the blue line to cut the village in two. [This needs to be addressed.] We decided not to cut the village. It was a mistake. The problem now – those living on Lebanese soil are Israeli citizens. **Dekel:** Barta'a, Baqa al-Sharqiyeh, Barqa al-Gharbiyyeh, Betil, Beit Safafa ... **Qurei:** This will be difficult. All Arabs in Israel will be against us. **Tal Becker:** We will need to address it somehow. <u>Divided. All Palestinian. All Israeli.</u>[29]

Media commentators at the time might have attributed this position—the endorsement of "population transfers"—to Yisrael Beiteinu, a right-wing nationalist party catering to Russian immigrants and headed by Avigdor Lieberman, the current foreign minister. Yet the Papers reveal that the same racist policies were endorsed and promoted by Tzipi Livni, a perceived "moderate" with whom the Palestinian Authority preferred dealing—a revelation that comes as a blow to the hope that the two sides can reach a historic compromise.

Tal Becker, who was chief policy advisor to foreign minister Livni, clearly felt on solid political ground when he stated the desired outcome in clear and unequivocal terms: "Divided. All Palestinian. All Israeli." Livni had conditioned the PA for it in talks on January 27, 2008:

> **Livni:** Does swap mean also the swap of the inhabitants? I know this is a problem for you. ... **Qurei:** ... We'll never accept any change in the reality of the life of the Arabs living in Israel or their transfer. They're

---

29 http://www.ajtransparency.com/files/3027.pdf

Israeli citizens. **Livni**: ... You didn't accept the annexation of settlement blocs and we never accepted 1967 borders. Therefore let's look at the maps. **Erekat:** First, we ask where the borders are. Abu Ala' says 1967 borders with minor modifications by value and reciprocity. Let's first agree on the principle and not the criterion. **Livni:** There are thousands of Israelis living in the West Bank and our capability to implement any agreement depends on us knowing where they'll end up at. Besides, 1967 borders are not sacred. **Erekat:** The armistice line according to 1949 agreement is sacred. **Livni:** In the end the whole matter isn't merely the value of exchange but the reality of those Israelis and where they live...The basis for the creation of the state of Israel is that it was created for the Jewish people. Your state will be the answer to all Palestinians including refugees. Putting an end to claims means fulfilling national rights for all.[30]

Taken together, it is clear that Livni, in her capacity as foreign minister, initiated negotiations on the fate of one-fifth of Israel's population—behind their backs, and with an inappropriate party. By refusing to refer to Arab-Israelis as "Israelis," and by emphasizing "Israel as the Jewish state," Livni was clearly intent on using the Annapolis talks to remove as many Arabs as possible from Israel.

It is important to note that any population transfer—even if negotiated by the Palestinian Authority, which has no standing or basis to represent Israel's Arab citizens—could constitute an act of ethnic cleansing under the definition provided by the United Nations. At a minimum, it contravenes the international safeguards put in place to preserve the rights of the 1948 Palestinian refugees, including UN Resolution 194.

Given the imbalance of power between occupied and occupier, international law and concepts of justice are the last refuges for Palestinian negotiators. But in the same discussions, their preferred interlocutor, Tzipi Livni, made it clear that she values neither:

Livni: I was the Minister of Justice. I am a lawyer ... But I am against law – international law in particular. Law in general.[31]

In spite of this, the senior PA leadership time and again demonstrated their affinity for negotiating with members of the Kadima Party—in particular, with Tzipi Livni. Ahmed Qurei even goes so far as

---

30 http://www.ajtransparency.com/files/2309.pdf
31 http://www.ajtransparency.com/files/2003.pdf

to tell Livni (in the run-up to the 2008 Kadima primaries) that, were he able, "I would vote for you."[32]

Support by the occupied for the occupier is a recurring theme throughout the Palestine Papers. Clearly Livni's belief in her powers of persuasion was audacious; she demanded that the Palestinians give up their rights willingly. Best reflected in the Livni quote below, it was an assertion made on more than one occasion, to various PLO negotiators:

> **Livni:** In order to create your state you have to agree in advance with Israel—you choose not to have the right of choice afterwards. These are the basic pillars.[33]

The tenor of Israel as a Jewish-only state set the tone for later discussions on the fate of Palestinian refugees. Of the more than 280 meetings held during the Annapolis process, the refugee file garnered the least enthusiasm and attention from the Palestinian Authority. While PLO executives were designated to chair various committees— from Culture of Peace to Legal and Security—there were no volunteers for the refugee file.

The Papers suggest this lack of concern was symptomatic of the PA's predetermination that the refugee file would be the biggest loser. Indeed, given the remarkable concessions entertained, it is no surprise that few officials were willing to put their names beside it.

Considered one of the most sensitive core issues, refugee claims strike at the competing narratives over Israel's creation, and raise the question of whether the state was created on the backs of Palestine's indigenous population.

Setting aside historical sensitivities, international law and UN Resolution 194 provide Palestinian refugees with an individual Right of Return (or "RoR"). It's a straightforward principle that was successfully applied in several other modern conflicts, from Kosovo to Bosnia to Rwanda. But because the Israelis have hardened their positions over time, the PA appeared to accept defeat. By the time of Annapolis, long gone were the heady days of the January 2001 talks between the PA and Israel at Taba. No longer were the Israelis willing to entertain allowing even 50,000 refugees the right to return for family unification.

---

32   http://www.ajtransparency.com/files/2826.pdf
33   http://www.ajtransparency.com/files/2657.pdf

Refugees were discussed on two parallel tracks during the Annapolis process. Tal Becker and Saeb Erekat held a "virtual" dialogue by exchanging technical drafts, while Mahmoud Abbas and Ehud Olmert negotiated privately. According to the PA's own internal records, the Olmert-Abbas track is best described as an effort to reduce the issue to a number: how many (or how few) Palestinians can be allowed to exercise their Right of Return?

An NSU advisor named Ziyad Clot was assigned to shadow Erekat on the rare occasion when refugees were discussed. According to an internal NSU email contained in the Papers, Clot expressed concerns about the way the PA was negotiating. He wrote how

> "President Abbas offered an extremely low proposal for the number of returnees to Israel a few weeks only after the start of the process. However, in the scope of the Erekat-Becker track, we have not given away anything despite the pressure put by the Israelis, and now the US, and despite a very awkward and dangerous process (these exchanges of papers between Becker & Erekat)."[34]

It is a challenge to determine "how low" the Palestinian Authority was willing to go on the refugee file – but the meticulous records kept within the Palestine Papers make it possible. They give abundant indication that Palestinian refugees were again about to become victimized, this time by their own people.

To accomplish this, the PA agreed to erode the right of return by anointing the United States and select Arab governments as "deciders" on the issue, perhaps to defray the enormous domestic political costs of compromising on refugees ("it's outside our hands!") – even though these third parties have their own agendas.

In my interview with Saeb Erekat, he insisted that the Palestinian Authority did adequately defend the Right of Return:

> **Swisher**: Was the refugee file in any way used as a bargaining chip? **Erekat**: No. **Swisher**: How did you guard from that? **Erekat**: I deal with all issues in accordance with international legality and international law and these are my basis for dealing with Israelis. **Swisher**: Had an agreement been reached, would the Palestinian Diaspora have had a vote or say? **Erekat**: Yes, absolutely. I mean once the refugees are—there's polling outside and that's their right. **Swisher**: And the

---

34   http://www.ajtransparency.com/files/4064.pdf

Israelis were clear on that? **Erekat**: They know it and they know the
negotiator with the PLO because the PLO represents all Palestinians.

But behind closed doors – during a meeting with the Belgian foreign
minister on March 23, 2007 – the PA's own records provide evidence of
how Erekat had once felt otherwise.

> **Erekat:** We will not give up refugees before permanent status nego-
> tiations ...
>
> I never said the Diaspora will vote. It's not going to happen. The
> referendum will be for Palestinians in Gaza, the West Bank and East
> Jerusalem. Can't do it in Lebanon. Can't do it in Jordan.[35]

A year after that telling remark, the PA would find itself fully
engaged in those much sought-after permanent-status talks. In the
early Annapolis talks, though, the only real point of agreement on
the refugee file was hardly a breakthrough: a shared recognition that
people "suffered" as a result of conflict.

This exchange from March 24, 2008, demonstrated one of Israel's
most frequently employed tactics: shifting the discussion away from
the more than 6 million Palestinians made stateless by Israel's territorial conquest and planned expulsions.

> **Livni:** What about the people who suffered from terror attacks, are
> you going to apologize? **Erekat:** We do. We condemn each one. **Livni:**
> People suffer during war. People suffer with their lives. They die. We
> can relate both of us to the suffering.[36]

The Papers show those converging ideas on "suffering" to be later
included in an offer conveyed by Ehud Olmert to Mahmoud Abbas. It
was delivered orally and without a traceable paper; and it was appall-
ingly vague, diluting even the most basic refugee rights. The PA later
summarized the offer in an August 31, 2008, confidential memo:

Refugees

1   Israel would <u>acknowledge the suffering of – but not responsibility
for – Palestinian refugees</u> (language is in the preamble). In parallel,
there must also be a mention of Israeli (or Jewish) suffering.

---

35   http://www.ajtransparency.com/files/5177.pdf
36   http://www.ajtransparency.com/files/2437.pdf

2   Israel would take in 1,000 refugees per year for a period of 5 years on "humanitarian" grounds. In addition, programs of "family reunification" would continue.

3   Israel would contribute to the compensation of the refugees through the mechanism and based on suffering.

4   Not clear what the heads of damage for compensation would be, just that there would be no acknowledgement of responsibility for the refugees, and that compensation, and not restitution or return (apart from the 5,000), would be the only remedy.[37]

On September 16, 2008, lawyers from the PLO's Negotiation Support Unit supplied Abbas with detailed questions for Olmert, which subsequently went unanswered:

> What does it mean to acknowledge the suffering of refugees, without reference to responsibility? How is that different from acknowledging the suffering of people as a result of, say, a natural disaster? How do you propose to deal with the issue of responsibility?
>
> If you recognise suffering, why do you refuse to deal with compensation for non-material damages?
>
> Why is the suffering of Israelis relevant to the refugee issue?
>
> Regarding the 1000 annually for 5 years: while we agree to negotiate the number of returnees in consideration of Israel's capacity of absorption, this offer is not serious and cannot be accepted.[38]

Apart from the Olmert-Abbas discussions, Erekat shared with Tal Becker his thoughts on where the real "progress" on refugees would be made—again reinforcing that the PA wanted to mortgage less contentious issues against the rights of the often voiceless Palestinian refugees:

> **Erekat**: The decisions will be left to the leaders. Ehud Olmert and Abu Mazen have been discussing the returns. I think we have worked constructively. The refugee issue is part of the package and linked to the resolution of the other files. We are set on a text. This will all fall together once there is the package. I am fine, unless there is any other question?[39]

---

37   http://www.ajtransparency.com/files/4736.pdf
38   http://www.ajtransparency.com/files/3294.pdf
39   http://www.ajtransparency.com/files/3651.pdf

As the Bush Administration was pressing the PA leadership hard to forgo the right of return, Erekat confided to Becker his strategy:

> **Erekat**: Recognition of responsibility is a bilateral issue. I don't want the Americans to be involved in this. <u>These are my bargaining chips</u>. **Becker**: Our respective narratives cannot be reconciled. You think you are the victims. We think we are the victims.[40]

Determining what number Olmert offered in the final months of the Annapolis process is difficult, but not impossible, to estimate. In a June 16, 2009, briefing for his legal advisors, Erekat stated how:

> **Erekat:** "Olmert accepted 1000 refugees annually for the next 10 years."[41]

Hardly a generous proposal – yet if one follows elsewhere in the Papers how Erekat described the progress during Annapolis on refugees to Senator Mitchell, one gets the impression it may have been close enough:

February 27, 2009

> **Erekat to Mitchell:** <u>On refugees, there were discussions on numbers that will return to Israel over a number of years. The deal is there</u>. With it you can develop the 'Obama plan' with your associates in Europe. Abbas can call for an emergency Arab/Islamic summit and submit to them the offer, and tell them: 'you decide with me.' <u>I think they will go with it, like with the Arab Peace Initiative</u> (which now nobody can talk about) ... 42

October 21, 2009

> **Erekat to Mitchell:** I want to point out I am answering in my personal capacity on these questions. Nineteen years after the start of the process, it is time for decisions. Negotiations have been exhausted. We have thousands of pages of minutes on each issue. The Palestinians know they will be a country with limitations. They won't be like Egypt or Jordan. They won't have an army, air force or navy, and will have a third party to monitor ... <u>Palestinians will need to know that 5 million refugees will not go back.</u> The number will be agreed as one of the options. <u>Also the number returning to their own state</u>

---

40 http://www.ajtransparency.com/files/3284.pdf
41 http://www.ajtransparency.com/files/4660.pdf
42 http://www.ajtransparency.com/files/4449.pdf

will depend on annual absorption capacity. There will be an international mechanism for resettling in other countries or in host states, and international mechanism for compensation. All these issues I've negotiated. They need decisions.[43]

Nearly a year later, on January 15, 2010 – even though there were no direct talks with the Netanyahu government, only "proximity talks" – Erekat gave an exhausted reply to Ambassador Hale:

Erekat: What is in that paper gives them the biggest Yerushalaim in Jewish history, symbolic number of refugees return, demilitarized state ... What more can I give?[44]

The answer, Erekat knows, is that he won't have to give anything more; the Americans and international community will do it for him. As the Annapolis process continued, the United States began to act aggressively to push the PA to drop refugee claims, as advocated in this July 16, 2008, exchange with Secretary Rice:

Rice: If you want to talk about responsibility it is the responsibility of the international community, not Israel. They created Israel. [**Zeinah Salahi** argues that Israeli actions post-statehood are clearly their responsibility. This is dismissed by Rice.] **Rice:** Responsibility is a loaded term. [Notes the example of reparations for slavery in the United States.] I've always objected to it. It's not forward looking. Would I personally be better off? I don't know. But I do support affirmative action. ... Bad things happen to people all around the world all the time. You need to look forward. The first compensation is a state. Second is that the world and Israel accepts that the Palestinians need help to get back on their feet.[45]

It is breathtaking to read these words of an American Secretary of State who appears to believe the regular denial by Israeli spokesmen of the 'ethnic cleansing' of the Palestinians, which has been exposed over the last fifteen years by the meticulous research of Israeli academics.

As we have already seen, the State of Israel brands itself a "Jewish State," hoping to use the creation of a Palestinian state to rid itself of its Arab and Muslim citizens. At the same time, the amount of land

---

43   http://www.ajtransparency.com/files/4899.pdf
44   http://www.ajtransparency.com/files/5012.pdf
45   http://www.ajtransparency.com/files/2942.pdf

available to Palestinians is constantly shrinking as a result of Israel's illegal, Jewish-only settlement construction.

And so the PA began to warn during the Annapolis process that it would impose its own restrictions on refugees wishing to live in the state of Palestine, subject to that state's "absorption capacity." As one PLO lawyer confided to me, the PA's leadership feared the West Bank could become a "New Gaza," an area overcrowded with people and lacking proper infrastructure.

The PA's concern – that Palestine, not Israel, would have to absorb the vast majority of refugees – was not unfounded. From the start of the Annapolis process, PA officials accepted that they could not move Israeli public opinion toward accepting a right of return. Livni summarized Israeli sentiment in this January 22, 2008, meeting with Abu Ala:

> **Livni:** I don't want to deceive anybody. There'll be no Israeli official whether from the Knesset or the government or even the public who will support the return of refugees to Israel. There are many people in the world who are ready to contribute to the issue of refugees, and I'm not talking about Saudi Arabia but about [Microsoft Founder Bill] Gates and his like.[46]

Perhaps more ambitious than recruiting Bill Gates, both Israel and the PA began to see the United States as final arbiter of the refugee calamity.

As in other post-conflict settlements, an international mechanism would be required to help implement the Right of Return for Palestinians. For Israelis, then, the goal became to have the United States act in their interest. The United States—rather than Israel—could sit with the concerned parties, namely the Palestinians and countries with refugee populations (like Jordan, Syria, and Lebanon). In other words, America would be the one to haggle with the Arabs and the international community over how and to what extent refugee rights would be fulfilled.

At least initially, Erekat expressed some concern about giving the United States a lead role on the refugee issue. Here's what he said in an August 28, 2008, meeting:

> **Erekat:** The "US leadership" you propose is problematic for us. We

---

46   http://www.ajtransparency.com/files/2304.pdf

have not agreed internally to it. There is some debate amongst us: some would favor such leadership; others are much more reluctant ... I don't say no to the US leadership. But it remains to be defined and I would need some guarantees. We don't want to alienate anybody. We met with the French. The EU may offer to contribute financially. The parties can agree on who will drive the international mechanism: the PLO, the US and Israeli will decide. But you have to understand that we are under enormous pressure, especially on this file. **Becker**: You can take the pressure. **Erekat**: Me, yes. But think about the others.[47]

Erekat took just three days to come around to the Israeli idea. But it did not pass without internal controversy. Erekat never shared with his legal team his intention to subcontract the refugee file to the United States. His fellow negotiators believed it was because Erekat knew they would oppose the move as a travesty for refugees. That quickly became evident in the meeting of August 31, 2008. After hashing out the general "articles" that define the refugee problem, Ziyad Clot (the lawyer accompanying Erekat) moved to start discussing the final parameters that would go in the actual "treaty." It would include critical details: how much money would be paid to refugees as compensation, for example, and the actual number of refugees who could return.

As soon as the discussion headed in this direction, the note taker observes Erekat leaving the room. The exchange, while technical, is worth quoting in full:

> [**Erekat** leaves the room to take a phone call]
>
> **Tal Becker**: Did we agree to "as detailed in the Treaty"?
>
> **Ziyad Clot**: No. We suggest replacing "Article" by "Treaty" here. It is in line with your demand to have the "Article" or the "Agreement" replaced by the "Treaty" elsewhere. The Treaty being the comprehensive legal instrument, we have to refer to it.
>
> **Becker**: (showing signs of irritation): So you have inserted a reference to the Treaty without our agreement?
>
> **Clot:** This is just a proposal ...
>
> **Becker**: All our obligations [meaning Israeli obligations] relating to refugees will be included in this Article. <u>We are not going to discuss refugees further after that. This is what we have agreed with Saeb.</u>

---

47   http://www.ajtransparency.com/files/3284.pdf

Clot: I am not sure I get your point.

Becker: This article deals with all the issues that are bilateral. <u>The Israelis will not have any further involvement in the refugee file after that. The process will then become multilateral. This is why we want the US to be involved. They will then lead the process.</u>

Clot: I thought the common understanding was that we were currently discussing the framework/the principles of the agreement on refugees and that a negotiation round on the details of the agreement would follow?

Becker: No, this is unrealistic. We have agreed on this with Saeb Erekat.

Clot: Well, if this is the case, it doesn't make any sense. The current document we are discussing is totally irrelevant without a complementary agreement on the details. In such case, all the commitments taken by Israel would become in reality vague engagements which could not be enforced as such. How could I know on the basis of this document what will be Israel's financial contribution? You will agree to pay some money, without taking any real commitment as to the amount, and then the international community will be asked to cover most of the expenses. Is it the idea? Technically, you will have a bilateral declaration of principles that will be imposed on the participants of a multilateral track? Do you expect us and other stakeholders to accept this? Have you thought about this seriously?

Becker (annoyed): The next process could also be trilateral [with the US].

Clot: If the two parties are serious about this option they should start thinking about the technical, legal, and practical implications of this choice. We should list all issues that are clearly bilateral and make sure they are agreed on before any next step is taken.

[Erekat comes back in the room. Clot explains what the Israelis have just explained and asks if we have agreed on their proposal regarding the process. No clear answer.][48]

Whether or not Erekat's PLO colleagues agreed with this compromise, the logic was apparent: a US-imposed verdict on the right of return would offer the Palestinian Authority a way to save face. Similarly, for the Israelis, it would allow them to tell the world they had negotiated in good faith – despite never acknowledging any responsibility and never agreeing to pay a single penny. They could thus uphold

---

48   http://www.ajtransparency.com/files/3284.pdf

their domestic slogan: that they admitted nothing and that no Palestinian refugees would ever have the right to return to their homes.

Given the close US-Israeli relationship, the jury would be rigged
from the start. With its invasion of Iraq and the displacement of
millions, the United States, with no apparent sense of irony, even
acknowledged its familiarity with handling the outcome of Arabs
forced to flee their homes. But America's trademark "creativity" would
hardly satisfy any semblance of justice sought by Palestine's refugees,
regardless of the wild solutions it imagined.

> **Rice**: Also, there is a question of if the compensation will go to the
> refugees or to the states. If the US is going to have a major role, we
> have a problem with funding the states for refugees. Jordan now we
> are paying for some of the Iraqi refugees, through helping to cover
> some of the costs ...
>
> ... Maybe we will be able to find countries that can contribute in kind.
> Chile, Argentina, etc. (i.e. give land) ... [49]

4. Security

With increased intensity, successive US administrations, with
European complicity, have pushed to ensure that the State of Palestine, if born, will emerge as a "pro-Western" body that is both authori-
tarian and repressive. To satisfy international pressure, the Palestinian
Authority has, according to its own records, killed its own people (both
independently and with Israeli forces), arrested thousands, tortured
Hamas members and other supporters of resistance, and suppressed
religious activity. This has come at the same time as America
outwardly committed its national resources, both through diplomacy
and war, to the idea of democracy promotion and human rights in the
Arab and Muslim world. Reporting on September 17, 2009, to Senator
Mitchell's staff on the PA's efforts to improve "security," Erekat made
the following admissions:

> **Erekat**: We have had to kill Palestinians to establish one authority,
> one gun and the rule of law. We continue to perform our obligations
> ... We have invested time and effort and even killed our own people
> to maintain order and the rule of law. The PM is doing everything

---

49   http://www.ajtransparency.com/files/2797.pdf

possible to build the institutions. We are not a country yet but we are the only ones in the Arab world who control the Zakat and the sermons in the mosques. We are getting our act together.[50]

Since 2001, the United States has sent as envoys a senator, a CIA director, an ambassador, and six generals with the mission of either "calming" the violence on the ground or, more recently, standing up Palestinian Security Forces to "provide law and order." The rationale for these various missions was supposedly premised on readying the Palestinian Authority as a capable partner able to enforce a peace agreement, as the United States and the Quartet were promising that a Palestinian state was around the corner:

In 2003, the Roadmap projected the creation of a Palestinian State by 2005.

In 2007, the Annapolis Summit envisioned Palestine by 2008. In 2010, the Obama Administration said Palestine would be created by 2011.

Just as that goal has proved elusive, the PA has nonetheless pursued a campaign against its own people as the Israeli occupation both intensified and expanded to levels that may have rendered Palestinian statehood impossible. The cumulative body of the Papers shows how the so-called mission of "establishing rule of law" has become a codeword for suppressing Hamas, the Islamist organization that won elections in 2006. The PA leadership has adopted these practices with the intent of ensuring its own political survival, motivated largely by the need to keep open the spigot of European and American funds channeled toward the favored Fateh Party. Apparently lost on the PA was the fact that never in the history of armed conflict has an occupied people achieved their liberation by abandoning all forms of resistance and collaborating with the occupier.

The Palestine Papers provide ample evidence to support these findings, revealing that the PA's *raison d'etre* has shifted from its founding purpose of liberating occupied Palestine to crushing its political rivals. Activities once considered inconceivable in a culture that is family- and clan-based have by 2011 become the norm. While repressive measures were encouraged during the Oslo process of the

---

50   http://www.ajtransparency.com/files/4827.pdf

1990s, following 9/11 and the so-called "Global War on Terror," they were vastly expanded and are today systemic.

From 2001 until present, the Palestinian Security Forces have gone from being accused by Israel and the West of complicity in terrorism against Israel to bringing terror against its own people. This was clearly reflected in a conversation between US Security Coordinator Lt. General Keith Dayton and Saeb Erekat on June 24, 2009.

> **Dayton**: By the way, the intelligence guys are good. The Israelis like them. They say they are giving as much as they are taking from them – but they are causing some problems for international donors because they are torturing people. Hamas does it.
>
> **Erekat:** That is not an excuse.
>
> **Dayton:** I've only started working on this very recently. I don't need to tell you who was working with them before.[51]

According to a September 2008 summary of a conversation between General Dayton and Prime Minister Salaam Fayyad, the Israeli occupying forces had begun to see the Palestinian Authority as a partner because of the latter's performance on American-inspired efforts in the West Bank areas they controlled:

> "Dayton noted the beginning of a shift in Israeli perception of Palestinian security performance. Salaam Fayyad concurred adding that Barak told him [IDF Chief of Staff General Gabi] Ashkenazi is no longer skeptical about the utility of cooperation with the PA on security matters."[52]

The Palestinian Authority laid out the extent of its cooperation with Israel in a confidential memo it gave Middle East envoy George Mitchell in June 2009. Among the actions the PA highlighted:

Arrested approximately 3,700 members of armed groups;

Summoned around 4,700 individuals for questioning about various offences, including affiliations with armed groups;

Confiscated over 1,100 weapons;

---

51   http://www.ajtransparency.com/files/4676.pdf
52   http://www.ajtransparency.com/files/3251.pdf

Seized over 2,500,000 NIS [shekels] belonging to armed groups;

Confiscated numerous materials used to incite violence.[53]

Israeli Foreign Minister Tzipi Livni noted on March 31, 2008, the extent of the close cooperation—a sharp departure from the height of the second intifada, just a few years earlier, when Palestinian Security Forces were themselves targeted by the Israelis.

> **Livni:** The situation in the West Bank is under control since we are there and because we are working together. We must prevent what took place in the Gaza Strip from taking place in the West Bank.[54]

The Papers corroborate the above as a sentiment shared between the officials responsible for maintaining said security cooperation. This May 2008 exchange is from a meeting in Tel Aviv between the PA's West Bank Police Chief Hazem Atallah, Amos Gilad, director of Israeli military intelligence, and Yohav Mordechai, the Shin Bet (Israel's General Security Service) official responsible for the Occupied Territories.

> **Gilad:** You have internal factional problems with Fayyad. **Yohav Mordechai**: [to Dajani] This is between us, don't write it down. **Rami Dajani**: These notes are confidential. ... **Atallah**: Jenin is the test that we are serious. In Qabatya today when someone shot at the NSF, they shot back. That is the way, they have to learn to respect the authority of the Palestinian security forces. I understand human rights, but this is not Switzerland. We need to take decisive measures. **Gilad**: I agree – freedom is not chaos ("fauda-stan"). It's like in the Quran: the straight path ... **Atallah**: Or else it's the fire.[55]

What in part took the Palestinian Security Forces from being hunted and killed by Israeli forces in 2002 to full partner and friend by 2008 was strong security collaboration, including an operational willingness by the Palestinian Authority to kill their own people—regardless of political faction—at a time when there were no credible political negotiations.

The seeds of this clandestine partnership were laid bare in a summer 2005 joint committee meeting on fugitives in Tel Aviv between Israeli Defense Minister Shaul Mofaz and PA Minister of

53   http://www.ajtransparency.com/files/4641.pdf
54   http://www.ajtransparency.com/files/2454.pdf
55   http://www.ajtransparency.com/files/2520.pdf

Interior Nasr Yusuf. Al Jazeera obtained handwritten notes in Arabic revealing their exchange on a plan to kill a Palestinian resistance fighter named Hassan Madhoun, a member of the Al Aqsa Martyrs Brigades from Gaza.[56]

> **Mofaz:** Hassan Madhoun—we know his address and (Preventative Security Organization Chief, Gaza) Rasheed abu Shabak knows that. Why don't you kill him? Hamas fired because of the elections and this is a challenge to you and a warning to Abu Mazen. **Yusuf:** We gave instructions to Rasheed [Abu Shabak] and will see. **Mofaz:** Since we spoke, he has been planning an operation, and that's 4 weeks ago, and we know that he wants to strike Qarni or Eretz. He is not Hamas and you can kill him. **Yusuf:** We work, the country is not easy, our capabilities are limited, and you haven't offered anything. **Mofaz:** I understand that nothing has been accomplished in the Strip. **Yusuf:** Don't you acknowledge the effort made? And what of the decline? **Mofaz:** There is an increase in violence. Non-adherence to Sharm. **Yusuf:** You have not implemented Sharm for 3 months, and if we continue at this pace, we would not get anywhere.[57]

The above cooperation could only have been executed with the endorsement of the PA leadership, including President Mahmoud Abbas, and other Executive Committee members of the dominant Palestinian Liberation Organization. Note this exchange between President Abbas and Prime Minister Ariel Sharon at the latter's Jerusalem residence in June 2005. Abbas noted:

> ... with pleasure that the fact that Sharon considered him a friend, and the fact that he too considered Sharon a friend, would serve them both in the days ahead.

> Abu Mazen said that Palestinians want peace, and hence, every bullet that is aimed in the direction of Israel is a bullet aimed at the Palestinians as well. It is neither in the Palestinian interest, nor in the Israeli interest, to persist with violence.[58]

The fact that Abbas considered Ariel Sharon – considered by many Palestinians as 'the Butcher of Shatilla' – as a friend and would

---

56 Madhoun was killed on November 1, 2005 by a missile fired from an Israeli Apache over the skies of Gaza. The attack also killed a wanted Hamas activist.
57 http://www.ajtransparency.com/files/5240.pdf
58 http://www.ajtransparency.com/files/5116.pdf

describe him as such in the presence of PA officials must have helped establish the climate of unwavering collaboration throughout the PLO's ranks. In fact, going by their own language in the Papers, it is clear the PA viewed Hamas as its real enemy, as opposed to Israel who was occupying and confiscating their lands. Consider this description by Ahmed Qurei to Tzipi Livni about the Al Aqsa Martyrs Brigades—a group Fateh supporters had once boasted as its die-hard resistance force against the Israeli occupier:

> **Abu Ala'**: Al-Aqsa Martyrs Brigade is part of Fateh movement and they agreed to be part of the current security apparatus, even though this was not my position when I was a prime minister. I wanted the Brigade to remain as it was to confront Hamas.[59]

With this level of cooperation, it's little wonder the Palestinian Authority was also receptive to outside training and advice, which the United States and its European allies were only too eager to provide. All that was needed was to memorialize the arrangement into a formal treaty—preferably in a secret annex—as suggested in this June 24, 2008, meeting:

> **Rice:** ... Then Palestinians will know what they need to do, etc. In our experience, fighting terrorism is about the civil and the military working together. **Qurei:** ... I commit myself to fight terror – but how is not to be in the agreement. **Rice:** I want to understand. We have this kind of an agreement with Iraq and with Afghanistan. Why would you not define what it means to fight terror? **Qurei:** We agree to fight it – but ten pages of details on it should not be in the agreement. **Dekel:** We have with Egypt a security appendix.
>
> **Livni**: [If it's about selling it to other people, we can put it in an annex]. **Qurei:** I don't want to hide my obligations! But I can't write in the agreement that we will close shops, etc.[60]

To understand better the scale of the PA's security relationship with Israel and the United States, I spoke on November 4, 2010, with Colonel P.J. Dermer, whose name appeared in the Papers in connection with his service as defense attaché at the US Embassy in Tel Aviv from 2005 to 2007.

---

59   http://www.ajtransparency.com/files/2312.pdf
60   http://www.ajtransparency.com/files/2797.pdf

Dermer: Washington wanted something done about Hamas. No doubt about it. Now whether they were going to get that done through Dayton, the Palestinians via the Dayton mission, is another question. Did it come on the table? Of course it did ... This is the post 9/11 era. Hamas was all things evil.[61]

The United States publicly describes its US Security Coordinator (USSC) mission as increasing the capacity and professionalism of the PA security forces, improving their command structure and lines of authority. But several of their private conversations, including this one between General Dayton and Saeb Erekat, show that tough PA action was at a premium—whether or not it came at the expense of long-term goals like unitary command structure.

Dayton: The same problems with the intelligence units. The Preventative Security Organization reports to the Minister of Interior, but the General Intelligence [Service] reports to the president. The police: Hazem Attalah works on his own – like he has his own Ministry of Interior. I've said "good for him" – at least he's doing things that need to be done.

Erekat: Hazem is great. I told the president to promote him. I nominated him to take on the security file in the permanent-status negotiations. I think he should be Minister of Interior. I supported him on that. But I can see how he is working on his own.[62]

Part of what further morphed the USSC's already ill-defined 2005 creation was the January 2006 electoral victory of the Hamas movement, and the subsequent formation of a National Unity Government between Fateh and Hamas. Colonel Dermer remembered the US government's reaction well:

Dermer: I watched the sheer reversal and terror coming out of Washington to Tel Aviv and Jerusalem—"Oh my God, what happened? Why didn't we know?" Number one. Number two, "We can't let this stand. We got to do something about Hamas." Out of the blue. And in the middle of all of this was the USSC. This was not a USSC issue. This was a political issue. But of course, with General Dayton being on the

---

61   In 2010, Dermer penned an important and authoritative scholarly article on his impressions of the PA security performance in the Journal of Palestine Studies. It can be found at http://www.palestine-studies.org/files/pdf/jps/10706.pdf.
62   http://www.ajtransparency.com/files/4676.pdf

ground, and this is a very bad habit of Washington—Washington has an age-old habit of having somebody on the ground for reason A, but the fact that he's there, he ends up getting reason B, C, and D out of nowhere—without any preparation, any training, any in-depth discussion, anything. The mere fact that you're on the ground means that we need you to tackle this.

At the highest levels of the US government—in both the Bush and Obama administrations—the Papers show it was made abundantly clear to senior PA officials that there was no acceptable Palestinian leadership *except* for Mahmoud Abbas and Prime Minister Salaam Fayyad. The latter was educated on this according to a November 2008 email recapping his discussion with then-Assistant Secretary of State David Welch and Jonathon Schwartz, the State Department Legal Advisor.

> **Welch**: The new U.S. Administration [of President Obama] expects to see the same Palestinian faces (Abu Mazen and Salaam Fayyad) if it is to continue funding the Palestinian Authority.[63]

Indeed, that level of commitment to specific Palestinian personalities continued, as shown in this October 2009 meeting between Secretary of State Hillary Clinton, Middle East envoy George Mitchell, and Saeb Erekat, at one of the many moments when President Abbas was contemplating resignation.

> **Hillary Clinton:** Abu Mazen not running in the election is not an option—there is no alternative to him.[64]

The United States also involved itself to the point of regulating internal PA tensions to ensure that neither Abbas nor Fayyad would upset the other's standing in their own eyes. Though General Dayton's remit was not supposed to be political, in September 2007 he used unequivocal terms to spell out the consequences of defying the United States:

> **Dayton**: There are rumors in the US that Fateh old guard are undermining Fayyad. As much as President Bush thinks Abu Mazen is important, without Fayyad, the US will lift its hand from the PA and give up on Abu Mazen.[65]

---

63 http://www.ajtransparency.com/files/4252.pdf
64 http://www.ajtransparency.com/files/4905.pdf
65 http://www.ajtransparency.com/en/document/1941

ANALYSIS

The disappointment US officials felt following the 2006 Hamas election victory is by now well known. What was less appreciated prior to release of the Papers, however, was the extent to which the Bush administration relied on the PA for information on a group it refused to meet with. This July 17, 2005, tutorial between Erekat and US Assistant Secretary David Welch tells it well, and even suggests the United States consulted the PA on how best to punish its political rival:

> **Ereket**: Hamas cannot win if we get our act together.
>
> **Welch**: Tell me why you object to Hamas winning.
>
> **Erekat:** They won in Qalqilya, where they prevented this young singer from performing. The real fight for a social way of life. We cannot be silent anymore. Islamic Jihad and Hamas – these are not political parties but act as a parallel authority.
>
> **Welch**: Is Islamic Jihad strong in the West Bank?
>
> **Erekat**: No.
>
> **Welch**: So, why isn't the PA acting against them here?
>
> **Erekat**: I talked to Nasr Yousef about this. He says he does not have the bullets to fight them for even 10 minutes.
>
> **Welch**: Are there any circumstances where you could define criteria for their participation [in the political process]?
>
> **Erekat**: They should not have guns.
>
> **Welch**: Do you know who is a member of Hamas and who is not?
>
> **Erekat**: No.
>
> **Welch**: Do they have a list?
>
> **Erekat**: Hamas is very organized and structured. They must keep some sort of list.
>
> **Welch**: What do you think of the EU's criteria for contacts with Hamas? (1) accept Israel's right to exist (2) renounce terrorism and violence (3) [in the meantime] contacts are solely for elections purposes.
>
> **Erekat**: I met with Ismail Hanieh and asked him, "Are you a political party or a parallel authority? If you're a political party, I'm happy to talk to you. But if you're a parallel authority, I cannot." If the Europeans can convince Hamas to respect the rule of law, this would be even better. A policy of zero-tolerance for multiple authorities is the most crucial.

Welch: Is there an effective way for the U.S. to orient its assistance programs so as not to support Hamas? For example, in a case where you know a mayor of a town is Hamas, how do you distinguish between helping the people of that town on one hand and the obvious political benefit to the Hamas mayor on the other?

Erekat: As long as you don't deny that assistance, you can always find others to coordinate it with – like the governor, for example.[66]

Despite crippling economic sanctions, political isolation, and Israel's punishing Cast Lead assault on the Gaza Strip, none of the US, Israeli, Egyptian and PA-led efforts to eliminate Hamas from Palestinian politics succeeded. Even with the election of President Obama and the appointment of George Mitchell as envoy, who had engaged with armed resistance groups during his experience as a mediator in the Northern Ireland conflict, the PA continued following America's lead down the same road of fighting Hamas, sapping its own energy and further dividing its people amid continued Israeli colonization. All of this came at a time when Fateh leaders were publicly calling for unity talks with Hamas, pledging to put their differences aside for the greater good of Palestine.

October 2, 2009

Mitchell: I talked to [Egyptian Intelligence Chief] Omar Suleiman last week. We discussed two issues: one, the right to call elections belongs to Abbas, it does not require Hamas agreement; two, whatever is agreed on security forces restructuring ... **Erekat:** Yes – it has to be consistent with the PA Basic Law. **Mitchell**: We made the argument more directly: the PA has done an outstanding job in the West Bank. We are strongly opposed to a situation that gives control over it to Hamas ...

Erekat: Just make sure that you see the material before they [the Egyptians] present it. You know Meshal has been working hard in Cairo.[67]

---

66   http://www.ajtransparency.com/files/5128.pdf
67   http:// www.ajtransparency.com/files/4844.pdf

5. Gaza and the Goldstone Report

Just as the Annapolis negotiations were concluding, in the winter of 2008-9, Israel began a deadly, three-week military offensive against the Gaza Strip. Dubbed "Operation Cast Lead," the air and ground assault killed more than 1,400 Palestinians, including at least 1,000 civilians, 400 of them children. Thirteen Israelis were also killed, including 3 civilians. A UN fact-finding commission headed by Judge Richard Goldstone accused both Israel and Palestinian armed groups of committing war crimes.

In defending their handling of the Gaza War, President Abbas has long held that the PA had warned Hamas—both in Gaza and through its Syrian-based leadership—that Israel was planning an attack on the Strip. Abbas maintained that his information was based on Israeli press reports rather than specific information. On November 5, 2010, Dr. Erekat recounted for me his mission to warn the Hamas leadership in the weeks leading up to the attack on Gaza:

> **Saeb Erekat:** I think Abu Mazen took his information from the plan that was published in the Israeli press about attacks from Gaza. There were plans, maps, charts published in the Israeli press and Abu Mazen met with Olmert and Olmert raised the issue of missiles from Gaza and so on and nobody told him. Look, we cannot solve this problem militarily under any circumstances. You tried in Lebanon, please don't do that in Gaza, please. It's a real catastrophe. Gaza has 1.5 million people and it will be a disaster that we cannot bear. The negotiations will go down. And he really spoke to him and spoke to President Bush later and then he sent me to Damascus. I saw General Mohammed Nassif in Damascus. He was my counterpart. I go to Damascus and Jordan and Egypt to share exactly what the negotiation is all about in all files. **Swisher:** What did you tell General Nassif? **Erekat:** Tell Hamas to renew the ceasefire, please. Please. **Swisher:** And was that based on specific information? **Erekat:** No. It was based on what we were ... what we heard from Olmert about the missiles and he cannot stay silent. And also what Abu Mazen read in the newspapers. They showed me plans and I took it with me from the Israeli newspapers. And then when I came back to Amman, I saw Abu Mazen and I told him they will help. He called President Assad personally on the phone and told him please -- this was the 10th or 11th of December. Just three weeks before the attacks against—aggression against Gaza. We tried to work very hard with the Egyptians. We called the Turks also

on this to convince Hamas to renew their ceasefire but unfortunately we failed. **Swisher:** So at no point did you have any specific information from the Israelis that an attack was imminent? They never came to you and briefed you – **Erekat:** We don't discuss these things, no.

In spite of Erakat's denials, the PA's own records tell a different story. In the presence of his American counterparts on October 21, 2009, Erekat is recorded as telling envoy Mitchell that it was the director of Israeli military intelligence, Amos Gilad, who alerted President Abbas prior to the Gaza attack:

> **Erekat:** Amos Gilad spoke to [Foreign Minister Avigdor] Lieberman – told them about the claim that Abu Mazen was colluding with them in the Gaza war. He went to Abu Mazen before the attack and asked him. Abu Mazen replied that he will not go to Gaza on an Israeli tank. Gilad testified about that. He was honest. So we can maintain the channel.[68]

The Papers also provide overwhelming evidence that Amos Gilad, who continues to serve the Israeli government as an advisor to Defense Minister Ehud Barak, held several conversations with PA negotiators on the situation in Gaza prior to Cast Lead.

In this Annapolis negotiation on March 31, 2008, with the PA present, Amos Gilad and then-Foreign Minister Tzipi Livni foreshadowed a tragedy in the making:

> **Livni:** Israel does not want Hamas. We cannot accept to have an Islamic regime on our borders. This contradicts our strategic vision.
>
> **Gilad:** My personal opinion, and I do not represent the government in this, is that sooner or later we will collide with Hamas because they are like Hezbollah, continue to build their military capacities. We will clash with them but we will not stay in the Gaza Strip.
>
> **Livni:** The last sentence represents the position of the government.
>
> **Qurei:** You said that Israel is not negotiating with Hamas, but how do you see Hamas if the situation continues as it is now?
>
> **Gilad:** The West Bank is coming and this is Hamas's strategic goal. We are not negotiating with them, but we allow the entry of food and fuel into the Gaza Strip for humanitarian reasons. My strategic advice for you is to be ready. It is like Achilles' heel; if the situation goes on as

---

68   http://www.ajtransparency.com/files/4899.pdf

it is for a year or two more, you will become weaker and Hamas will have control over the West Bank. They in Hamas understand the situation and they are fearful ... [69]

The Israelis had earlier raised with Qurei and other PA officials specific ways that the siege in Gaza could be tightened in order to undermine Hamas. In fact, in a February 4, 2008, meeting, it was Qurei who actually suggested the Israelis "re-occupy" portions of the Strip. Just ten days earlier, Hamas had blown a hole in the Rafah crossing in order to allow its starving residents to cross into Egypt to buy food and supplies. A glimpse of how Israel and the PA reacted during their Annapolis talks:

Livni: Did the opening of the borders appear to be a victory for Hamas?

Qurei: Yes, they appeared to have ended the siege.

Livni: The Egyptians don't do enough, and we're sure they can do much more.

Qurei: What can you do about Philadelphia Crossing?

Livni: We're not there.

Qurei: You've re-occupied the West Bank, and you can occupy the crossing if you want.

Livni: We can re-occupy the Gaza Strip. What is your position?

Qurei: Our strategic position is that we want a state in the West Bank and the Strip with a safe passage.[70]

Qurei was not the only senior PLO Executive Committee member complaining that sanctions against the Strip were not strong enough. In that same series of October 2009 meetings. Erekat recounted to Mitchell his disagreements with Amos Gilad—as well as the Egyptian government—on Gaza policy.

Erekat: Senator. I am just briefing you on my meetings with the Israelis. I am not giving you a message. They were good meetings. I told AG: you are Egypt's man. You know the Egyptians. 11 kms! What's going on with you and the US, the $23 million and ditches – it's business as usual in the tunnels – the Hamas economy ... AG started laughing!

---

69   http://www.ajtransparency.com/files/2454.pdf
70   http://www.ajtransparency.com/files/2312.pdf

Mitchell: What did he say?

Erekat: They don't want to say anything negative about Egypt. It's their strategic relation with them. But they make me pay the price. I am no longer there. I am not alone responsible for the coup d'etat in Gaza.[71]

The injustices by the PA against the people of Gaza only intensified following Israel's Cast Lead. On September 15, 2009, Judge Richard Goldstone presented the Goldstone Fact Finding Report to the international community, recommending that both parties initiate credible and independent investigations into suspected war crimes. On October 2, 2009, the Palestinian Authority controversially took part in a move to delay a resolution vote to endorse the Goldstone findings in the Geneva-based UN Human Rights Council.

The PA had come under considerable pressure in the weeks preceding the October 2 vote. Amid widespread public backlash at the PA decision, in both the West Bank and Gaza, the PA went on to investigate their own causes for dropping the vote, later admitting they had made "mistakes." Here is how Saeb Erakat described it in his interview with me:

Swisher: Of course there was a lot of controversy generated after the Gaza war and the Goldstone report and the PLO was criticized for yielding on the UN Human Rights Council's investigation into Judge Goldstone's finding. What was your role in that and what kind of pressures were you facing from the Americans to drop the Goldstone investigation? **Erekat**: I had no role. **Swisher**: Did the Americans ever raise it with you? **Erekat**: I was in Washington at that time and I don't recall that people here raised the issue. It was their team in Geneva that were dealing with the issue. **Swisher**: Senator Mitchell and his team were not pressuring you in any way -- **Erekat**: I'm not -- I did not even talk about it, but the point -- **Swisher**: Not even in private? **Erekat**: Not in private. There is nothing called private.

Once again, the Papers suggest a different set of facts. On October 2, 2009—the date the PA dropped the Goldstone resolution vote in Geneva—Erakat was in Washington attending meetings with the Obama Administration. The Papers reveal the PA had been seeking from Obama a "Terms of Reference" aimed at restarting peace talks with Israel. However, to obtain the terms it wanted—namely, a refer-

---

71   http://www.ajtransparency.com/files/4905.pdf

ence to the 1967 borders as a starting point in the discussion—some actions by the PA would also be required.

So envoy George Mitchell's team presented Erekat with a diplomatic plan known as a "Non Paper," a document not on official US letterhead and one that both parties could deny ever receiving.

Under the heading of "Palestinian Authority Steps," this three-page action list posted the following demand:

> "The PA will help to promote a positive atmosphere conducive to negotiations; in particular during negotiations it will refrain from pursuing or supporting any initiative directly or indirectly in international legal forums that would undermine that atmosphere."[72]

Seeking a ladder to climb down from the widespread international criticism, the PA promised an internal investigation, requesting UN officials to re-examine the Goldstone report. The UN would provide a forum that would give its New York–based diplomats a chance to make televised publicized speeches in support of Goldstone, at a time when many Palestinians around the world believed the PA had done a wholesale selling out of Palestinian rights.

On October 12, from his office in Jericho, Dr. Erekat lobbied the European Union Special Representative Marc Otte to help the PA recover its badly damaged image.

> **Erekat:** Then there is all the Goldstone business. Help us by voting in favour of it, and let it take its course. Support us in Geneva and in the UN Security Council. Benjamin Netanyahu has started again his "no partner" strategy. Abu Mazen is convinced of this. Israel leaked the deferral of the Goldstone report.[73]

The following day, on October 13, 2009, Erekat had this exchange with Robert Serry, the UN Secretary-General's Personal Representative to the PLO.

> **Erekat:** I appreciate what you did ... on Goldstone ... Security Council tomorrow (October 14th). **Serry:** The Security Council will be just a talk. Geneva is the important forum now. The majority in the Security Council want to follow the procedure to go through the [UN] HRC

---

72 http://www.ajtransparency.com/files/4845.pdf
73 http://www.ajtransparency.com/files/4868.pdf

before the [UN] Security Council.[74]

Even though, as Serry noted, the procedurally correct course of action was to pursue Goldstone through the UN Human Rights Council—which the PA had already abandoned—the opportunity for the PA to give speeches on the UN floor clearly had a political appeal. So on October 14, the UN General Assembly began Goldstone talks—nearly 50 presentations—including from the PLO Ambassador to the UN, now supportive of the investigation. On Friday, October 16, the matter was brought to a vote. There was little surprise that the US and 5 others vetoed the resolution, preventing the case from advancing to the UN Security Council, and ultimately, the International Criminal Court.

The following week, on October 21, Erekat was back in Washington for a meeting with Obama National Security Advisor Jim Jones and Special Envoy for the Central Region Dennis Ross. The Papers reveal the following exchange:

> **Jones**: We got the message and we will act on it with urgency. And thank you for what you did a couple weeks ago; it was very coura- geous.

It is hard to imagine what the US National Security Advisor would have thanked Erekat for, given that US policy was publicly opposed to the Goldstone investigation.

Erekat's own legal staff was unaware of whatever backroom deals had been made on Goldstone, though the Papers do provide a poignant legal critique by the NSU of George Mitchell's October 2, 2009 "non-paper" demanding the Goldstone case be dropped. Dated October 18, is worth quoting in full, as the PA could not claim that it did not have solid legal advice:

> As the Palestinian cause is anchored in justice and international law, neither the PNA, nor any party, should be called upon to relinquish its fundamental right to seek recourse and remedies for illegal acts in any legitimate international or domestic legal forum. The inter- national community has regularly demanded that Palestinians use non-violent means of conflict resolution, which would now also be foreclosed if such a demand is made. If the United States and the

---

74   http://www.ajtransparency.com/files/4882.pdf

international community consider that such non-violent avenues are not helpful at this time (despite successful precedents such as the case of Apartheid South Africa), then they need to guarantee a credible political process that would provide Palestinians an alternative manner of securing their rights.

In the quest for a just, durable and peaceful solution to the conflict, ongoing injustices must be properly addressed, and victims must be provided with just and effective remedies. Accountability for humanitarian and human rights violations is not an obstacle to negotiations, but rather a requirement for any such negotiations to truly succeed. For Israel and Palestine to live side by side in peace and security, past and ongoing grievances need to be addressed; unresolved injustices will continue to impact on the lives of the victims and are bound to resurface in the future.[75]

Reacting to the draft in an October 21, 2009, meeting at the State Department, Mitchell offered the following response:

Mitchell: Much of what I read is not controversial. **Erekat**: I disagree for example on the PA steps and not going to international bodies. **Mitchell**: This is only during negotiations. **Erekat**: They won't refrain from doing the illegal things that they do. If they refrain, OK, but they won't. This is my only weapon. We have actions by settlers, attacks, provocations, Al Aqsa, home demolitions, families thrown out of their homes. Either we retaliate in a civilized manner or through violence. Which one should we choose? On going to the UN we always coordinate with you. It's our only weapon. Don't take it away from us. **Mitchell**: But if you have good faith negotiations ... **Erekat**: They have a different interpretation of good faith, if you ever dealt with the Israelis. **Mitchell**: I would agree with Israel if you were negotiating and bringing actions against them it would be in bad faith. **Erekat**: If they don't take illegal measures, I have no complaint. You think I complain for nothing! You know even rabbits have defense mechanisms. Lets say they throw more families out of their homes. They defied you on this, and the UN. **Mitchell**: You can go for a public statement. The ICC is a different thing. **Erekat**: I might go to the General Assembly. **Mitchell**: You would go to the GA if two families are thrown out? **Erekat**: Maybe if it's 50 families.[76]

Erekat makes clear he would go to the UN General Assembly, where speeches can be made, if fifty families were evicted. But the PA would

---

75 http://www.ajtransparency.com/files/4891.pdf
76 http://www.ajtransparency.com/files/4899.pdf

not cast a procedural vote in the Human Rights Council to initiate an investigation into the deaths of more than 1,400 of its people in Gaza.

The Papers also show that the PA sought other possible scapegoats for the Goldstone deferral: to the fifty-seven-member Organization of the Islamic Conference, the non-aligned movement, and top unspecified "Arab states." While they declined to be specific in public, PA officials expressed deep outrage and betrayal to senior members of the Obama administration. In the Papers, Erekat accused some of the PA's (and America's) closest Arab allies, namely, Egypt, Jordan, and Saudi Arabia, of fully collaborating in the decision to postpone the vote.

Erekat told me the Goldstone postponement was agreed by consensus.

> **Swisher:** President Abbas, did he have conversations on it [Goldstone]?
> **Erekat:** I think President Abbas was in touch with his ambassador in Geneva and the consensus was made and it was deferred and we have Abu Mazen showing the tape actually. Now when hell broke loose, overall had—what's going on? Everybody was asserting themselves, all Arab ambassadors that were there, all of them, denied that they were part of the deferral. I said, fine.

That corroborates what Erekat had to say to US Special Envoy Senator George Mitchell behind closed doors on October 20, 2009. Here Erekat revealed the PA's sense of betrayal and outrage, suggesting that other American allies had all along been complicit.

> **Mitchell:** We know how they treated you. **Erekat:** [Egyptian Foreign Minister Ahmed] Abul-Gheit was candid. He said in public "Goldstone finished you. You're finished." Then he goes to Jordan on the 5th with [Jordanian Foreign Minister] Nasser Joudeh, and dares to say Egypt had no knowledge. Then hell broke loose—because this was Egypt ... **Mitchell:** It's not true? **Erekat:** Of course not. [Egyptian Ambassador to the UN] Hisham Bader was in the meeting. They were consulted. We are not even a member. It was the Pakistani who read the resolution on behalf of the three groups. Instead they said Abu Mazen sold out – and the story about Wataniya. I know life's not fair – but this was despicable. The Emir of Qatar going on the phone personally, calling intellectuals telling them to attack Abu Mazen – calling Azmi Bishara and Abdul-Bari Atwan. This is because Abu Mazen wouldn't go and do reconciliation in Qatar like the Lebanese. But there is nothing you can do with Qatar ... **Mitchell:** We do talk to them. **Erekat:** I know it's about interests and your base. They do the

opposite of what you tell them. On Goldstone, we have an internal investigation. It's not about individuals. We could resign if needed. Abu Mazen said the decision was with consultation of all who were there. No one objected. Now they even deny the mere fact they were there ...

Now, we don't want to surprise you. I saw the Israelis, Shimon Peres, on the 4th. Two days ago I met with Amos Gilad and Etan Dangot — delivered a strong message. I told them the hell with you. After nineteen years we are still being taken on a ride. Now you insinuate about Goldstone. You think you can punish Abu Mazen! In no time you will have Aziz Dweik as your partner. Nineteen years of promises and you haven't made up your minds what you want to do with us. Lieberman is too precious — while you have Livni there, the head of the largest Zionist party. Instead you will get Qatar and Iran. Maybe Abdallah can drive Meshal and bring him to you. That's it. Nineteen years. We delivered on our Road Map obligations. Even Yuval Diskin raises his hat on security. But no, they can't even give a six-month freeze to give me a fig leaf to see, to find out, what we can do ... on swaps, but no. You don't see me on the same ship. Your focus is on PR, quick news, and we're cost free. You know my word is nothing compared to you, in Congress. What good am I if I'm the joke of my wife, if I'm so weak.[77]

The passion and the anger and the frustration that other Palestinians might have expressed sooner was coming out at last. But it seems it was too little, too late to save the so-called Peace Talks, which since that time sank into the sands of Israeli intransigence and U.S. acquiescence.

---

77 http://www.ajtransparency.com/files/4905.pdf

The
Palestine Papers

To retrieve these papers as PDF files go to the Al Jazeera web address
printed at the bottom of the first page of each document.

Initials used in the Papers

Initials	Definition
AMA	Agreement on Movement and Access
API	Arab Peace Initiative
BATNA	Best alternative to a negotiated agreement
CBM	Confidence-building measure
CEC	Central Elections Committee
GOI	Government of Israel
I&P	Israeli and Palestinian clauses compared
KSCP	Kerem Shalom crossing point
LO	Liaison office
MB	Muslim Brotherhood
MF	Multi-national force
MFA	Israeli ministry of foreign affairs
NAD	Negotiations affairs department
NSU	Negotiation support unit
NUG	National unity government
PA	Palestinian Authority
PG	Presidential Guard
PLC	Palestinian Leadership Council
PS	Permanent status
PSN	Permanent status negotiations
RCP	Rafah crossing point
RM	Road map
SPB	State with provisional borders
SSR	Security sector reform
SWG	Security working group
TOR	Terms of reference
WG	Working group

	Names of participants, identified by initials
AA	Abu Ala' (Ahmed Qurei)
AB	Azem Bishara
AG	Amos Gilad
AM	Abu Mazen (Mahmoud Abbas)
ARY	Gen. Abdel Razzaq Yahia
BM	Ban Ki-moon
BO	Barack Obama
CR	Condoleezza Rice
DH	David Hale
DR	Dennis Ross
DW	David Welch
GM	George Mitchell
HC	Hillary Clinton
JS	Jonathon Schwartz
KD	Gen. Keith Dayton
KE	Khaled el-Gindy
MD	Mohammad Dahlan
MO	Marc Otte
MR	Mara Rudman
PP	Lt. Gen. Pietro Pistolese
RD	Rami Dajani
RN	Gen. Raji Najami
SA	Samih al-Abed
SE	Saeb Erekat
SF	Salam Fayyad
ST	Shalom Tourgeman
TB	Tal Becker
TL	Tzipi Livni
UD	Udi Dekel
YAR	Yasser Abed Rabbo
ZC	Ziyad Clot
ZS	Zeina Salahi

Meeting Summary
Erekat – Dayton
July 24th, 2007

Attendance: *USSC:*   Gen. Keith Dayton (KD),
Col Lane Lance (LL),
Neil (US consulate),
Tamara (translator)

           Palestinian: Saeb Erekat (SE)
Rami Dajani,
Nizar Farsakh

SE: AM wants to discuss PS issues only and leave all the rest to SF.

       The money the US is thinking of giving is too little. In Wye River Clinton coughed $450 million.

KD: I agree it is peanuts but the money simply is not there with all what is going on in Iraq. MoI is assembling a good team and Blair said he has ways of getting funding.

SE: last 6 weeks we've had the least amount of money transferrals from Arab states. Someone has to tell them something. Egypt is allowing the tunnels to continue. What's this business with the Saudis too? Bandar strikes a deal then Abdallah outmanoeuvres him. These regimes depend on you, how can you

KD: the Saudis do not like Hanieh, Mishal or AM at the moment.

SE: if you work separately from Blair and from the State Department and without AM or SF then all what you do will evaporate.

LL: Blair told us that his idea is to have a security plan within a governance plan within a political plan.

KD: your security forces needed training and organization not ammunition.

       On Bader forces, I do not support it. It is a bad idea. They went down from 2000 to 600 because they were not paid. Their training is zero. And Palestinians in the West Bank see them as Jordanians. I told ARY this and he agrees that these people do not understand the WB and we need people who do.

LL: we put up a plan for a 4-month senior leader course on strategic planning. International experts would come and train in Amman.

SE: do it in Jericho.

KD: Olmert's NSC advisor asked me who replaces Dahlan? Who's the new strong man? And I told him: 'didn't you learn the lesson?' we no longer will deal with strong men, only the minster of interior.

SE: AM asked for cars from the UAE. What are those for?

KD: I know nothing about this. This is like the Bader Brigades, everyone thinks it is a bad idea and he's raising it in every meeting. Who whispers in AM's ear? We need to have a meeting with him.

SE: I suggest you take ARY with you.

Minutes from 7th Negotiation Team Meeting
(In Preparation for Annapolis)
Monday, 12th November 2007, 3h00pm
Crowne Plaza Hotel, West Jerusalem

Attendees:
Palestinian
- Ahmed Querei (AA)
- Yaser Abd Rabbo (YAR)
- Akram Haniyeh (AH)
- Dr. Saadi Kronz (SK)
- Zeinah Salahi (ZS)
- Dr. Saeb Erekat (SE)

Israeli
- FM Tzipi Livni (TL)
- Yoram Turbovich (YT)
- Shalom Turjeman (ST)
- Gen Amos Gilad (AG)
- DG Abromovich (Abr)
- Tal Becker (TB) (Arrived late)
- Alon Bar (AB) (Head of Policy Staff of the Foreign Ministry)

Detailed minutes:

TL:
- [Notes that all parties need to leave early today. TL needs to leave to defend a vote of no confidence in the Knesset due to the negotiations process. AA had to leave to a meeting in Ramallah. She noted that the next meeting should be longer than two hours. She suggests the next day as the best time for the next meeting.]
- Today we should focus on what the issues are and outline where agreement is, and not address what the disagreement is over. We should leave that until the next meeting.
- Tomorrow while we are sitting we can start to draft.
- [Discussion over timing of the meeting tomorrow. Five pm is agreed. Side discussion over possible locations for the meeting.]

AA:
- [Makes point that he was denied from entering Jerusalem yesterday, and that this greatly concerns the Palestinians.]
- I am afraid soon that I will need a visa to enter Jerusalem!

TL:

1

- If we have some items that are agreed we can start drafting tomorrow. Let's not discuss what was not agreed today.
- On the preamble [TL then highlights the key points from the Israeli perspective of the preambular language that was read in earlier meetings. She notes specifically:
  - the Bush vision,
  - the principle of two states for two peoples,
  - language referring to the fact that a future agreement will address all outstanding issues,
  - that the two states will be the homelands of their respective peoples and fulfill their national aspirations, Israel a state for the Jewish people, and Palestine for the Palestinians,
  - the importance of implementation of the Roadmap ["RM"] by both sides.]

SE:

- So basically your preamble [as read at earlier meetings].

TL:

- Not the language. I'm just trying to understand what is not agreed [in principle].

AA:

- There are many things that we don't agree with.

SE:

- We agreed not to exchange drafts.

AA:

- We see three elements in the preamble:
- The Terms of Reference ["TOR"], which will include good words, address the future;
- The two state solution – I think we agreed on this;
- Implementation of the RM. We talked about the first phase – we have the five points.

TL:

- But we couldn't reach and understanding on the TOR? You want to put all the future points in the preamble?

AA:

- Second point, is the core issues;
- Third point is the day after Annapolis – negotiations, the process, timeline etc.

TL:

- We added the role of the international community and the Arab world.

AA:

- We have no problem with these.

2

TL:

- But we have to outline what we agreed. These are the basic parameters/outline of the future agreement. On the TOR -- you say yours, we say ours. We can try to find the common ground.
- 242, 338
- RM and previous agreements
- President Bush's vision [clarifies that this is the vision – not the speech]
- 3 quartet principles – is this agreed?

AH:

- We agreed to present these in another way.

SK:

- This is about the Hamas government!

AA:

- The RM
- The Arab Peace Initiative ["API"] [TL: this is not agreed]
- International Law
- International legitimacy [TL: what does this mean?] Resolutions 242, 338, 1397, 1515, 194
- President Bush's vision

TL:

- President Bush's vision is agreed.
- Now we have the agreed and the not agreed.
- I don't want to go into detail on each one today.
- Now the TORs – agreed and not agreed.
- The two-state solution – this refers to two states for two peoples. We suggested that we refer to it as a fundamental principle. The goal is two nation states, Israel and Palestine living side by side in peace and security [repeats homeland for its people language, that these states would fulfill the national aspirations of their people in their own territory, Palestine for Palestinians, Israel for Jews.] This is what we want. Now what is agreed and what is not?

AH:

- First of all I noticed that Olmert hinted in the Knesset that Palestinians approved, and that Abu Mazen approved [the Jewish state language]. It's not true!

ST:

- I was with him. He didn't say that!

AH:

- That is what is reported in the press.

3

AA:

- This point is fundamental for you. Not to have it is fundamental for us.

TL:

- I read four lines – I want to know what is agreed and what is not.

AA:

- It's not for the Iraqis or the Kuwaitis – we don't need it. Two states with full sovereignty [and all the other attributes of statehood].

TL:

- Why establish a Palestinian state? Because you want self determination which we respect. The conflict is based on [achieving] your national aspirations for your people. [The two] nation states are to give an answer to these aspirations.

YAR:

- Beyond the words we see the problems. First – we don't want to interfere in the nature of the state. We don't want to join the Zionist movement. We want to leave the Arab national movement!

AA:

- [Suggesting language acknowledging the suffering of the people.]

TL:

- But it's not about individual suffering. Line by line [what are the problems] – I really don't understand.

YAR:

- We can't interfere with the nature of the states. [Sovereign states are sovereign states and can do whatever they'd like with their states.] We are sovereign people and don't want to interfere with yours even if you let us! It's your decision – we recognize your state however you want [to define it yourselves].

TL:

- You are referring to the last line as a Jewish state.

YAR:

- No – until we solve the issue of refugees we don't want any sentence to complicate our life. We don't want our intellectuals to debate the true meaning of that sentence.

TL:

- But you want something that says at the end of the road [our goal is] to create a Palestinian state? [The creation of the state is connected to the principle of giving an answer to the national aspirations of the people.] When we talk about the core

4

issues – it's not like we'll erase the refugees. We'll talk about it. [TL again tries to walk through her language sentence by sentence.] So what is the meaning of a state?

AA:

- For Palestinians, to alleviate the suffering – achieve national rights -- we are not here to describe for each state what to do.

TL:

- So what's not agreed is the nature of the state?

AA:

- [Sovereignty over all of the territory and natural resources, viability, independence, etc. this is the language with which we can describe states.]

TL:

- I understand we both know what we are talking about. I just want to list [i.e. what is agreed and what is not agreed] this meeting. You have problems agreeing to the nature of the state of Israel.

YAR:

- We are not against what Israel describes itself as. We just don't want to say it -- we have citizens of Jordanian citizenship. It will create problems. [Continues to explain the problematic nature of defining the nature of a state.]

AA:

- We want a two state solution. [Reiterates traditional language on this, side by side... etc.]

TL:

- Two states for two people.

AA:

- What if we import other people?

TL:

- We respect your right for a state of your own. You should respect mine. Two states for two people. Two nation states. If you cannot say that a Palestinian state answers the national aspirations of the Palestinian people...

AA:

- In a permanent agreement we can say whatever we want. Now we are preparing for Annapolis. Now we are talking about a two state solution. We can elaborate in a permanent agreement. If you want a one state solution, we can discuss that.

AH:

5

- [Raises engagement metaphor.]

SE:

- How can we describe a state without describing its borders!

TL:

- We can say [this description will come to fruition] once we have borders.

SE:

- We have six core issues to solve – Jerusalem, Refugees, Borders, Settlements, Water and of course Security. We cannot solve the problems in a preamble.

TL:

- If we can't say two states for two people then we have a problem. This is not a core issue.

AA:

- There is two states or one state [i.e. there are only two solutions to the conflict].

TL:

- There is also two states with one on the other side of the Jordan [River].

YAR:

- Or three states – Gaza.

AA:

- The two state solution is what we agreed. Since this means sovereignty – two states – we don't want to describe the two states!

TL:

- There is no two states if there is no [two states for] two people.

SE:

- If we want a confederation with Jordan – how is that your business?

TL:

- The historic reconciliation is based on two states for two people. Once we do that you can do whatever you want!

AA:

- In an agreement we don't need it.
- [Notes that he received a visitor today that asked him what a Jewish sate means – did it mean that 1.5million Palestinians would be deported from Israel?] Also – we need to decide refugees.

TL:

6

- This is not about the refugees. 20% [of the state] is Palestinian so [if you ask me] it doesn't affect refugees if it can be 20 or 21. Refugees [will be dealt with as one of] the core issues. Refugees is one of the core issues. Also there are those that say that you don't represent the Israeli Palestinians!

AH:
- Aren't you asking for an end of claims in a permanent agreement?

TL:
- But if a Palestinian state will not answer the questions… we are not talking about end of claims [with this issue].

AA:
- If you insist on this it forces Palestinians back to the one state [solution].

[TL receives a phone call from her son who has recently gotten his first call to the army. She reiterates the importance of making peace for precisely that reason, although it may be too late for her son already.]

AA:
- Our aspirations we will speak about it to our peoples. It is not necessary to speak about it [in the document].

TL:
- This was not agreed at all.
- What you are doing now [is a huge mistake] it's like rejecting the partition plan!

AA:
- 181? If you want we'll put it on the table.

TL:
- But without this sentence – you have your problems we have ours. [Makes point that she can explain away some of the problems by saying that negotiations on the core issues come after Annapolis, etc. implying that this issue cannot be so easily explained away.]

AH:
- [In] the peace treaty there will be a recognition of each state…

TL:
- But this is like agreeing to talk with no idea what the vision is!

YAR:
- Postpone it…

TL:

7

82

- Ok, the RM. Three principles. We have a problem which is the committee.

AA:

- When will the committee meet? [Joking.]

TL:

- We agreed to the Americans the principles that implementation of both sides starting now, that the Americans will be the judge, and that any future agreements are subject to the RM. You asked for the trilateral committee, and we did not agree.

AA:

- Why didn't you agree parallel?

TL:

- Some things in the RM [are not parallel.] [TL repeats arguments over the sequentiality of some of the obligations in the RM. She also notes again that the Israeli side did not agree immediate and parallel.] To be fair, I did say that since the Americans are the judge they can invite anyone they want to any meeting; if we are invited we will come. But we disagree to the trilateral committee. [Continues to recap the three principles again.]

[Discussion on the language in the RM and the utility and logic of using it as an absolute TOR continues – for example, SE raises the question where does the principle of "subject to" appear in the RM.]

AA:

- When will the Israeli government take a decision to freeze all settlement activity and reopen Jerusalem institutions? It doesn't need a bulldozer or anything! [Continues to press Israelis on a concrete and immediate commitment to implement their RM obligations.]

TL:

- In the document we will [sign to our intention] to implement fully and completely the RM.

AA:

- This is just words – we need deeds!

TL:

- Before Annapolis we'll discuss what we can do. [We'll discuss] other CBMs…

AH:

- So not before Annapolis?

TL:

8

- We will discuss. We are discussing now. This will be signed right before Annapolis. [You can decide not to sign it if it doesn't meet your needs.] After it's signed you can ask me when we will start. We are willing to sign that we are ready to fully and completely implement the RM. Once we sign this you can ask me when [and we can fight about the timing of each other's obligations. You don't see us asking when you will complete each security obligation? Then we can ask you about] your security obligations. [TL continues along these lines.]

[SE hands out a paper listing some of the tenders that have happened since 2004 to refute TL's assertion in the last meeting that there had been no tenders or money towards settlements except Maale Addumim since a government decision in 2004.]

TL:

- The day after, the international community, the Arab world, and the core issues. How do you see the reference to the core issue – since Annapolis will launch negotiations…

AA:

- I told you – for example on borders. The 1967 border. We can discuss [the possibility of] minor modifications, the percentage, that [any swaps] will not prejudice territorial contiguity or national resources….

TL:

- Since we are talking about the day after – should we try to reference these issues the day before? Or leave all of them to the day after? To try to find an understanding on each of the core issues [now] will be a mistake.

AA:

- [Notes that the importance of addressing the core issues now is to understand the direction that the negotiations will go in post Annapolis and what kind of an agreement we are working towards.]

SE:

- In our meeting with Olmert he said he needed indicators on each of the core issues. What does this mean?

ST:

- He said that there will be a list of issues that will be dealt with. The substantive discussion on each of the core issues [will be] post-Annapolis.

SE:

- [Asks for further clarification.]

ST:

- He also said that there would be no solution in the Annapolis statement.

9

TL:

- We need to be pragmatic. In the past there was an understanding on the need to agree the core issues, to meet in Annapolis, and then implement the RM.
- Then there was a change in the process. Then Israel agreed to do something that they did not agree before – to launch [negotiations on the] core issues post-Annapolis. [So if we address the core issues in the Annapolis statement,] there will be no post- Annapolis.

AA:

- First we agree the four main issues in the document: first the preamble, second the core issues, third the day after Annapolis, fourth the timetable, fifth (you added this) the international community. Let's go through our position again, so there is no misunderstanding. [Notes again the Palestinian position on the two state solution, the five US points on the RM, the timetable of 7-8 months to be concluded within the Bush term (and the process to include a committee to follow the negotiations).] On the core issues – do you want to hear our position now? Or later?

TL:

- Tomorrow. But it's about being pragmatic about time. [Recaps all of the Israeli positions on the above again.] On the core issues – each and every party should ask and answer itself – whether it's feasible and whether you want [to include them in the document now] because [addressing core issues] means hard compromises on both sides. We have two options – in two weeks we launch real permanent status negotiations, or we fight over it now. [TL makes the point that whatever is agreed now will be attacked by the public on both sides.]

[TL leaves to attend the no-confidence vote in the Knesset.]

[It was agreed that the next meeting of the teams would be held on Tuesday at five pm, location to be determined.]

10

Minutes from 8th Negotiation Team Meeting
(In Preparation for Annapolis)
Tuesday, 13th November 2007, 5h00pm
Mount Zion Hotel, West Jerusalem

Attendees:
Palestinian
- Ahmed Querei (AA)
- Yaser Abd Rabbo (YAR)
- Akram Haniyeh (AH)
- Dr. Saadi Kronz (SK)
- Zeinah Salahi (ZS)
- Dr. Saeb Erekat (SE)

Israeli
- FM Tzipi Livni (TL)
- Yoram Turbovich (YT)
- Shalom Turjeman (ST)
- Gen Amos Gilad (AG)
- DG Abromovich (Abr)
- Tal Becker (TB)

Detailed minutes:

TL:
- I would like to suggest that we will continue according to what I tried to at the beginning of the session yesterday, but unfortunately while doing so we ended up in some sort of a discussion. At the end of today's meeting the minimum that is required is some sense of the six or seven points that you stated that need to be in the document. Just [a] list [of] what is agreed or not agreed. Put aside the core issues for now, just have a list of agreed and not agreed, in points. If we have this agreement… let's not include the areas of disagreement now.

AA:
- [Suggests an I and P paper]

TL:
- Ok I think that this is a very good idea about all of the issues. I think that when this comes to the core issues [however] this is problematic. Let's start with all the other issues then go from there. Because when we get to the core issues you will start with yours I will start with ours [i.e. positions]. This is our duty to do, so but it will not help us to do so now.

[Discussion continues on this a bit more.]

1

THE PAPERS

TL:
- I think that [putting down all of this for the non-core issues] is important because this part is more about process. When it comes to the core issues, putting the basic positions of the Israelis and the Palestinians will not help. Therefore let's start with the others.

AA:
- We can finish tonight the subjects – the preamble. What are the components. Not the language or the nice words etc. We should focus on three things in the preamble. One is the terms of reference ["TOR"]. The three core elements in addition to the [nice] language. One is the TOR. Second is the 2 state solution. Third is the Roadmap ["RM"]. Is there anything to be added to the preamble?

TL:
- No – it's ok. And what we called before some good words. The basic idea of where we are going. End of conflict, [the goal is] to find a way to do so... something like this.
- So if you want to summarize the positions, this is something we did in our former conversation. When it comes to the TOR we want reference to 242, 338, the RM and other agreements agreed between the two sides. You added, and this is the problem, the API, international law, 1515, 1397, and 194. And we wanted the three principles of the Quartet.

SE:
- Do you have differences on 1515 and 1397?

TL:
- Yes.

AA:
- Basically you want 242 and 338?

TL:
- Yes... basically we can refer to the RM as it is. The RM and previous agreements as adopted by both sides. President Bush's vision -- I forgot it before. The 3 principles of the Quartet. [AA asking clarification questions throughout.]
- Do you agree these?

AH:
- The three principles... we cannot include it as it is.

[It was agreed by both sides that we can find another place/way to include the three Quartet principles. TL suggested the same for the API. She reiterated the point that

2

including the API is like including the Israeli declaration of independence – both are similarly one sided in their view of a resolution to the conflict.]

TL:

- Ok. I would suggest we find a place for the API, not as part of the TOR but in another place.

AA:

- I think that this is a mistake for Israel. It is the only real compromise from the Arab world.

TL:

- We can find another place for it… it is not part of the TOR.

AA:

- This is a main principle. Part of the TOR. This is what will make the Arab states come.

[Recap the points.]

AA:

- International law?

TL:

- NO. I was the Minister of Justice. I am a lawyer…But I am against law -- international law in particular. Law in general.
- If we want to make the agreement smaller, can we just drop some of these issues? Like international law, this will make the agreements easier.

[TL made the point that Palestinians don't really need international law. Palestinians protest this assertion. AA raises examples of where it is important, such as water, and that it is key for the parties to agree what the permanent status agreements will be based on. Abr says that the agreement will be whatever is agreed at the table. At one point during this discussion, SE raises a problem with the "as adopted" language with respect to the Roadmap and previous agreements, noting that this would encompass the Israeli reservations which is not acceptable to the Palestinian side.]

AA:

- Second is about the two state solution.

TL:

- Two states is the ultimate goal of the process. But also part of the TOR.
- Each state is the answer to the natural aspirations of its people.

SE:

3

- [Raises RM language regarding unequivocal duty to accept each state as is. Reads from the RM.]

TL:

- To say the idea that two nation states contradicts the RM...

SE:

- [But we've never denied Israel's right to define itself.]
- If you want to call your state the Jewish State of Israel you can call it what you want. [Notes examples of Iran and Saudi Arabia.]

TL:

- I said basically that our position is a reference to the fact that each state is an answer to the national aspirations of their people.

AH:

- There was an article in Haaretz saying that Palestinians would be stupid if they accept this [i.e. the Jewish state].

TL:

- Someone wrote the Palestinians?

AA:

- I want to say two state solution living side by side in peace security stability and prosperity, Palestinian democratic state independent with sovereignty, viable with East Jerusalem as its capital.

TB:

- That's all? [Sarcastically.]

AA:

- Yes that's our position.
- Two state solution living side by side in peace security stability and prosperity, Palestinian democratic state independent with sovereignty, viable with East Jerusalem as its capital.
- This is what we want to have. This small sentence.

TL:

- Since we are talking about two states, and since we agree that we shouldn't refer to internal things for each and every state...
- I just want to say something. [Responding to a sarcastic question about whether the problem with the Palestinian suggested formulation is because Israel does not want a democratic state.] Not that there is a reference to being a democracy. [AA: if you don't like it...] No, there are those that would like it a lot. Our idea is to refer to two states for two peoples. Or two nation states, Palestine and Israel living side by side in peace and security with each state constituting the homeland

4

for its people and the fulfillment of their national aspirations and self determination...

AH:

- This refers to the Israeli people?

TL:

- [Visibly angered.] I think that we can use another session – about what it means to be a Jew and that it is more than just a religion. But if you want to take us back to 1947 -- it won't help. Each state constituting the homeland for its people and the fulfillment of their national aspirations and self determination in their own territory. Israel the state of the Jewish people -- and I would like to emphasize the meaning of "its people" is the Jewish people -- with Jerusalem the united and undivided capital of Israel and of the Jewish people for 3007 years... [The Palestinian team protests.] You asked for it. [AA: We said East Jerusalem!] ...and Palestine for the Palestinian people. We did not want to say that there is a "Palestinian people" but we've accepted your right to self determination. Now I have to say, before we continue, in order to continue we have to put out Jerusalem from your statement and from our place. We have enough differences, without putting another one out there.

AA:

- Why is it different?

TL:

- The whole idea of the document is to launch negotiations on final status issues, one of them is Jerusalem. I know what is the Palestinian demand. You know the Israeli position. If we want a joint statement we should find common ground. And Jerusalem is one of the most sensitive issues. Jerusalem is one of the core of the core of the core issues.
- In the preamble anyway adding the issue of Jerusalem cannot lead to something [that we will agree]. If this is trying to do a tradeoff between Jerusalem and the national aspirations it is not the same at all.
- I didn't ask for something that relates to my own self. I didn't ask for recognizing something that is the internal decision of Israel. Israel can do so, it is a sovereign state. [We want you to recognize it.] The whole idea of the conflict is ... the entire point is the establishment of the Jewish state. And yet we still have a conflict between us. We used to think it is because the Jews and the Arabs... but now the Palestinians... we used to say that we have no right to define the Palestinian people as a people. They can define it themselves. In 1947 it was between Jews and Arabs, and then [at that point the purpose] from the Israeli side to [was] say that the Palestinians are Arabs and not [Palestinians – it was an excuse not to create a Palestinian state. We've passed that point in time and I'm not going to raise it. The whole conflict between the Jordan River and the Mediterranean Sea is not the idea of creating a democratic state that is viable etc. It is to divide it into two.] For each state to create its own problem. Then we can ask ourselves is it

5

viable, what is the nature of the two states. In order to end the conflict we have to say that this is the basis. I know that your problem is saying this is problematic because of the refugees. During the final status negotiations we will have an answer to the refugees. You know my position. Even having a Jewish state -- it doesn't say anything about your demands. …. Without it, why should we create a Palestinian state?

AA:

- Can I have a minute to talk about the conflict?

TL:

- There is something that is shorter. I can read something with different wording.
- That the ultimate goal is constituting the homeland for the Jewish people and the Palestinian people respectively, and the fulfillment of their national aspirations and self determination in their own territory.
- And we take Jerusalem off the preamble.

SE:

- I noted that. We took it out. That is your position we take honestly what you said.

AA:

- That is your position… in 1947 the UN issued its famous resolution to create two states for the Arabs and the Jews. In 1948, 194 came. [That whole time people were pushing for a one state solution – one secular state.] This was in 1968. From that date until 1988 this was the Palestinian position. In 1988 – the PNC of the PLO agreed the two state solution.

TL:

- What did you say in 1988? What is written in your decisions 1988?

AA:

- The acceptance of 242 and 338.
- And then we came to the negotiations – Jerusalem is part of the occupied territories since 1967. When we speak about East Jerusalem, when we talk about the core issues we will speak about the core issues in such a way that will keep all of the issues on Jerusalem [for later] when you say that East Jerusalem will be the capital of Palestine [we are addressing just the territorial element. Jerusalem can be divided into two elements – territory and arrangements. On arrangements there are many other aspects -- more than ten or eleven to discuss later.]

TL:

- I would like to ask something. There are two things you referred to. One is Jerusalem and the other is two states for two people. For Jerusalem, I want to state the obvious. [Talking about any core issue in the preamble cannot happen because we won't reach an agreement on the preamble, on any core issue. We know your opinion.]

6

AA:
- [Refers to 181.]

TL:
- 181 is a matter of borders.
- If you say that two states for two people – [and that] the problem is that the borders are not defined yet [we can define it to come into effect once the borders are defined].
- This closes the circle. Two states for two people - then [include a] reference to the future Palestinian state. Without the borders agreed upon it constitutes nothing. By saying that the borders will be agreed [you protect yourself]. The vision is to end the conflict.

AA:
- Ok – let's [move on].

[Discussion on technical procedure for drafting the joint document.]

TL:
- [Reads from 1988 Palestinian Declaration of Independence.] "Palestine is a state for Palestinians wherever they may be."

AA:
- [You have your position, we have ours.] Let's come to the RM. We have the 5 points.

TL:
- You know our position. At least delete immediate and parallel. And we want to change the trilateral committee to something that will refer to the American judge and say that the American judge can invite whomever they want to.

[Reference to Yediot article on trilateral committee.]

AA:
- You want the trilateral committee to be a bilateral committee?

TL:
- No – we accept the Americans as the judge. And the judge can invite whomever they like. We can have trilateral meetings, but not a trilateral committee. ... I think that the Americans can live with it.

AA:
- [Recaps Israeli position. Short side discussion on it.]

AG:

7

- I took part in all the meetings of the trilateral committee. Dayton, Moscovitz, CIA, Wolfe, State Department... Except the White House I think all the [departments] of the US shared this comment. After the good morning, it was like court – the verdict was written before. Everyone spoke to the history, the record, and not the security. With Dayton, instead of dealing with security we dealt with prestige. We dealt with a power point war. By the way I think you won the power point war but we lost everything. We want to deal with security. In all the committees the idea was to impress the Americans and not to deal with security. The first committee is deteriorating. What we need here is some flexible mechanism that will deal with security if we are serious about security.

YAR:

- What is the mechanism you will suggest?

AH:

- We are not dealing with security only.

AA:

- We have many mechanisms that we want to activate that deal with more than just security. We are committed to all the bilateral mechanisms [between us that deal with economics, security, etc.] we are talking about the first phase of the RM. [We all have problems with it.] We want a trilateral committee to follow up on the commitments of both sides. This is why we need it to be parallel and immediate. This is why we need Israel to say tomorrow that we will freeze all settlement activity. [AH: This has nothing to do with security] Also we need to reopen the Jerusalem institutions which have been closed since 2004? [Side discussion on date of the closure] 2001. Also what is the problem to say that we will start to dismantle the outposts? That the decision [is] taken. To start. [Emphasizes seriousness of Palestinian efforts on security reform. If we succeed in Nablus we will move to Jenin. Also stresses Palestinian commitment and understanding to Israeli security and Palestinian security. We need it. You need it. We need the trilateral committee for this.]

ST:

- How is it different from what is in the RM, which includes a monitoring mechanism, and which we accept?

AA:

- We want something to follow up on [the obligations of both sides].

AG:

- [You are dealing with many issues. None of this deals with security as we define it. None of them are dealing with Hamas. Other major security issues. You are far away from dealing seriously with security. There is no intelligence cooperation about terror. And that is what happened in Gaza. And instead of dealing with terror – you showed us power point presentations that showed us

8

how you behaved beautifully and did nothing about security. And we paid for this failure with hundreds of deaths. We don't want the trilateral meetings to focus on issues like settlements, etc. We need something to deal with real security issues.]

SE:
- [This is the logic of having the US as the judge. To tell Palestinians if they are not serious, and to guide them along.]

AG:
- [But you saw what happened with Dayton!]

TL:
- We understand your concern [that we will use the RM as an excuse and with the difference of opinion over internal sequencing in the phasing. To deal with your concerns we agreed to the American judge. Another thing – the judge will refer to the implementation of the obligations of both sides, not just the Palestinian obligations.] Because of the [past experience of our MOD, our experience has been] that it doesn't help. And since the 3rd party can invite to the meetings anyone he wants... And therefore [knowing the Americans if you ask them to call a meeting with all the three sides, they will do so. Therefore this should be sufficient to answer your concerns and it is easier to accept for us.] Anyway when it comes to the Israeli implementation of the RM, to find out whether we froze the settlements or not -- it is a decision – we don't need a trilateral committee or meetings on this. [The Americans can call us in on this in one day.] Anyway the trilateral committee doesn't help on these things. [TL raises the issue of CBMs again, and asks to defer all of this until the creation of a list of CBMs that sends the right message to the Palestinians.]

AA:
- If you allow me to [explain] and to ask for an explanation. You know that all of our problems come from two things. One is territory, the other is the freedom of the people. [These have not been achieved. I respect AG when he says that [total security reform] has not happened...]

TL:
- At the end of the day it is our decision and not [inaudible].

AA:
- Exactly. And since 2003 – do you need to expand [the settlements]? [TL: No.] But it has continued. I can give you maps, etc. We need freedom of the people and the territory. Because of these concerns – this is the real concern. I recognize that your concern is security. [Continues along same lines and the seriousness of Palestinians with respect to security.]

SE:

9

- Can I add to what AA said? I will take the points that AG said, not to satisfy you but to satisfy the [Palestinian] people. The RM states that Palestinians and Israelis will resume security cooperation based on the Tenet plan. [Describes the Tenet work plan, which includes a trilateral committee.] AA is basing his argument that everything that we are doing on security is in line with this.

ST:

- So if it is there why do you need to say it?

SE:

- [Because it is not functioning and I need it give it a fresh start.]

TL:

- Basically the RM refers to the cooperation between the two sides and doesn't say anything about the trilateral committee [SE protests]. I don't want to reinvent the wheel. [We accept the RM as it is. There will be bilateral and trilateral meetings. I don't know why it is so problematic to accept but this is our position.]

[Discussion continues on the importance of the trilateral committee and the seriousness of the Palestinians on security. AH notes that it is insulting that Israel is not acknowledging the seriousness of Palestinians with respect to security. Look at what Palestinians are doing with Hamas!]

TL:

- I'd like to say something to AA about the settlements. Just like you said you understand our security needs. I understand the sentiments of the Palestinians when they see the settlements being built. The meaning from the Palestinian perspective is that Israel takes more land, that the Palestinian state will be impossible, the Israel policy is to take more and more land day after day and that at the end of the day we'll say that it is impossible we already have the land and cannot create the state. [It was the policy of the government for a really long time. Now it is still the policy of some of the parties, but not the government. On the borders – we have a distinctions between blocs of settlements and individual settlements. Some are not even in our interest to expand. This is why we haven't built new settlements. This is why it is important -- the dismantling of outposts is important for us as a government but this creates some difficulties as well. If it interests you the way Israelis see the situation… In the past there are those that felt that each day that passes while we are holding part of the land is another victory because we are holding the land. We made our choice – the most important thing is not more Jews living in all of the land, but the most important thing is the existence of Israel as a Jewish and democratic state. And for this we decided that we needed to divide the land and to live in a smaller, Jewish and democratic state. And by doing so to give the Palestinians the [right to self determination]. [Since 2004 we stopped subsidies to settlements. As Minister of Housing we refused to be in Kiryat Arba and other sensitive places because it is against the internal structure in Israel. It is not in our interest to keep taking on

10

one hand and to talk peace on the other. But you have not seen expansion beyond the existing settlements.]

ST:

- What is happening is through private sector.

TL:

- There has not been the confiscation of land. [Palestinian side protests at this comment, and notes the confiscations that happened one the same days as the first negotiation sessions.] Well there is the matter of the Wall.
- So let's continue. Would you like to continue to other issues?

YAR:

- Well did we close the issue of security, settlements, etc…?
- [Israeli side says no.]
- But I really wanted to ask just for the sake of clarity. The conclusion I get is that you want to make security on your own without our cooperation or anything.

YT:

- I will phrase what AG said. At the moment Gaza is a country of terror. You regret it and we regret it. In the WB there is a very good cooperation between you and us, headed by Salam Fayyad who we tremendously respect, [that has started but this takes time. AG said it was too early to judge the results or whether this reform has taken root. It is a good beginning. It is not that we don't want cooperation – we do. We agreed the American judge. The only difference we have is over the procedure.]

YAR:

- We are not talking about all issues. There will be bilateral daily issues between us. We are talking about the first phase of the RM. [Continues to explain.] There are two levels. [The trilateral and the bilateral do not contradict each other.]

TL:

- [Asks why the Pals think that the formulation she suggested is less good than the trilateral committee.]

YAR:

- Because we want a serious mechanism. Because you connected this to the implementation of the entire peace treaty in the future. Therefore we want a different mechanism where you and the US will not just come occasionally to check in.

YT:

- You are preaching to the converted. [We agree – the difference here is just procedural. The objective person is a serious achievement for you.]

11

[Discussion continues on this.]

AA:

- I just want to say one thing – back to the settlements – we don't want the territory and the people to be kidnapped. The settlements there are real and [there is] too much expansion. Second we are talking about settlement expansion – we are not talking just about the government expansion, but also the private sector.

TL:

- But you need to understand something about the process itself. When the government has [issued] the tender in the past it means that the private sector won the tender and then it has the rights on the land. They are entitled to work on the land that they purchased. Even in talking in terms of freezing the settlements – I'd like you to put some parameters a list on what is the most problematic from your perspective. New settlements is the most. Expanding the settlements is the second.

AA:

- In 1995 [raises the issue of the construction lines].

SE:

- What defines a settlement freeze, including natural growth. [Makes point that it doesn't matter whether it is private or public, etc. The RM is clearly a freeze -- period -- without distinction.] We all have our internal difficulties.

ST:

- Natural growth – what does it mean? If a family has a baby can it live in the settlement?

[SE begins to answer. TL interrupts to say: I respect your right to SD, respect my right to a Jewish state.]

SE:

- If a child is born he has many alternatives. [AA's son, on the other hand, living in Abu Dis cannot even build a bathroom.]

TL:

- You refer to the RM and the obligations on both sides. Your obligations on security will take some time. There are certain things that are crucial because there are things that make the settlements bigger, because it takes some of the land. I would like to share with you some of our problems – it's not an excuse.
- The private sector– they have some rights in some places
- There are other places where they started. The child is born and the tractors are there on the ground. It takes some time, but they are there on the ground.

12

- It is not internal political issues – I think that we need also to understand – because the last thing that we want is to say something and you will say that you are even in violation with your own statement.
- You understand our position – we are not trying to expand to give you less in the end. Now we have to deal with what is on the ground. [We want to know what exactly it means if Israel takes this decision -- what exactly this will mean.]

[AA raises construction lines concept again. Discussion continues. TL again asks for help in defining a freeze.]

AA:

- Can we speak about the timetable? What we propose is that the peace treaty will be in President Bush's term. We put a date that is seven or eight months.

TL:

- When is Bush's term?

AH:

- January 2009 [elaborates].

TL:

- [Why do you say less than the full term?]

[Palestinians respond that you need a buffer zone of time and a target date. Discussion continues repeating the logic of the timetable from earlier meetings and whether or not a timeline was agreed. SE clarifies that timetable is to ensure commitment to achieve an agreement and not just to exert best efforts.]

AA:

- I want to talk about the day-after Annapolis. Let's say that the day after Annapolis there will be negotiations, and we will start immediately with teams to deal with all issues of the PS negotiations – not just the six issues – to form a steering committee on all the committees, etc. there will be a committee, each to meet with the delegations, the parties, each three months to evaluate [progress].

ST:

- The Arab League? [joking]

AA:

- Amr Musa. [joking] To evaluate -- to see progress. After six months, we propose an international conference according to the RM.

TL:

- What do you mean according to the RM?

AA:

13

98

- The RM calls for two.

TL:

- You can refer to meetings – please don't refer to the RM [with respect to the international conference].

[Joking about possible locations of international conference.]

AA:

- Fourth is the timetable. If you have anything else – maybe we can talk about the agenda of the negotiations.

[Palestinian side suggests one day after the meeting be dedicated to the first day of negotiations. TL thinks it is a good idea but has to check.]

TL:

- The statement will be adopted by the executive committee before or after Annapolis?

[Palestinian side responds before.]

[Discussion returns to the day after. YT and ST leave.]

TL:

- Now I am talking about what you suggested on the timetable. It was understood by Olmert that Abu Mazen agreed [to no timetable]. Since Olmert referred to the timetable in his speech, we can quote what was in his speech.

SE:

- [Notes again for the record that Abu Mazen did not agree this. Discussion on this continues. Abr also leaves.]
- Are we meeting tomorrow?

TL:

- My teams have left for two days, but we can meet the two of us or the four of us… [Referring to herself, TB, AA and SE]

TL:

- [Reads from Olmert speech.] "There is a chance that we can reach real accomplishments, perhaps even before the end of President Bush's term in office."
- Now referring to the day after, there are a lot of words that can represent seriousness [that should be included – I said that we need to ask about the first meeting, it sounds like a good idea.] We are not in favor of these follow up committees [especially if we don't know who they are].

14

- I'd like to refer now to an easy thing – the role of the international community and the Arab world.
- We would also like to refer to [fact that] the process is a bilateral one. That there is no substitute for the bilateral process. We recognize that the international community in general and the regional and Arab and Muslim states in particular have a critical role to play in supporting the bilateral process as well as any agreement negotiated between the parties.
- And now we have some ideas about the support of the international community.
- International support to the legitimate PA – maybe this is the point where we can refer to the 3 Quartet conditions.
- I think that there should be a reference to the capacity building, economic development, a reference to Tony Blair's mission or something.
- I would like to see something about the determined efforts to confront extremism, incitement, intolerance, weapons smuggling, cutting public and private funding to terror. All these things that we need especially from the Arab world to do so. I don't know if the Arab world will have a problem with this.

YAR:

- We don't want anyone to think it is directed against them.

AA:

- I think that there are international resolutions on this.

TL:

- [This is a way for the Arabs to be involved. Now this is where we can refer to the API] and to say something about the need to improve the regional ties and to promote regional cooperation [and to launch the multilateral committees] and until we have the real CBMs – I know it is a vague idea – I would like the Arab world to take steps -- as we take steps towards the Palestinians they take steps towards Israel [to help Israel help the Palestinians]. I know if the CBMs will not be serious – they will not do so.

TB:

- The three core parts are:
- [Support for the bilateral process, fighting extremism and the API as part of regional cooperation.]

TL:

- [Notes that from their perspective the good parts of the API refer to peace and normalization with Israel at the end of the Road. She repeats that the goal of peace with the Palestinians is for its own sake, not for normalization. But the API includes parameters for the resolution of the core issues which is problematic for Israelis and cannot be part of the bilateral process between Pals and Israelis.] There are relevant references in the RM as it is. [Notes if you want a more concrete reference beyond what is in the RM to the API, this is the place to include it. Including the rest of the API is like including the Israeli declaration of

15

independence, which is also a one sided perspective on what peace should be.] I would like to add one last thing. [Refers to her trip to Lisbon and a discussion with Amr Musa.] He said about the need to promote a process and a bilateral track which is important. Then he said that we have our own proposal and this is the API. So this is a proposal and not part of the bilateral…

AA:
- [Refers to 242] and that no party has the right to acquire territory by force. Egypt – you've withdrawn from every meter. Syria – they are ready and have [basically agreed the borders]. Why are you trying to make the Palestinians pay the price for all of this? Putting the API in this context does that.

TL:
- Of course we will have our future discussions on all these points.

AA:
- So if Israel is ready to withdraw completely from the Golan Heights…

[Refers to previous discussions on the Syrian track. AA notes that the API deals with regional peace and not just the Palestinian track; normalization with the Arab world is not cheap. TL responds that she respects the peace with the Palestinians very much and that including it in the TOR is basically like including its parameters as the parameters on the core issues themselves.]

SE:
- [Reads from six references to the Arab states in the RM. Reads again the language on the API and regional peace, no funding, restore pre-intifada links, viable multilateral engagement… etc.] But this all comes in the context of a comprehensive peace with the Arabs. [In 2003 the Arab and Islamic countries all met in Tehran and adopted the API. We cannot go to them now and try to get them to take these steps piecemeal or fragmented steps outside the concept of the comprehensive peace. The Arab states have all accepted the RM.]

TL:
- I understand the sensitivity – that many want Annapolis to be part of the regional peace initiative [Syria etc.].

YAR:
- If the Syrians don't behave themselves in Lebanon for one week no one will care about them in the regional track.

TL:
- My understanding from discussions [with Jordanians etc.] is that the Arab league is very sensitive. If the problem is to put the discussions in the regional peace context – [I need to think of what the best way to do this is]. [Reiterates that the problem is that the API tries to resolve all the open issues on both sides.]

16

Meeting Minutes

Jerusalem/Sheraton Plaza
22 January 2008
15:30 – 17:00

Attendants

Palestinian side:
- Ahmad Qrei' (Abu Ala')
- Dr. Saeb Erekat
- Salah Ilayan

Israeli side:
- Tzipi Livni
- Tal Beker

Livni: I met with Shas Minister Eli Yishay to persuade him not to withdraw from the government coalition, and every week he asks about our progress in the negotiations. I told him nothing has been agreed on.

During our last meeting I listened to your vision about borders and Jerusalem, and we'd like to continue our talk about borders and security. What about inviting two separate teams to work under our supervision on these two subjects? We've to agree on the issue of the borders, and we need to look to the Israelis behind the wall and to the Palestinians inside the borders.

We asked Dr. Saeb and Tal during our last meeting to discuss together these issues but we were not clear about our expectations from them. We'll ask specialized people from both sides to start negotiations about the borders and to review the maps. But before we do this, there are principles that we've to agree on regarding settlement blocs and exchange of land. I mentioned in the last meeting that talk about a ratio of land exchange won't help, and then I said we had to look at the maps in order to identify and know the areas that will be evacuated.

Abu Ala': For this reason I want Dr. Saeb and Tal to discuss the matter together before enlarging the circle.

Livni: I'm not sure Tal's able to address such issue.

Abu Ala': They can ask for the assistance of specialized people, but for the sake of confidentiality they must both discuss the issue together and perhaps design a structure. Then we can work within the frame of this structure.

Livni: Then Dr. Saeb and Tal will design the structure.

www.ajtransparency.com/files/2304.pdf

Saeb: We're ready upon your guidance to start work.

Livni: I'd rather have work begin next week because this week isn't appropriate due to the issuance of Winograd Report next Wednesday. But parallel to this we need to think about means to involve the international community in the process especially with regard to the issue of refugees.

Abu Ala': We want Jordan Syria, Lebanon and Egypt for the issues of refugees, water, the environment and borders.

Livni: As for the water issue, I know that you were close to reaching an agreement in Camp David.

Abu Ala': This isn't true. The water issue is complex. There's the issue of surface water and the Jordan River is the most important source of surface water in the West Bank. There's also the issue of underground water in the western basin and the north-eastern basin in the West Bank. In Gaza strip there's the issue of the underground coastal water reservoir.

As for the refugees, when we start serious talks about this issue, we'll see there are promising horizons that the multi-lateral talks can address. In the final analysis, it's not you or me who decides to re-launch multi-lateral talks but the US and the Quartet.

Livni: Then what you're saying is that we don't need to start multi-lateral talks before bilateral issues start to move ahead.

Abu Ala': We've no problem starting multi-lateral talks, but we want Saudi Arabia and the Arab League to be involved. For example, there's the issue of compensation. How can we discuss compensation before reaching an agreement on the issue of refugees.

Saeb: With regards to water, there's the issue of the Jordan River. Palestinian farmers used to benefit from the water of the Jordan River before 1967, but later Israel imposed restrictions on water use and declared adjacent territories military zones. In addition, Israel diverted most of the water of the Jordan River from Lake Tiberias to the Negev Desert. There are also the issues of the Dead Sea and Bahrain Canal. There are issues that need to be coordinated with neighboring Arab countries.

Abu Ala': Before we talk about going to Arab countries, we need to agree together first. There are issues that we can discuss together, while other issues need to be discussed with neighboring Arab countries.

The multilateral track aims at achieving progress on the bilateral level, but we don't deal with multi-lateral negotiations issues on the basis of the same criterion.

Livni: Then we'll work on putting the structure, borders and security. As for water and the environment, perhaps we can invite specialized people like we did with the issues of borders and security.

As for the refugees, frankly the Israeli position is that the creation of a Palestinian state is the answer to the refugee issue. I know that you don't accept this at the present time. I believe we can say that after finding an organized solution to the problem of refugees, we can discuss issues of compensation for host countries so that you won't seem to have agreed on things you didn't want to agree on, things that may embarrass you. We can discuss the issue of compensating host countries and the issue of refugees resettlement during multi-lateral talks.

Abu Ala': Let's be clear. The multilateral track isn't a source of decision. In group work sessions anybody can say whatever they want, but the importance of the multi-lateral track is to support the bilateral track which is the place where decisions can be taken. The issues of compensation, return and resettlement will be confidentially discussed with host countries.

Livni: Who do you think should talk with Jordan, for instance?

Abu Ala': The US, Europe and the Quartet. Later we may engage Syria and Lebanon in the talks for the resettlement or return of refugees.

Livni: I don't want to deceive anybody. There'll be no Israeli official whether from the Knesset or the government or even the public who will support the return of refugees to Israel. There are many people in the world who are ready to contribute to the issue of refuges, and I'm not talking about Saudi Arabia but about Gates and his like.

Abu Ala': I don't want the multilateral track to find a solution, but we can talk about the rehabilitation of refugees in camps as well as other issues related to them and to the improvement of their living conditions.

Livni: What should we ask the multilateral track to do?

Abu Ala': We don't decide. We can ask the multilateral track to conduct a study on the issue.

Livni: Let's give it something to start with.

Abu Ala': There are people who create problems in the multilateral track. I know this since I was the general coordinator of Palestinian delegations in the multi-lateral negotiations work groups.

Saeb: Let Tal check the number of refugees you can absorb.

Abu Ala': Our position is clear in this respect, and it's the right of return and compensation for those who decide not to return, in accordance with the UN General Assembly resolution #194. When we begin to talk about the refugees issue then we'll talk about everything frankly and clearly.

Livni: We've to think about how to involve the international community in this case.

Abu Ala': Let's leave this matter to Saeb and Tal.

Livni: Another thing we can start to think about in order for it to part of the agreement is the steps towards creating a state.

Abu Ala': We can start with People to People Program.

Livni: I want to hear about your vision about Jerusalem because I want to learn.

Abu Ala': There are many issues to discuss especially the modalities. Another thing is the land since Jerusalem is part of the Palestinian territories occupied in 1967. If we reach an agreement on the land, then negotiations can address the issue of modalities that have to be applied to all issues in a manner satisfactory to all concerned parties. I think the issue of Jerusalem will have been solved when I'll be able to tour any part in East and West Jerusalem in my car and feel that it's really mine. Both the western and eastern parts of the city should be open to all and all arrangements taken should not affect negatively on the daily life of the people.

Everything in Jerusalem starts from the Old City, which is the most important thing in this respect.

We've also to talk about issues of electricity, water, sewage, municipal services, the infrastructure, roads, tourism, economy, and security.

We've to talk about the situation of Jerusalem: Will it be an open city or a divided city? And how will we deal with the holy places? We want an open city because I can't imagine there'll be zigzags on the borders.

Livni: For our security needs, we want real borders.

Abu Ala': Then East Jerusalem will have to be the capital of the Palestinian state where there'll be full Palestinian sovereignty like any other capital in the world. But I said dividing the city will be a problem.

Livni: What d'you mean by an open city?

Abu Ala': To have Israeli check up for those coming into the city from the Israeli side, and a Palestinian check up for those coming into the city from the Palestinian side, with different models of coordination and cooperation in municipal services related to the infrastructure, roads, electricity, water, sewage and the removal of waste material. I'm here talking about both east and west Jerusalem; but we can talk also about East Jerusalem according to 1967 borders and not greater Jerusalem.

Saeb: We want a rare situation: Yeroshalim as the capital of Israel, and al-Quds as the capital of Palestine.

There are 250,000 Palestinians living in Jerusalem, and I don't think you want to keep control of them.

When we talk about dividing the city, we don't simply talk about check up, but about planning and organization. It's not logical for a Jews to construct a building that has 20 floors while an Arab is allowed to build three floors only. Talking about municipal services, tourism, security, the infrastructure, water, electricity, planning and organization, does not mean that the city is not divided.

Abu Ala': the solution requires creative ideas without division of sovereignty.

Saeb: Sovereignty is tantamount to the organization of relations.

Livni: How d'you see the future of the holy places not only in Jerusalem but also in the West Bank?

Saeb: In Jericho we allow and welcome people to visit the Jewish synagogue. Likewise, we'll welcome any individual to visit the al-Ibrahimi Mosque, Rachel's Tomb, Joseph's Tomb, and other holy places.

Sovereignty isn't belief or ideas or doctrines, but it's related to laws and regulations.

The Israelis said in Camp David they didn't want to build the Temple beneath the al-Aqsa Mosque, but they wanted to keep and guarantee their values there. There's a relation between religion and nationalism, and we respect your traditions and values.

Livni: D'you want to divide the land between the river and the sea?

Saeb: We want to return to Resolution 181.

Livni: This doesn't represent demographic division as it stands today.

Saeb: It did represent demographic division 60 years ago.

Abu Ala': We'll defeat Hamas if we reach an agreement, and this will be our response to their claim that gaining back our land can be achieved through resistance only.

Livni: An agreement requires compatibility.

Abu Ala': Surely.

Saeb: Give me a just agreement and you'll get the support of 80% of the Palestinians.

Livni: What about the future of Gaza?

Abu Ala': We'll talk also about the relation between the West Bank and Gaza. They'll be linked with a safe passage. This matter was discussed earlier.

Livni: We'll meet next Monday, but until then what's Saeb and Tal's homework.

Abu Ala': Putting the structure -- borders -- security.

Livni: What about the multilateral track?

Abu Ala': We'll start when the time becomes ripe. We'll start with easy issues such as the environment and water.

Meeting Minutes

Jerusalem
27 January 2008
09:00 – 11:00

Attendants

Palestinian side:
- Ahmad Qrei' (Abu Ala')
- Dr. Saeb Erekat
- Salah Ilayan

Israeli side:
- Tzepi Livni
- Tal Beker
- Alon Bar

Livni: What's your vision to end the conflict and establish a Palestinian state?

Abu Ala': Before beginning serious talk, we should clean the table of all violations and obstacles that impede the easy flow of negotiations without exception, especially the siege, incursions, assassinations, killings, and arrests in the West Bank and the Gaza Strip. The closure that has been recently imposed on Gaza and the disruption of fuel and basic goods is a serious act that can in no way be accepted or disregarded. The act is a breach of all international customs and agreements. Additionally, it presages a human tragedy.

Under no condition can we accept the continuation of settlement activities on West Bank territories occupied in 1967 including occupied East Jerusalem. We can't accept the Israeli forceful measures taken in this respect, particularly the settlement expansion on Jabal Abu Ghneim and Ma'ale Edomim settlement, plus the settlements built in Jerusalem and its outskirts. The declaration of Jerusalem mayor to build 7300 residential units in five settlements in East Jerusalem is also unacceptable. We can't continue to negotiate in light of the Israeli policies and violations.

Negotiating issues whose future Israel has already determined by imposing new realities on the ground is meaningless. We'll never accept the construction of the wall, settlement expansion, keeping settlement outposts, and the continued closure of institutions in Jerusalem.

This calls for a meeting of the tri-lateral committee to put a program and a timetable for the implementation of the first phase of Road Map Plan.

Livni: What's your position about removing settlement outposts and moving them into existing settlements? Will you denounce this act or keep silent about it?

Abu Ala': All settlement outposts and all settlement activities on Palestinian territories are illegitimate. The outposts should be removed in accordance with Road Map Plan, since we're talking about a final settlement. We've always refused the transfer of settlements that were in Gaza into the West Bank.

We can't go on with the negotiations in light of these policies and practices, and if we're serious about reaching a comprehensive peace agreement, we must conduct intensive talks.

Besides, we can't disregard our past experiences in the final status negotiations that took place in Stockholm, Camp David, and Taba. We must take them into consideration as a springboard for serious work.

The formation of committees to do research on each issue separately is the best way to give each case its due right. If this isn't feasible, I suggest, in addition to our periodical meetings, giving Dr. Saeb, from our side, and Tal, from your side, more privileges to look into the core of all issues without making any public statement and far-off from the mass media.

Livni: I agree, perhaps we can hold two meetings during next week.

Abu Ala': The understandings President Abu Mazen has reached with Prime Minister Olmert must be considered and be part of the process.

Livni: I met will all previous Israeli negotiators and I don't want to waste time because there are differences in their opinions and assessment for what had happened before.

Abu Ala': Should we, for instance, take Clinton's parameters in consideration without saying whether we accept them or not?

Livni: We can take them into consideration but what's important is to talk about what's happening now.

Abu Ala': I'm not saying they are the terms of reference for the peace process but to take them into consideration.

Livni: All will take them into consideration. Did you develop a vision for the modalities of the solution, because I want to have a better understanding?

Abu Ala': Since we're talking about putting an end to conflict and reaching a comprehensive peace treaty and not a declaration of principles, our understanding of the solution is that it has to address all issues of conflict, to put solutions, and to respond to all issues that might surface. The main issues are those of borders, land, Jerusalem, settlements, refugees, security, and water. In addition, though, there are other issues and details.

Livni: I agree to this.

Abu Ala': If we reach a solution to all these issues, we'll reach a peace agreement. These issues are the future and they'll determine whether the Palestinian state will be viable.

Livni: What do you mean by a viable state?

Abu Ala': A state that has adequate land space that is geographically contiguous and is able to absorb all civilians of whom refugees are a part. Such a state will have the respect of its neighbors and have full control of its own water resources, borders and holy places. It has also to be capable of developing its own economy.

Saeb: Road Map Plan says the goal of the negotiations is to end the Israeli occupation that began in 1967 and to establish a democratic and independent viable Palestinian state coexisting side by side with Israel and other neighbors in peace and security. By addressing the issues mentioned above, we can develop a framework to achieve this end.

Livni: I said the goal is to put an end to the Israeli occupation that began in 1967 and end the claims. Will you conduct a referendum inside and outside on the agreement that we'll reach?

Abu Ala': Yes.

Livni: Won't you have problems as a result of this?

Abu Ala': The problem that we'll face is Israel's desire to cut off part of the West Bank and annex it to Israel. As for the refugees, if the Arabs will be part of the solution there will be no problem in this issue. We've to engage countries that host the refugees directly or indirectly.

Livni: How can we engage Jordan, for instance? Will Jordan accept to be part of the process?

Abu Ala': We'll coordinate together. Even the Syrians want to be part of the process, and they don't want to sit with you to discuss the matter but with us.

Livni: Can we use Canada in this matter since it's the sponsor of the work groups on refugees in the multi-lateral talks?

Abu Ala': Not now. Multi-lateral talks won't look for a solution to the refugee problem, but they'll help in the bilateral track. Let's begin with the water and environment committees.

Livni: What about borders?

Abu Ala': The minimum that we could accept is the 1967 Green Line borders, and any modifications, which will be for a very little ratio, will be reciprocal in value by the ratio of 1:1. If we reach an agreement about the borders and the land, then we'll be able to solve many problems. The problem of settlements will be resolved if we agree on the borders of the Palestinian state and land. What remains then is to determine the future of settlements in the territories and which will be part of the Palestinian state. We'll negotiate to dismantle them or keep them or give Palestinian citizenship to those who'll be willing to live under Palestinian law. In addition, we'll be able to resolve the problems of environment and water.

With regard to Jerusalem, the city is part of Palestinian land occupied in 1967. It's an issue that has two parts: the core of the issue is the land, and the modalities. If we reach an agreement on the land, negotiations can take place to determine the modalities that will have to be implemented. If we agree to keep Jerusalem an open city and a capital for two states, then we discuss the issue of municipal services, security and means of access to the holy places, plus other issues. All the unilateral measures Israel had taken in Jerusalem are not acceptable.

Livni: We have standards when we talk about land. The annexation of settlement blocs is not an ideological case but a reality on the ground. When we voted for the evacuation of settlements in Gaza, we were talking about the evacuation of 7000 settlers. But when we talk about settlements in the West Bank, we're actually talking about tens of thousands of settlers who live in settlement blocs. This will affect our decision regarding borders.

The holy places are a complex and sensitive issue, not merely in Jerusalem but also in Hebron and elsewhere.

There are two criteria in relation to security: (1) security on the borders; and (2) security from your side.

There are also the issues of the Jordan Valley and crossings and these will affect our position regarding borders.

In Israel we talk about a comprehensive solution and the acceptance or refusal of anything depends on our security needs. If our security needs are fulfilled, then all other issues, except the sensitive issue of Jerusalem, can be solved. When we talk about security needs, we must say that the Palestinian state should be demilitarized.

Does 'swap' mean also the swap of the inhabitants? I know this is a problem for you.

Abu Ala': We don't say 'demilitarized' but 'limitedly militarized'.

Saeb: This is part of the negotiations.

Livni: D'you think it's possible to invite people specialized in security to our meetings? Or d'you think they need to meet by themselves?

Abu Ala': I prefer to have a special committee to reach an agreement on the security issue.

Livni: For example, we invite Amos Gilead from our side and whoever you want from your side to participate in our meetings. Then they meet together to discuss security issues such as monitoring of crossings, airport, seaport.

Abu Ala': The deployment of international forces.

Saeb: Regional water, air space, electromagnetic field.

Livni: Alert stations, deployment of emergency forces.

Abu Ala': With regards to borders, we didn't approve the annexation of settlement blocs in any previous negotiations, and we can't accept them as a reality situation. We'll deal rather with each case separately, and the same goes for the wall. We'll never accept any change in the reality of the life of the Arabs living in Israel or their transfer. They're Israeli citizens.

Saeb: We know your position and you know ours with regard to all issues, and in the end we'd like to reach a package deal.

Livni: You didn't accept the annexation of settlement blocs and we never accepted 1967 borders. Therefore let's look at the maps.

Saeb: First, we ask where the borders are. Abu Ala' says 1967 borders with minor modifications by value and reciprocity. Let's first agree on the principle and not the criterion.

Livni: There are thousands of Israelis living in the West Bank and our capability to implement any agreement depends on us knowing where they'll end up at. Besides, 1967 borders are not sacred.

Saeb: The armistice line according to 1949 agreement is sacred.

Livni: In the end the whole matter isn't merely the value of exchange but the reality of those Israelis and where they live.

Abu Ala': For example, I can't accept Ma'ale Edomim settlement as a reality because it divides the West Bank, and the same goes for Giv'at Ze'ev settlement.

Saeb: There are many secrets of the negotiations that we've not divulged. One day the Israeli agreed to evacuate 130 settlements in the West Bank, including Kiryat Arba'.

Livni: I can't talk about ratios. If we say, for example, 2%, I may say I want Ma'ale Edomim and the old city of Jerusalem. Thus we don't want a principle that isn't feasible and waste time on details. Eventually, the government will give evacuation orders to the army. By looking at the maps, we want to know the places that will be evacuated.

Saeb: What's the area of the territories on which settlement blocs are built?

Livni: I don't' know.

Saeb: We don't mind to have settlers live as Palestinian citizens who have all rights under the Palestinian law.

Abu Ala': Take into consideration that peace is peace, and thus deal with us as you've dealt with Jordanians and Egyptians to whom you returned all their land until the last centimeter. The same thing will happen with Syria when you reach a peace agreement with her.

Saeb: Whoever will be able to reach an agreement to solve this conflict will be the most important figure in the region after Jesus Christ!

Livni: Israel was established to become a national home for Jews from all over the world. The Jew gets the citizenship as soon as he steps in Israel, and therefore don't say anything about the nature of Israel as I don't wish to interfere in the nature of your state. The conflict we're trying to solve is between two peoples. They used to say there were no Palestinian people; my father used to say so too. They used to say Palestinians were Arabs so let them find a solution in an Arab country. The basis for the creation of the state of Israel is that it was created for the Jewish people. Your state will be the answer to all Palestinians including refugees. Putting an end to claims means fulfilling national rights for all.

The next meeting was scheduled to take place in Jerusalem at 15:30 on Sunday, January 27.

Meeting Minutes

Jerusalem/Sheraton Plaza
4 February 2008 '
12:00 – 14:00

Attendants

Palestinian side:
- Ahmad Qrei' (Abu Ala')
- Dr. Saeb Erekat
- Salah Ilayan

Israeli side:
- Tzepi Livni
- Tal Beker

Livni: Did you hear about the suicide attack? Al-Aqsa Martyrs Brigade, affiliated with Fateh, declared its responsibility for the attack. I am talking with representatives of a movement that has claimed responsibility for the attack. What steps will you take?

Abu Ala': D'you want to show your anger? We're angry too.

Livni: I said I'll not halt negotiations because of this incident.

Saeb: I wouldn't say Fateh or Hamas until things are clear.

Abu Ala': The attack took place in Israel not in an area under Palestinian control. It took place in Dimonah, one of the most sensitive areas in Israel. The main issue here is that the perpetrators acted against the peace process; whether they're Fateh or Hamas isn't important.

Livni: What's Fateh doing with regard to Al-Aqsa Martyrs Brigade?

Saeb: They have been contained after they pledged to hand over all their arms to the Palestinian security apparatuses and refrain from carrying out any military action. Whoever didn't sign is outside the organization. The fault of Israel is that there were many who've committed themselves but Israel assassinated them.

We strongly condemn this attack and you've to be patient until it becomes clear who the perpetrators are. Hamas uses Fateh's name.

Abu Ala': Those who act against what Fateh's doing are against Fateh and against Abu Mazen.

Livni: Can you do anything against those who are against Fateh and the leadership?

Saeb: Al-Aqsa Martyrs Brigade, the Popular Front, and the Unified Resistance Squad declared their responsibility for the attack, but I'm sure Al-Aqsa Martyrs Brigade will denounce it. All use the name of Al-Aqsa Martyrs Brigade.

Livni: What's the relation between Fateh and Al-Aqsa Martyrs Brigade? Is it possible to issue a communiqué that Fateh is opposed to Al-Aqsa Martyrs Brigade and condemn their actions?

Abu Ala': Al-Aqsa Martyrs Brigade is part of Fateh movement and they agreed to be part of the current security apparatus, even though this was not my position when I was a prime minister. I wanted the Brigade to remain as it was to confront Hamas. Some are funded by Hamas, Hizbollah, and others.

Livni: Does the Brigade have a leadership?

Saeb: Whoever pays is their leader.

Abu Ala': Some didn't sign the commitment and remained outside and Fateh doesn't pay them. After the opening of the passage, Hizbollah paid Hamas and them. Hizbollah smuggled money and arms and people to the Gaza Strip.

Livni: My question is that what if another Goldstein killed Palestinians, God forbid, and Kadima Party claimed responsibility? I'd have gone out and said that Kadima is against the perpetrator of the attack.

Abu Ala': We've always been opposed to such actions because they're not only against Fateh but against our national interest as well.

Livni: Can you say they're not part of Fateh?

Saeb: I'm sure the President will handle the matter well.

Livni: Not by condemnation only. We say he can always condemn but he's incompetent. We want more than just condemnation.

Saeb: Yesterday a communiqué was issued in the name of al-Aqsa Martyrs Brigade calling for killing Salam Fayad. Another communiqué released by Al-Aqsa Martyrs Brigade was issued in which the Brigade denies any relation with the previous communiqué. The Brigade is divided.

Livni: What about the Gaza Strip?

Abu Ala': I accompanied President Abu Mazen in his trip to Cairo and we met with Minister Omar Suleiman and President Mobarak. It's become clear to the Egyptians that opening the borders isn't a game and what Hamas endangers Egyptian national security.

President Mobarak said they'll close down the borders after Sunday and whoever is caught on Egyptian territories will be considered illegal.

They want to work in accordance with the agreement signed in 2005, but Hamas refused this. They said harsh words to him and President Mobarak refused to meet with them. Minister Omar Suleiman met with them instead without any media coverage. The Egyptian told Hamas this was the last time they'd allow them to do such thing.

In Gaza the Egyptian position is taken seriously. Rafah is the only passage they've after you've closed the borders with Israel and thrown the ball into the Egyptian court.

Livni: The ball didn't come from Israel, but from Egypt to Gaza. How can we stop it?

Abu Ala': But it reached the hands of Hamas and you know how to stop it if you want.

Livni: The ball has to be caught in Egypt.

Abu ala': I didn't hear from you a stormy protest.

Livni: It seems that each party is working for its own benefit without any coordination; I mean the Israelis, Palestinians, and Egyptians.

Abu Ala': I've great doubts about your position towards the Gaza Strip.

Livni: Put every thing on the table and be clear and plain.

Abu Ala': You're supporting Hamas to segregate Gaza because your aim is separation.

Livni: The content of our work is to establish two states from the sea to the river, the state of Israel and the state of Palestine in the West Bank and the Gaza Strip. We withdrew from the Strip.

Abu Ala': But you're still occupying the Gaza Strip.

Livni: How?

Abu Ala': You control the entire Gaza Strip.

Livni: We'll never concede anything with regard to our security needs. Our position is not to allow for the establishment of two Hamases in the Gaza Strip. We'll not give legitimacy to Hamas and we'll stop the smuggling of money and arms from Egypt. Did the opening of the borders appear to be a victory for Hamas?

Abu Ala': Yes, they appeared to have ended the siege.

Livni: The Egyptians don't do enough, and we're sure they can do much more.

Abu Ala': What can you do about Philadelphia Crossing?

Livni: We're not there.

Abu Ala': You've re-occupied the West Bank, and you can occupy the crossing if you want.

Livni: We can re-occupy the Gaza Strip. What is your position?

Abu Ala': Our strategic position is that we want a state in the West Bank and the Strip with a safe passage.

Livni: By the way, the safe passage is a sensitive issue and we'll discuss it later.

Abu Ala': The borders of the Palestinian state with Egypt, Jordan, and Israel. What we want is to return to Gaza Strip not defeated but as a legitimate authority.

Livni: How?

Abu Ala': Hamas must not feel that it's achieving daily victories, sometimes with Israel and sometimes with Egypt, and Al-Jazeera Channel praises these victories. I hope Hamas will be defeated, not militarily I mean because we didn't try this; we didn't engage in a civil war. President Abu Mazen was wise enough not to give orders to Fateh members to use arms, otherwise we'd have had many casualties.

The Arabs are starting to understand the danger that is threatening them.

Palestinian control over Rafah Crossing will be a defeat for them, I mean Israel and Egypt and of course the Europeans because they're part of the agreement. This will change the situation because they didn't have freedom of movement.

Israel has to allow the entry of fuel and all basic goods. It was wrong of you not to let fuel and basic goods into Gaza. We've to work to compel Hamas to review its policies. They don't work for their own interest but for the interest of Iran and sometimes Syria. Iran wants to use Hamas and Hizbollah in case it's attacked.

Livni: How would the situation change? Through elections?

Abu Ala': Elections come later and that's why we refused to talk. We asked for the return of the situation to its previous state and for respecting our obligations. Then we can have elections.

Livni: D'you have doubts that we want to separate the Gaza Strip? Is this considered a threat or a victory for Hamas?

Abu Ala': D'you remember Rabin's saying: "I hope to sleep and wake up and see that the sea has swallowed Gaza."

Livni: We've a saying too. When you want to curse somebody you tell him "Go to hell" but we shorten it and say "Go to Gaza."

Abu Ala': What will affect Hamas is Rafah Crossing if work is resumed in accordance with the agreement signed in 2005.

Livni: Is their dream to establish a state in Gaza?

Abu Ala': Yes, and they will apply Islamic Shari'a and export their regime to neighboring countries.

Saeb: The battle with Hamas is unending. We've two schools: one says that the establishment of a state can be achieved through negotiations, and the other says that we've tried negotiations and they're an illusion; only resistance can lead to the establishment of a state.

When you besiege the Strip and cut off electricity and you see them cry over a sick child in candlelight—this is kind of victory they're seeking. They don't care about the suffering of the people.

What will destroy Hamas is for us to reach an agreement. They wager on our failure.

If you decide as some Israeli politicians blinded by anger sometimes behave and separate the Gaza Strip—this will be a victory for Hamas.

Abu Ala': To reach an agreement with us will be an accomplishment not because we're good people, but we're the only option for peace.

Livni: Agreement requires compatibility. If we agree, will we be able to market our agreement or will Hamas use it against you?

Abu Ala': If we're convinced about the agreement then we'll know how to convince people about it.

Livni: Saeb and Tal have completed work on the structure and this is good because through it we know where we're heading.
These are the main issues and we can add more issues, if there are any.

Structure of an Agreement

1. Preamble
2. General Provisions
3. Borders
4. Settlements
5. Passage Agreements
6. Security
7. Refugees
8. Jerusalem – I (Holy Places)
9. Water and Environment
10. Economic relations **& Infrastructure**
11. Civil Spheres and Arrangements Regarding Infrastructure
    State to State Relation
12. Legal Relations
13. Culture of Peace – People to People
    Civil society & Culture of Peace
14. Steps towards **the Establishment of** the Palestinian State and Implementation
    Arrangements
15. Coordination and Cooperation and Dispute Resolution Mechanism
16. End of Conflict, p. (Reparations) and Finality of Claims
17. Prisoners
18. Final Clauses

Abu Ala': The best place to discuss the holy places is State to State Relations.

Livni: I've an objection to Reparations which doesn't appear in any previous agreement. You can put it forward but I'll object to it since I can't ask you to bring back to life those who were killed in terrorist attacks. We're talking about the future and not the past.

Abu Ala': We did put it forward during our talks with Shlomo Ben Ami.

Tal: But it was never one day a major issue.

Abu Ala': Why don't we put it for discussion?

Livni: Putting it for discussion means we agree to it. During the past session I suggested reviving multi-lateral negotiations in issues that don't embarrass you or us. I'd like also to make another suggestion but you don't have to respond now. I believe it's possible to activate work groups in issues of water, environment and economic growth.

Abu Ala': Let's start with water since the US is the sponsor of this work group, as well as of regional security and arms control.

Livni: What about if we ask two specialized people from each party to present their suggestions to us regarding what we see proper for the activation of multilateral talks

Abu Ala': It's not you or me who decides. I've talked with Condoleeza Rice.

Livni: What about inviting Russia to the follow up conference of Annapolis Conference? Do we really need such a conference? What will we say in this meeting?

Abu Ala': It may be good to bring Syria in!

Livni: Do you want us to talk with Syria? We've always believed that you don't prefer our talk to have two tracks.

I'll talk to Condoleeza Rice about multilateral talks.

I want to bring specialized people in the field of borders, water, and security to our meetings but not all at one time. After we hear what they've to say we'll ask them to work among themselves because there's a lot to do and this will take time.

Abu Ala': Let's convince ourselves first that we're achieving something. Let's let Saeb and Tal start talks about the preambles and general regulations, and we start talks about borders and security.

Livni: I suggest to have people specialized in maps to talk about borders, settlements and security.

I've some ideas about settlements and we want to see what will happen with regard to options: if we decide to evacuate settlements what will happen to the assets; what about the future of civilians (setters) if we decide to have some settlements within the borders of the Palestinian state; what will happen to the Palestinians if we decide to annex some settlements to Israel; lease.

Abu Ala': I suggest that Saeb and Tal put the drafts for borders, settlement and security.

Livni: In the presence of specialized people and we bring one with us to the meeting for each case.

Abu Ala': Strategically, we want security for our sake first and you've your security needs as well. We'll sit together and discuss the matter over.

I won't convince you with what I've decided strategically; and you won't convince me with what you've decided either.

Minutes from Secuity Session
Post Annapolis
Thursday, 28th February 2008, 5:30pm
Office of Ms. Tzipi Livni, Tel Aviv

Attendees:
Palestinian

- Ahmed Querei (AA)
- Dr. Saeb Erekat (SE)
- Brig. Gen. Hazem Atallah (HA)
- Salah el-Alayan (SA)
- Rami Dajani (RD)

Israeli

- FM Tzipi Livni (TL)
- Gen. (ret.) Amos Gilad (AG)
- Tal Becker ? (TB)
- Udi Dekel (UD)

Meeting Summary (*not verbatim*):

TL:

- [On Gaza] If rocket attacks continue, more will be killed. We were forced to leave Gaza, but maybe will have to go back. Our public is demanding we do something about the situation.
- How does Gaza affect the West Bank street?

AA:

- People are worried: Where will this lead? But Hamas does not have a problem with it.

TL:

- For them it's resistance ... so giving them more power?

AA:

- Steadfastness – resistance. All this is promoted by TV channels, and stories of conspiracies against them.

TL:

- This [present situation] is going to be continued. Effectiveness of measures is not the question. Some will need to be taken into consideration, but impossible to just do nothing and hope that nothing happens.

AA:

1

- Are you ready for a real ceasefire?

TL:
- Hamas will strengthen and build its forces more. Speaking openly, what we do in Gaza is because they target Israel. They know the equation. Once they stop we stop and they know it. When there is quiet, they build up power. So we need not only to stop the rockets but also smuggling of weapons. Negotiating with Hamas strengthens them and weakens you.

AA:
- But to continue with this situation?

AG:
- Negotiating with "Hamastan" will harm both of us. They will continue smuggling military and terror, building power.
- Even if we accept ceasefire, it cannot include West Bank because we need freedom to act to prevent suicide attacks.
- Rockets are aimed not only to murder, but also to terrorize – so even one is not acceptable.
- Hizbollah is involved in Gaza, and Egypt is doing what it is doing. They are sensitive to Muslim Brotherhood at home so they are feeding the monster. There is coordination with Egyptian government officials – not only corruption. They are riding the tiger but the tiger bites. When Aljazeera reported everyone cheered against the great Egypt.

AA:
- But this is like a children's game – attacks and counterattacks.

AG:
- But we have stopped a spectacular act of terror. We are trying our best not to hurt civilians, using better technology.
- Hamas is not only a terror organization, they are using prisons, torture. They want to establish Hamastan and extend it to the West Bank.

TL:
- What are Hamas' parameters for success in Gaza?

AA:
- Steadfastness in the face of the occupier with no peace process working. They invest in events like massing at the border and demonstrations when people are killed. They know how to use this.

SE:
- Yesterday I asked a question about *tahdi'a*. We need to stop the killing on both sides. Sure that Hamas won't respond. The idea was to bring Omar Suleiman here to work on a complete ceasefire. Now he is not coming because of events.

2

- The major problems on a regional scale, between Iran and Europe play a role. Arab summit may not be held. Situation with Syria and Iran precludes attack in the North. Only options are inside Lebanon and from Gaza.

AG:

- Regarding Omar Suleiman, maybe he delayed because he is afraid we will attack while he is here. It will hurt him – would look like collaborator. It is significant that Hamas can delay visit of Egypt's Number Two.

AA:

- We are here to discuss the future: security after establishment of a Palestinian state – not the present.

AG:

- But we are inspired by the present… to understand the future.

TL:

- One way or another we have to address the situation in Gaza.

SE:

- You don't need to worry about Gaza in this discussion. You are protected by Annapolis. Implementation is subject to …

TL:

- Yes

AG:

- You find a solution in international force, but we believe in partnership between us in security, as for example we have with Jordan. Such partnership cannot exist without reliable security forces. There are two main lessons from the past: the Jordan Valley in the 1970s, and the Philadelphi corridor in hands of Palestinians.
- It is difficult to understand why Egyptians are acting this way now – supporting strategic threats to the peace camp. They need to manage Hamas, together with Muslim Brotherhood, these are their strategic rivals with agenda to radicalize and destabilize and take over the region. So the Egyptians conclude to live with the threat by feeding the monster with weapons.
- Situation in Gaza is changing constantly because Iran is investing heavily. Iran has a new line of product: simple missiles with 17km range that are easy to assemble (they come in 4 parts). These will widen the belt of terror, so the GoI won't tolerate it. Like in the Jordan Valley in the 70s, open to all gangs of terror.

HA:

- They are primitive home made rockets.

AG:

- No. The range is most important. Assembled not home-made.

3

- Jordanians almost lost the kingdom... you know well that in Jordan things can change quickly. Jordan needs a stable cooperative counterpart on the western side.
- You ask to take control. This will be problematic for Israel – to give it to you or an international force. International force lacks both intelligence and capabilities – these are not parades in Rome. They need to be able to investigate, arrest, run courts, which runs well in Jordan. But Jordan may not be able to continue with it if situation changes dramatically on the western side..

TL:

- Question is how can we keep the same effectiveness under new arrangements ...

AG:

- It [Jordan Valley] is one security entity as we witnessed in the 70s.

AA:

- Times are different now.

AG:

- Security is the same.
- Our assessment is that Iran is eager to open channels: through Hizbollah to Gaza, and through southern Iraq to Jordan and the West Bank. They have established infrastructure in south of Iraq. In Jordan it is difficult because it is strong, but still contacts are developing. So we need to prepare for these threats.

TL:

- So we need effectiveness on future Palestinian-Jordanian border, and in Gaza, effectiveness on Egypt border.

AG:

- It is not only Iran, there are others in Iraq – al Qaeda.

AA:

- It is not their priority.

SE:

- So they can put bombs in Amman hotels and not be able to touch you because of border arrangements?

AG:

- [mentions name of suspect as case in point] We gave the name to Dahlan and he refused to act. So we took him by force. Al Qaeda is eager to penetrate. Dughmush are their representatives ... Jabal Hilal. They try in Jordan – if there is no sense of deterrence they will keep trying.

TL:

4

- So at the crossings, you need effective supervision of what and who is coming and going. You don't want Al Qaeda coming.

AA:

- This is our responsibility.

AG:

- Cooperation is needed and should be based on real criteria and real security. Now we don't have that. Your agencies are penetrated. If present capabilities continue …

AA:

- Please think differently. Situation will be different after end of the occupation. Right now everyone is suffering. In the future we can deal with each other as equals.
- But if you continue to think of tomorrow like today, we won't be able to agree.
- So we need a strong agreement with strong support, respect and implementation.
- We have no objection to having a third party to give you confidence, and we will build our own strong police, with mechanisms to be supported.
- If you maintain arrangements that keeps it like the occupation, this will create problems, for example if you control our crossings.
- The situation today is different from 20 years ago. Threats are more sophisticated. You can easily fire missiles from Tehran.

HA:

- In a future independent state, people will have something to protect and die for – they will have to protect their dream.

TL:

- We need a prescription, which like any medicine, is not fool-proof and will have some negative side effects. Like when you treat a patient, you expect side effects.
- So some of the things we discuss can affect the feeling that you describe. But we need efficiency, while respecting your need for freedom and dignity. On the other hand, some things we need because we cannot just rely on people's perception.
- I was optimistic during the disengagement. I remember the discussions with Wolfensohn on greenhouses, infrastructure, prosperity etc. Instead we got a slap – all of us – so I am trying to learn from the past.
- We have certain needs. Maybe in the future they won't be needed. It is problematic because there is a period of time before the creation of the state (which we all support), but the situation will not change the day after.
- Some Palestinians hate us, and maybe they have reasons.
- Effectiveness of your forces now is not reliable
- We can give list [unclear]. AG will address this.. Some aspects you will say this affects independence and sovereignty but this is a question of feeling – the difference between what is agreed and what is forced.

5

125

- I know the importance of symbols and can think of ways of doing what is needed without affecting the symbols.
- Some of these parameters can also be removed after the creation of the state – they are transitional arrangements.
- You may say this is putting us in a vicious cycle – of anger and mistrust, but let's refer to each need and see how problematic it is.
- On international forces: Israel does not have an answer yet, but we know they are not effective and don't want to have a situation of another war.

AA:

- Why do you say they are not effective?

TL:

- Europeans are not going to come the Middle East to die for our peace.

AA:

- They have been effective elsewhere – in Bosnia for example.

TL:

- We can talk about air strikes …

AA:

- Who gave independence to Kosovo?

SE:

- [To TL] Your assumptions are not true – they are not objective and tested against reality. Your 'truth' is that failure in Gaza was because of us. It was unilateralism that destroyed us – it was the Israeli mistakes. But you don't admit your mistakes. You blame me for everything.

TL:

- Unfortunately, I blame myself … AG said we need cooperation and I agree …

AG:

- Not exactly. I said cooperation between reliable, effective, credible partner, but right now we don't consider you a partner.

SE:

- We are speaking about the future. We have Dayton, EU BAM and others helping us improve performance. We are trying to get there. However, I know that you will protect yourself and won't need me to protect you.
- But, don't make assumptions about Jordan and security. If your assumption is that we failed Gaza so you can't trust us in the West Bank, that you don't want to gamble with Jordan …

TL:

6

- Since you are not good to take care of security now, the West Bank can be a threat to me. So we need to take measures; we can do them before statehood.
- Since I believe that at the end of the day the government on the other side needs to be effective, legitimate and able to fight terror (which is lacking in the region – Gaza, Lebanon) we need to address this issue.
- We can work in different ways: for example, here are parameters on what you are strong enough or not to do now, or, put on the table issues that can help the process. We are willing to take some risk.
- So, I said "no army" – a demilitarized state. You said "internal security"

AA:
- We are willing to consider limited arms.

SE:
- This is a contradiction. Why did we differentiate between the Road Map and permanent status. You have a guarantee that building the forces comes before implementation. So don't tell me at the same time to put parameters.

TL:
- You were at Camp David. Do you expect the state to have an army?

SE:
- No.

TL:
- Without these measures we cannot afford another state between Jordan.

AA:
- It is not clear what we are talking about. We are supposed to be discussing the future concept, this is an open discussion – no agenda. This is important for both sides. We both agree that we need a comprehensive and detailed agreement satisfactory to both. So, let us ask what are the issues. We can explore these issues. AG and HA and others can do this.

TL:
- They can have a meeting next week …

AA:
- Then come back. [internal discussion between TL and AG]

AG:
- No problem to have the meeting, but since SE thinks there is contradiction it is better to discuss here before making a list.

AA:
- Give me titles. What do you want? Enough with general concept.

7

TL:

- Next week's meeting will have concrete expression of the concepts and will explore disagreements, but AG still feels we need to discuss the concepts here.
- [To HA] You will share your vision. I hope you don't believe that we will just have borders … and that's it.

HA:

- No. These misunderstandings cause problems. I will talk about the past before the future.
- Before the intifada, the forces worked well. The officers had discipline, they had a reason to work well.

TL:

- But can you explain Gaza? I can't understand … the mood of the people. We left. How come they continue to fight? It's not about whether there was coordination – which is something technical.

HA:

- Hamas used the withdrawal for propaganda: signs comparing results of 10 years of negotiations with those of struggle.

TL:

- I heard this and used this point internally to argue that unilateralism was a mistake.

HA:

- At the same time, I cannot forget what happened to the security forces during the intifada. They were destroyed. It was clear until then that the fight was against Hamas and Jihad. With Israeli attacks came infiltration of the services by Hamas.
- We are now cleaning the services. It's a campaign for the future. We are recruiting and training young people who will work according to the law – to maintain law and order.

TL:

- We can take care of our security but do not want a failed state next to us. How do you see the role of the international force? To help with the construction?

HA:

- The internationals are already doing this. It is moving slowly but we are training in Jordan with help of Dayton. Third party can definitely help building the forces.

TL:

- Regarding Philadelphi – whether or not it was a mistake to leave it. If indeed it was a mistake, since Egypt is not effective like Jordan, can our agreement provide for Israeli presence in Philadelphi?

8

AA:

- Palestine will be independent but can coordinate. Agreement should reflect that with a commitment to security.
- Therefore regarding parameters I believe security is part of regional vision. Other neighbours don't have a problem -- regional security is interconnected.

TL:

- What is the idea of working with Gen. Dayton?

HA:

- Building up and improving the NSF, police and Presidential Guard.

TL:

- What is their role?

HA:

- Law enforcement. Problem was due to delays, but now it is going well. We are building new units and carrying out the program of retirement, the target being a young organization. So right now, if we want to deploy 2 battalions, the capacity is becoming available with newly trained people. There are 4 more battalions to be completed.
- At the same time EU COPSS is training the police force.
- Let me talk about the future shape of Palestinian security.

TL:

- So you've talked about the present, now the future.

HA:

- Plan to develop the security services is based on a defensive security strategy. The main function will be to protect the population and the territory.

TL:

- What does territory mean?

AA:

- Palestine – 67 borders.

HA:

- Protection requires knowing where the borders are first ... and preventing smuggling and infiltration.

TL:

- This means an army.

HA:

9

- No. It can be done in different ways. Army is only one way. Border guards and international force are other ways.

TL:

- Guarding from what?

HA:

- From everything, like infiltration – like the problem in Gaza now. We are talking about sovereignty. Every country needs to protect its borders.
- Another function of the security forces will be maintaining law and order and carrying out law enforcement duties.
- This is something we are testing ourselves with right now in Nablus – next it will be Hebron.
- Again functions are to defend borders and to fight crime and terrorism.

TL:

- We have an understanding of threats, so when you talk about borders, smuggling is fine, but external threats .. are you talking about a foreign army? If it is to defend against foreign attacks, then we have a big gap.

HA:

- No one is thinking of building an army to fight Israel. We are talking about something more than police and less than an army.

TL:

- This is something you can discuss later with AG.

AA:

- I'm afraid we are going into details that may not be necessary in a peace agreement.
- You need to say a strong police…

TL:

- Demilitarized state.

HA:

- There is no such thing. There is no example of it anywhere in the world. There are demilitarized zones, not states.

TL:

- We live in a small space.

SE:

- So Palestine will be a buffer zone? A demilitarized zone?

HA:

10

- We need strong security forces, as AA said. With enough ability to carry out their functions.
- Now we have serious problems just bringing in bullet proof vests.
- Security forces need appropriate weapons. So for example, not tanks, but armoured scout cars.

AA:
- Not demilitarized but limited.

TL:
- [discusses "limited" with AG] "Limited" seems to be no tanks, no airforce, no artillery, no missiles…

AG:
- Demilitarization is a meaningful term. It is not an NSU term. Limited: *Mahdud*. Regarding NSF the 1995 Interim Agreement limited them to 45,000. Now after fall of Saddam, may seem like less threat, but including Iran in the equation, the chances of destabilization, nuclear threat have increased. Now there is Shiite-stan in south Iraq, Hizbollah in Lebanon and Hamas in Gaza. Hostile military coalitions are possible – given geographic data.
- So it is understood that demilitarization must be a pillar, especially as it related to hostile alliances.

HA:
- Can any country maintain security by itself without any regional cooperation?

AG:
- Consider the Dayton plan. It took two years to send one battalion to one country with real training. Egypt training was a real problem.

HA:
- That was a shame.

SE:
- There is an Arabic proverb: You don't cut the snake's tail, rather you cut the head.

AG:
- About Dayton: it is a good idea. We should test it. We are watching carefully, testing the future by beginning in the present.

HA:
- Then why don't you help us?

AG:
- We have facilitated Dayton's work.

11

HA:
- There are still problems – for example with funding.

AG:
- You want money from us?

TL:
- You got 7 billion in Paris.

HA:
- That is all on paper.

AG:
- Regarding the future, there is the possibility of hostile alliances – we need demilitarization and no hostile alliances.

AA:
- You want a Palestinian state or a military base …

TL:
- So next week you [HA and AG] meet. Sunday or Monday?
- [To HA] This work is important. As decision-makers we have problems that are historical. Our publics are not supportive because of risks to our security. Some risks we can take, but some things we must address.

12

Meeting Minutes
On Borders

Jerusalem
Inpal Hotel (Larome)
8 April 2008
11:30 – 13:30

Attendees:

Palestinian side:
- Ahmad Qurei' (Abu Ala')
- Dr. Saeb Erekat
- Dr. Samih Al-Abed
- Salah Ilayan
- Zeinah Salahi

Israeli side:
- Tzipi Livni
- Udi Dekel
- Tal Becker
- Dani Terza

Livni: I would like to say one thing before reviewing the maps. I know that what you will see will make you feel like we are taking it away from you. You will say that we are taking your hands and your legs, but I hope you will look at what there is on the other side. We are in need of it not because we want your land but because we do not wish to evacuate people from their homes. We are talking about 250,000 settlers living in the West Bank and we would like them all to remain living in a small area. I know that every inch hurts you.

None of us has touched the heart of the other yet (Jerusalem).

Before the presentation, I would like to understand one thing. Abu Ala' talks about 1.5% for swap and Abu Mazen about 2%.

Abu Ala': Abu Mazen revoked. He does not want any percentage for swap.

Livni: Does this percentage have any basis, or is it simply a generous donation from you?

Abu Ala': Even though we do not acknowledge the realities on the ground imposed by Israel, the concession we made in Camp David is our willingness for swap by reciprocity and value. There was no talk about settlement bloss. There is talk about settlements in Israel only. We have never recognized these settlement blocs and therefore we suggested swap for a reasonable percentage and not a greedy swap, provided that we discuss how and where swap should take place. If you had asked today, we would have never agreed on swap.

Livni: I want to tell you about your needs and then translate them into a percentage. I will try to explain to you that it is need and not greed. If we do not annex them and if there is bloodshed after the establishment of the state then you will be forced to see our soldiers. This is something we do not want. We try to give an answer by reducing friction between both sides.

We will present our needs since we are still in the negotiation stage, and then experts will work to minimize them in some areas.

Abu Ala': I cannot accept these principles. It is like taking all your money and then negotiate on how much to return to you. The beginning is half the end.

The basis is 1967 borders. You and the whole world including UN resolutions number 242 and 338 recognize this. Then we can talk about modifications. I will look at the percentage if it is 1% or 2%, but if it is more I will not look any more.

Livni: Then you already object.

Udi: The first meeting on economy was good do not spoil it.

Samih: The first depends on what is achieved here about the land.

Saeb: You presented your position. We will listen but only remember our position as it was presented by Abu Ala'. The 1967 borders are the basis for the two-state solution; and we can discuss swap.

No negotiation track in the world will be successful if this track will fail. The aim is to serve the interest of both sides and reach a win-win situation. The more realistic we are in our proposition, the more progress we will achieve.

Livni: I do not want to present to you what causes you grief and misery.

Abu Ala': You said yesterday in a press statement that you have red lines. You answered this when you were asked whether we also have red lines that we cannot give up.

Next meeting they can continue to discuss many things, including means to remove settlements and others.

You have come with what you want and we have come with what is realistic. We hope they will continue to meet.

Terza: Of course, there will be the safe passage between the West Bank and the Gaza Strip. There is no need to bring this up.

Livni: Look, this is the answer to smothering the West Bank with Ma'ale Adumim. The distance between Ma'ale Adumim and the Jordan Valley is 17 kilometers, and the distance between Tulkarem and the Green Line is 14 kilometers.

The instructions I gave for putting the maps are:
- to include the largest possible number of Israelis;
- to exclude Palestinians;
- to include constructed areas or areas under construction;
- to exclude areas that have been organized;
- to take into account security needs;
- to link between them and Israel.

Terza: This is the line for the terms of reference.

Livni: What you call 1967 line.

Abu Ala': She cannot even say the word!

Terza: This is Gosh Etzyon area and it includes the settlements of Kfar Etzyon, Bitar 'Illit, Ephrat, Daniel, Alon Shafot, Teqoa.

It includes all constructed areas in addition to plans currently under construction.

Abu Ala': Does this mean that any area where there are no Palestinians should be given to Israel?

Terza: The area of Gosh Etzyon is about 544 square kilometers.

Saeb: What about the green area on the map?

Livni: I asked myself this question, and my answer was that it is for connection to create a vital zone. The problem here is topography.

Terza: Its area is 3.5 square kilometers and the population in Etzyon bloc is 50,000 people.

Livni: There are a number of small settlements for which we have to find an answer in the agreement.

The population in Gosh Etzyon is 50,000 people representing less that 1% of the West Bank area.

Let us now look at Ma'ale Adumim.

Terza: It includes Ma'ale Adumim, Kfar Adumim, Almon, Mitzape Yeriho, Alon, Kidar, and the industrial settlement of Mishor Adumim, and its area is 85 square kilometers. The population is 40,000 people and represents 1% of the West Bank area.

Livni: Today there are roads for the Palestinians and roads for the Israelis and all the roads are under Israeli control. We are talking about the next day and not the situation today, since we are living in the same area. In the future there will be roads in Palestine and each side will have sovereignty over its roads.

Saeb: What about the areas around Jerusalem?

Livni: We will discus this when we talk about the issue of Jerusalem.

Terza: Modi'in'Illit is 11 square kilometers and its population is 45,000 people.

28,000 people live in Ariel alone and the population living in surrounding settlements (Ariel bloc) which are like fingers (the fingers of Ariel and Kadumim) is 70,000 people and its area is 131 square kilometers.

Livni: I know what you are going to say: these fingers will pluck out your eyes. There are some small settlements that I exclude such as the ones near Nablus, for example.

There is no Israeli leader who will sign an agreement that does not include Ariel.

Abu Ala': And there is no Palestinian leader who will sign an agreement that includes Ariel.

Livni: Let us be fair. You referred to 1967 line. We have not talked about Jerusalem yet. There are some Palestinian villages that are located on both sides of the 1967 line about which we need to have an answer, such as Beit Safafa, Barta'a, Baqa al-Sharqiyeh and Baqa al-Gharbiyyeh. There are also some settlements that were built behind 1967 line but expanded inside 1967 line illegally, such as Uranit settlement south of Hebron.

Abu Ala': First, we cannot accept this proposition and I am sorry to hear it. This solution is not the two-state solution. It is the five-state solution: a state in Gaza, a state in Jerusalem, a state for settlers, a Palestinian state and an Israeli state. I do not think this will be the basis for any discussion.

Shlomo Ben Ami wanted to propose this to me but I told him no. Look how much Ma'ale Adumim has expanded since you suggested the swap. Thus if you want to be realistic and are concerned about the continuation of this channel, you have to come up with a realistic proposition.

I cannot look at you needs but I can look at swap by a realistic percentage.

If you want to terminate the PA with this proposition, we will leave it for our future generations to demand our rights.

Terza: Ma'ale Adumim was 64 kilometers in Taba.

Livni: At any rate, Taba is not a term of reference.

Saeb: I mentioned earlier that the establishment of the Palestinian state is the answer to the issue of 5 million Palestinian refugees, but this does not mean that you should make this state smaller.

Will what you need be swapped?

Livni: We do not create a state for every refugee but we create a concept. This is what happened in Israel when the state was created. The Jews came to the state and not to the land. There are things on the ground that you hate but they are there.

There is enough chance to reduce the needs that we have proposed.

Saeb: Will you compensate us for what you will take?

Livni: We will talk about the type of compensation.

I know that your position is for 1:1 swap. I said I cannot accept this percentage, but we will negotiate.

I know that Abu Mazen has proposed this to Olmert but Olmert refused it. I know that you have your ideas and I suggest that during next meeting you propose them.

Abu Ala': I agreed to listen to your propositions because I thought you would come with realistic propositions.

In light of these circumstances and these unrealistic propositions, I see that the only solution is a bi-national state where Moslems, Christians and Jews live together.

In Israel they do not realize our needs.

Is our demand for 1967 borders too much for us?

Livni: I did not say it is too much for you.

Abu Ala': Is it because settlers have come and settled in our land? Many countries occupied other countries and set up colonies but in then end they left them. The Soviet Union is the best example. They colonized many Islamic countries in Central Asia and left everything. There are many other examples from the world that shows this.

Livni: What you are saying is that there are no settlements you can live with?

Abu Ala': For the sake of the Palestinian state I may be ready to swap for small percentage.

Livni: I am not telling you to take this proposition or leave it, but what I am saying is that these are our needs.

Abu Ala': In Oslo we said that everything should take place gradually.

Livni: I do not like gradation.

Abu Ala': Now I do not like it but it was the only possible choice in Israel.

In one of the meetings with Abu Ammar and in my presence, Rabin said he would set up a fence around each settlement 50 meters far from the farthest house in it.

I said: Does this mean organization?

He said, "This is a decision."

If negotiations continue and Olmert goes on with the implementation of settlement construction including Jerusalem then 15% of the territories will be cut out.

For us the territories mean the West Bank and the Gaza Strip, including Jerusalem, the Dead Sea and No Man's Land. This is what the final agreement should include, and in this way all Palestinian claims about territories come to an end.

Livni: Why will No Man's Land go for you?

Abu Ala': And it is not yours. We can negotiate on it.

Livni: The gap is not big. It is about 350 – 450 square kilometers. Future generations will blame us and never forgive us if we lose this opportunity because of this gap.

Abu Ala': Then like what I said. The solution is a bi-national state from the sea to the river.

Livni: I suggest that during next meeting you present your ideas about this subject.

Meeting Minutes
On Borders

Jerusalem, King David Hotel
4 May 2008
20:45-21:30

Attendees:

Palestinians side: Ahmad Qurei (Abu Ala')
- Dr. Saeb Erekat
- Dr. Samih al-Abed
- Khaled Elgindi
- Salah Ilayan
- Zeinah Salahi

Israeli side: Tzipi Livni
- Udi Dekel
- Tal Becker
- Dani Terza

Livni: Based on what I have heard in the trilateral meeting with Condoleeza Rice, I believe that your offer will not be exciting.

Saeb: I hope you will like what will be proposed to you. Abu Ala' will begin identifying principles on whose bases we have drawn the maps.

Abu Ala': Our definition of the land includes the following: (1) 1967 borders which includes all the land Israel occupied in 1967 whose total area is 6,238 square kilometers; (2) the West Bank including No Man's Land and East Jerusalem, the Jordan Valley, etc.; (3) the Gaza Strip; (4) the Dead Sea.

Livni: Part of the Dead Sea.

Abu Ala': Part of the Dead Sea.

Livni: Is this a concession?

Abu Ala': - A big one for that matter.

- The safe passage
- Sea borders
- 1967 borders are the only basis for the two-state solution, Palestinians have made a historic concession by accepting 242 UN Resolution for the two-state solution. By accepting the resolution, Palestinians have recognized the state of Israel,

which was in fact a viable, contiguous and sovereign state along 1967 borders with 78% of the area of historic Palestine.

- Both of us agree that the settlement enterprise has a very negative effect and that the evacuation of settlements is for the good of both sides. Settlements confiscate large areas of Palestinian land, deprive Palestinians of many development spheres, impede communication and destroy Palestinian economy. Settlements were meant to artificially change the demographic structure and change realities on the ground, as well as to ensure that no viable Palestinian state would evolve. Now that you have accepted the idea of a Palestinian state, such a state must be geographically contiguous, viable and sovereign. But in order to make this a reality, the Israeli settlements must be evacuated. The issue is not whether evacuation should take place, but which settlements should be removed in order to be able to implement the two-state solution. Unlike the Palestinian state, the removal of settlements will not affect the viability of the state of Israel or its contiguity or security. Besides, if any of the settlers wish to live under Palestinian sovereignty, they have to be subject to the Palestinian law.

- For us, all settlements are illegal and their construction was a violation of the international law, and thus they should be evacuated. We are not the only ones who think this; this is also acknowledged by the rest of the international community. On the other hand, we understand that in order to reach a two-state solution in spite of all the Israeli measures that were taken in order to change realities on the ground, there is common interest in keeping some settlements. This is the concession that we make for the purpose of meeting your legitimate interests and making the two-state solution feasible. Thus any amendments on 1967 borders – the main basis for a two-state solution – should also meet our interests and keep geographical contiguity, viability and sovereignty of the state within the context of swap by the ratio of 1:1, with the same value and size.

Livni: Do you have any suggestions about the areas for swap?

Abu Ala': - You will see that on the maps.

- In order to meet Palestinian interests, swap of land with the same value and size and by the ration of 1:1 should take into account the following factors: (1) Any settlement included in the swap should not impede geographical contiguity especially with and within Jerusalem. This partially means that any settlement swapped to Israel should be near 1967 line. Therefore, any settlement swapped to Israel should be dealt with individually not as settlement blocs or individual houses. (2) All areas should be equal; in other words, all areas included in the swap should be in the same area (that is, land in Jerusalem for land in Jerusalem). (3) Areas swapped 'from' should not impede Palestinian development, and areas swapped 'to' should support Palestinian development, in accordance with the plans, and allow for urban expansion of Palestinian cities and towns. (4) The value of agricultural land should be preserved. (5) The Palestinian state must have adequate land, capabilities and resources to absorb Palestinian refugees who do not prefer to return to Israel, and those who hope to return to Palestine. (6) Areas

of religious, cultural and historical significance for the Palestinians should not be included in the swap. (7) In any swap, there should be access to quality water and other water interests. (8) Civilians will not be included in any swap; in other words, land inhabited by Palestinians will not be subject for swap. (9) Empty land shall not be swapped to Israel. (10) Security is not a condition for land swap because there will always be borders between Palestine and Israel. (For example, no agreement will provide strategic depth because of Qalqilya and Tulkarem, etc.). Peace is the only means to provide Palestinians and Israelis alike with peace.
- On the basis of these factors, some settlements cannot be included in swap under any condition, including the settlements of Maa'le Adumim, Giv'at Ze'ev, Har Homa (Abu Ghneim), and Ariel. These negotiations are not a market, and the issue is not that of numbers for compromise and or disagreements. We want to meet the interests of both sides.
- We suggested that 63% of all settlers be included in less than 2%. This suggestion meets the interests of all parties.

Livni: Is this with Jerusalem or without it?

Abu Ala': With Jerusalem.

Saeb: After reviewing your proposition during last meeting, we reviewed the areas and took into account your needs. Accordingly, we put suggestions in a manner that meets the interests of both sides.

Abu Ala': Dr. Samih will start the presentation.

Samih: - We tried in the proposition that we will present to you to be more fair than the proposition that was presented to us.

- Negotiations about land:
    - o 1967 line is the only basis.
    - o Swap by the ratio of 1:1 with the same size and value.
    - o Comprehensive, including Jerusalem, the Jordan Valley, etc.

Livni: What do you mean by the same value?

Abu Ala': If annexation was in Jerusalem area then swap will take place in Jerusalem area.

Tal: How can we measure this? Land has the same value.

Livni: Or is it only a slogan?

Samih: It is not a slogan. I do not wish to have land in the Dunhiyyeh desert area for land in Jerusalem, for example.

Saeb: The value of the land determines how the other side will benefit from it.

Livni: Will the Safe Passage have the same value of what is going to be annexed to Israel?

Samih: You are talking about the Safe Passage, but the value of the Jewish Quarter in Jerusalem is inestimable.

Livni: I understand that it is difficult to calculate the value.

Khaled: It is also important to see that we are talking here about all the areas. In other words, we cannot agree only on part of the borders because it is impossible to know the meaning of the part without knowing the nature of all the borders.

Livni: You mentioned Jerusalem. Do you think this is our hidden agenda?

Samih: Interests:

- **Palestinian interests:**

  o Political recognition.

Livni: I hope you will say the same thing when you talk about our interests.

Samih: Wait and we will come to that.

  o Sovereignty and control.
  o Viability and geographical contiguity.
  o Jerusalem.
  o Security

- Israeli interest:

  o Reduction of political and financial cost.
  o Jerusalem.
  o Security.

- 1967 borders.

  - East Jerusalem (square km)
  - No Man's Land (Latroun, Jerusalem)

Livni: Latroun was not occupied. Anyways, this is your position.

Samih: - Part of the Dead Sea.

- The Gaza Strip.

Other land related issues:

- Land contiguity (Safe Passage).
- Water borders.

Swap:

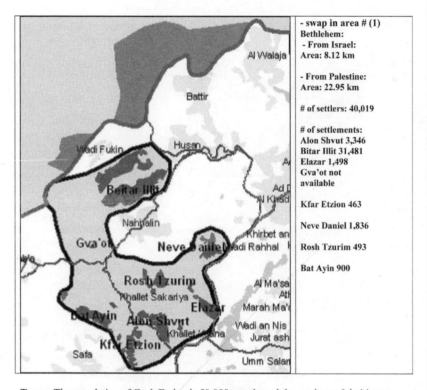

- swap in area # (1)
Bethlehem:
- From Israel:
Area: 8.12 km

- From Palestine:
Area: 22.95 km

# of settlers: 40,019

# of settlements:
Alon Shvut 3,346
Bitar Illit 31,481
Elazar 1,498
Gva'ot not
available

Kfar Etzion 463

Neve Daniel 1,836

Rosh Tzurim 493

Bat Ayin 900

Terza: The population of Gush Etzion is 50,000 people and the road near Jaba' is not included in the swap.

Livni: The problem is the road to Gush Etzion.

Samih: As you can see, there is a large area of empty land, and we think that Batir can be a suitable area for crossing and trade and others. As you probably know, there was a railroad there.

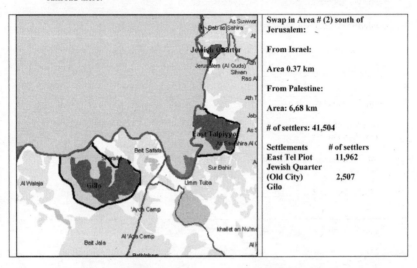

Swap in Area # (2) south of Jerusalem:

From Israel:

Area 0.37 km

From Palestine:

Area: 6,68 km

# of settlers: 41,504

Settlements	# of settlers
East Tel Piot	11,962
Jewish Quarter (Old City)	2,507
Gilo	

Livni: Doesn't Har Homa exist?

Khaled: The interest is to reconnect Jerusalem and Bethlehem. Such reconnection has a social, religious, economic and tourist significance. It is even more important than the connection between Jerusalem and Ramallah. The area is also important for the expansion of Beit Safafa which has become an isolated town between Gilo and Har Homa settlements.

Abu Ala': To address natural growth.

Livni: Now we are talking about natural growth?!

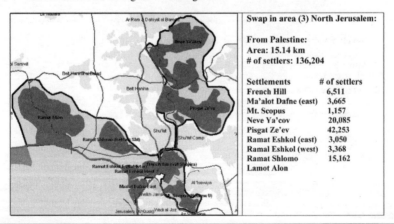

Swap in area (3) North Jerusalem:

From Palestine:
Area: 15.14 km
# of settlers: 136,204

Settlements	# of settlers
French Hill	6,511
Ma'alot Dafne (east)	3,665
Mt. Scopus	1,157
Neve Ya'cov	20,085
Pisgat Ze'ev	42,253
Ramat Eshkol (east)	3,050
Ramal Eshkol (west)	3,368
Ramat Shlomo	15,162
Lamot Alon	

Samih: There is empty land, but do not rush. Do not go tomorrow to take it and build a new settlement.

Saeb: We are building for you the largest Jerusalem in history.

Khaled: This area was the most difficult to delineate.

Tal: How can Pisgat Ze'ev settlement be connected with the French Hill?

Samih: A bridge can be built to connect them.

Swap in area (4):

From Israel:
Area: 9.06 km

From Palestine:
Area: 1.66 km

# of settlers: 2,673

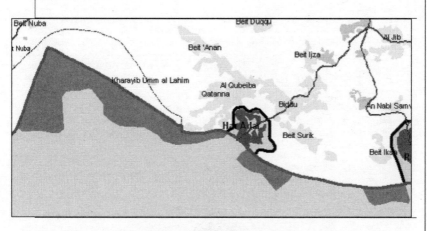

Dekel: You have overstepped everything. Is it on your side or our side?

Abu Ala': It is on our side with Ma'ale Adumim and Ariel.

Terza: There is a kibbutz on this side near Beit Iksa.

Samih; Not exactly.

Saeb: The intention is not to take even one Israeli.

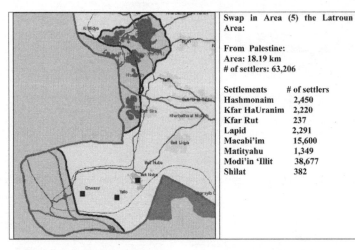

Swap in Area (5) the Latroun Area:

From Palestine:
Area: 18.19 km
# of settlers: 63,206

Settlements	# of settlers
Hashmonaim	2,450
Kfar HaUranim	2,220
Kfar Rut	237
Lapid	2,291
Macabi'im	15,600
Matityahu	1,349
Modi'in 'Illit	38,677
Shilat	382

Samih: We have drawn the line in a manner that keeps for you the main road connecting Tel Aviv and Jerusalem. Latroun Monastery is important for us but it is with you because the road is important for you. We have taken into account your interest by keeping connection between Tel Aviv and Jerusalem.

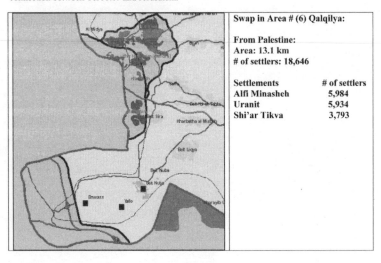

Swap in Area # (6) Qalqilya:

From Palestine:
Area: 13.1 km
# of settlers: 18,646

Settlements	# of settlers
Alfi Minasheh	5,984
Uranit	5,934
Shi'ar Tikva	3,793

Khaled: The interest here is to maintain geographical contiguity between Palestinian areas. It will be difficult to include more settlements without creating Palestinian enclaves.

Livni: This area and more to the left is the most complicated. Where is the Turkish enterprise located?

Terza: Not here; it is in al-Muqeibleh.

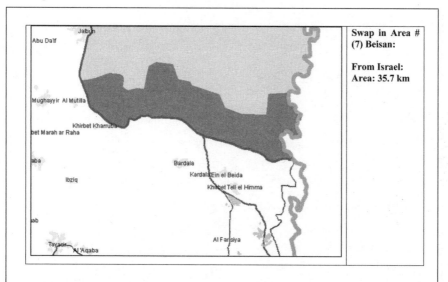

| | Swap in Area # (7) Beisan: |
| | From Israel: Area: 35.7 km |

Terza: Again, there is a kibbutz in this area.

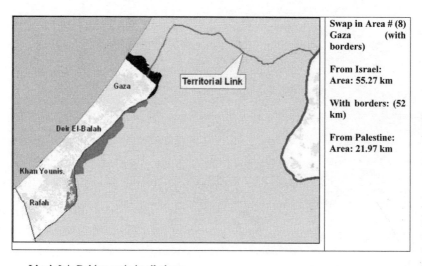

	Swap in Area # (8) Gaza (with borders)
	From Israel: Area: 55.27 km
	With borders: (52 km)
	From Palestine: Area: 21.97 km

Livni: It is Dahlan again in all places.

Samih: Leaving the northern area from the Gaza Strip until Wadi Herbia as part of the swap with the area of Abassan al-Kabira and al-Saghira; in addition to the eastern area as part of the swap.

Livni: This area is approved of with the Egyptians.

Khaled: We know that the northern area has been swapped for the area of Abassan al-Kabira and al-Saghira.

Samih: We want to verify and stabilize this on the maps.

Khaled: According to 1950 Modus Vivendi agreement, the armistice line has been changed. The whole matter depends on who has access to reliable data on this subject.

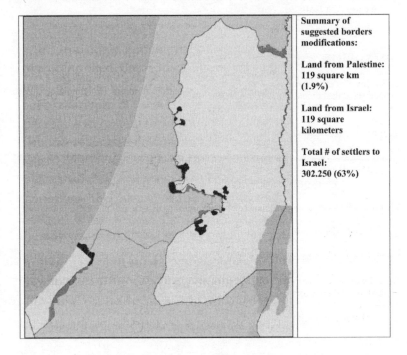

Summary of suggested borders modifications:

Land from Palestine: 119 square km (1.9%)

Land from Israel: 119 square kilometers

Total # of settlers to Israel: 302.250 (63%)

Livni: It is clear that Ma'ale Adumim, Giva't Ze'ev, Har Homa and Ariel do not exist.

Samih: Real peace cannot be reached with an 18-km long enclave inside Palestine. We do not want to create problems in the future. We do not wish to hurt peace.

Saeb: Can you imagine that you accept for the sake of peace to have Jews as citizens with full rights in Palestine like Arab Israelis?

Livni: But how can I provide Israelis living in Palestine with security?

Saeb: Can you imagine that I have changed my DNA and accepted a situation in which Jews become citizens having the rights that I and my wife have. Can you imagine that this will happen one day?

Dekel: I do not have such fancy.

Livni: I have to think about this. I do not know. You have proposed something, but I believe we have to be creative. My problem is that of security. Some said to me that there would be violence among my people if I evacuated them, but the pressure will be less if I give the right to choose. I cannot bear the responsibility of their life in case they are exposed to danger and then the army will have to interfere. It is a legitimate question but we need to think about it.

Dekel: What is missing here is Ma'ale Adumim, Har Homa, separation between the Jewish clusters in Jerusalem, Gush Itzyon, Giv'at Ze'ev, and Ariel.

Livni: What will you take for the Safe Passage?

Saeb: 5 square km, but if we use another track the area will be smaller.

Livni: If we suggested something else you would have stood up and shouted. You have to understand the complexity of this issue. Perhaps you would appreciate their interests more. In Ariel also some areas have to be annexed.

Samih: We have done our best to include the largest number of settlers.

Livni: I want to say that we do not like this suggestion because it does not meet our demands, and probably it was not easy for you to think about it but I really appreciate it. I think we have a reason to continue.

Abu Ala': We understand how hard it was for you as well.

Saeb: In Jerusalem it was hard for us but we decided to give you.

Livni: Can we have the maps?

Saeb: I want to say something. I am from the leadership headed by Abu Mazen and the leadership does not accept the facts on the ground.

Livni: That is why I said what I have said.

Saeb: This is not the Koran. Gabriel did not come down from heaven and revealed it to us. We have taken your interests and concerns into account, but not all. This is the first time in Palestinian-Israeli history in which such a suggestion is officially made. What we are doing no one will do for us, not the Americans or the Europeans.

Livni: I know about this.

Saeb: And since you have not given us your suggestions …

Abu Ala': Not for this reason only.

Saeb: We will examine the matter. We have lots of internal complications. I wish that you would give Abu Ala' a chance to decide. But you deserve to have a copy of it. What matters is that we have begun to participate and cooperate.

Abu Ala': We will think, and you think, too.

Livni: Perhaps the next thing we will do, after knowing the position of each of us, is to have the experts sit together and discuss the gaps and differences between the two maps.

Abu Ala': They have to do this.

Terza: We only need to have the file and there is no need for the map.

Livni: I suggest that you sit together, review and discuss the map. You may also want to correct parts of it such as the kibbutz that Terza said they exist in area for swap.

Saeb: We have no intention to include any Israeli.

Livni: The question is how to be creative.

Saeb: Do you want to sit together tomorrow and exchange maps?

Livni: Once again, I appreciate how hard it was for you to make this suggestion.

Abu Ala': We want to achieve progress in the issue of security, and we also want to start with the issue of refugees.

Summary Minutes from Security Meeting
May 6 2008 at 2:15 pm – 4:00 pm
Dan Hotel, Tel Aviv

1   **<u>Attendees</u>:**

2   *Palestinian*

3   • Maj. Gen. Hazem Atallah [HA]

4   • NSU: Rami Dajani [RD]

5   *Israeli*

6   • Gen. Amos Gilad [AG]

7   • Poly [P]

8   • David [D]

9   • Dany Kornbluth [DK]

2

1   *[Note: The meeting took place during a lunch hosted by the Israeli side. The discussion*

2   *was informal and not structured. Most of the meeting was in Arabic; therefore the*

3   *English notes may not always capture the full meaning of the proceedings]*

4

5   AG: Tell me about the meeting in Berlin.

6

7   HA: It was a good meeting. We presented 14 detailed projects needed to support the

8   police. It is positive because we are aiming to serve the people, and improve their lives

9   through these projects. Before there were problems because the security apparatuses

10   and their support was often for political purposes, and was manipulated by the

11   international community, instead of serving the population.

12   We presented the security concept, which you already know, that is a strong police

13   force supported by NSF (with special units) and intelligence.

14

15   AG: What are the projects?

16

17   HA: For example: riot control, special operations, criminal investigation capacity,

18   laboratories (testing equipment), rebuilding the destroyed infrastructure (eg. stations).

19   The budget is around $120 Million.

20

21   P: Why is there a delay in opening the police stations? The prime minister gave his

22   approval – it was already agreed.

23

24   HA: There is no money available yet – problems of bureaucracy.

2

THE PAPERS

1   [AG likens PA to Ottoman bureaucracy]

2

3   P: This is a problem. The OK was given a few weeks ago.

4

5   HA: The spending was approved by the prime minister. The ministry of finance has

6   not yet paid out the funds.

7   From your side there are cars still stuck at Ashdod.

8

9   P: Which cars? From Dayton?

10

11   HA: No, cars the PA bought [description]

12

13   P: We will look into it. But, before you get the $120 million, and do these projects,

14   what are you doing now?

15

16   HA: Organising, planning, putting the police force in order. For example, in the past

17   each station did its own paperwork, each had its own way of working.

18

19   AG: I am glad to hear this. A plan – this is important. Someone is thinking. This is

20   the same with Dr Fayyad. He has a plan. Implementation in the field …

21

22   HA: Dr Fayyad works well in the field. As a civilian, he has had a strong dialogue

23   with the security people.

24

4

1   AG: You have internal factional problems with Fayyad.

2

3   P: [to RD] This is between us, don't write it down.

4

5   RD: These notes are confidential.

6

7   HA: At first there were some problems, but since he started getting results,

8   opposition to him is down. The bottom line is performance – how he delivers.

9

10   P: But there is a Fatah issue – that he has a policy of not appointing Fatah people.

11

12   HA: No. He has a policy of appointing people with credentials, degrees, expertise. It

13   so happens that many Fatah people don't qualify.

14

15   P: He also goes "on the field" often…

16

17   HA: Yes, a lot. He visited with the security officers in Jenin and had lunch with

18   them. He's been to Biddu, Beit Surik …

19

20   P: Unlike Abu Mazen – other than Bethlehem and Jericho, he hasn't gone on the

21   field.

22

23   HA: Jenin is the test that we are serious. In Qabatya today when someone shot at the

24   NSF, they shot back. That is the way, they have to learn to respect the authority of the

4

THE PAPERS

1   Palestinian security forces. I understand human rights, but this is not Switzerland. We

2   need to take decisive measures.

3

4   AG: I agree – freedom is not chaos ("fauda-stan"). It's like in the Quran: the straight

5   path …

6

7   HA: Or else it's the fire.

8

9   P: Black and white. No grey. After 3 days in Jenin – only 1 gun collected.

10   [discussion on details of intelligence and security coordination]

11

12   P: Changing those people who don't work properly is important. In Nablus, we

13   tried intelligence coordination. You know it didn't work. All they did was warn and

14   negotiate and make deals. For 4 days we did not intervene in Jenin. We gave you a

15   chance.

16

17   HA: Jenin is different from Nablus.

18

19   P: Take the example of Abu [Ghalioun?] cadre of Islamic Jihad in Jenin Camp.

20   They are still negotiating with him and his relatives, instead of taking action –

21

22   HA: We need to deal with it. AM has given clear orders to take action.

23   [Discussion on former Police Chief Kamal Sheikh – P alleging he had ties with Hamas]

24

6

1   P: How are your relations with the other security agencies?

2

3   HA: Good but some are envious, because we are working transparently regarding

4   funding; some are used to dealing under the table.

5

6   [AG asked about AM's health, requesting that HA relay his best wishes to the

7   president]

8

9   HA: We have weapons still in Jordan that we need to bring in (990 Kalashnikov, 1

10   million bullets, 350 pistols) – the Serbia ones.

11

12   AG: Noted. What do you think of the developments on borders negotiations?

13

14   HA: I don't know. How come you are saying in the media that there is progress on

15   security as well?

16

17   AG: I believe they said "tangible progress".

18

19   P: You told AG you didn't want an army.

20

21   AG: On the borders Rami might tell us.

22   I assure you there are no secret channels on security. Rumors are common in the

23   Middle East.

24

6

1	P: How do you assess the security situation today?
2	
3	HA: There is definitely some improvement over the last few months.
4	[Discussion over details of people in various positions and their work]
5	
6	P: All this is good. How is your fight against "civilian" Hamas: the offices, people
7	in municipalities etc. This is a serious threat.
8	
9	HA: I don't work at political level, but I agree we need to deal with this.
10	
11	P: Hamas needs to be declared illegal by your President. So far it is only the
12	militants that are illegal.
13	[P says he just received SMS that people have taken over police station in Jenin – HA
14	says this is not true after checking by phone – discussion on Jebril Rajoub going to
15	Jenin to intervene]
16	
17	HA: There is also the request for tear gas canisters. You previously gave us these,
18	back in 96.
19	P: We gave some to you for Balata 2 weeks ago. What do you need them for?
20	
21	HA: Riot control. We want to avoid a situation where the security agencies may be
22	forced to fire on unarmed civilians.
23	
24	P: Are you actually controlling riots?

1

2   HA: Yes. It is needed to control certain situations [gives example]

3   There is also equipment donated by Canada for riot control. They need to be allowed in

4   ASAP.

5

6   AG: For Dayton?

7

8   HA: EU COPPS [provides description].

9

10   [Discussion of US envoys and their missions]

11

12   RD: There is still the issue of your response to our presentation. You said last

13   meeting you will consider it.

14

15   AG: I thought we were going to hear more from you.

16

17   RD: You were going to present …

18

19   [AG side conversation in Hebrew with DK]

20

21   AG: It is late now, perhaps we can set another meeting to continue. Next week?

22   Monday or Tuesday?

23

1	RD: It's better to fix a meeting agenda in advance. I can send a draft to Danny. This
2	way we can specify the issues and organise the meeting better.
3	
4	AG: I agree with the agenda. [instructs DK on following up the matter]
5	Are there any papers or documents you can hand over to us? It does not have to be
6	official.
7	
8	RD: No. But we take your request under advisement. We will study it for next time.
9	
10	P: Will you bring other people [as per previous discussion with HA] to the next
11	meeting?
12	
13	HA: Not to this meeting. It is a political decision.
14	
15	P: Maybe we can set two consecutive meetings?
16	
17	HA and RD: Will consider this possibility.
18	
19	END

MEETING MINUTES

Attendees: **Blair:**   Tony Blair (TB)
                             Rob Danine (RD)

              Pals: Salam Fayyad (SF)
                             Nizar Farsakh, NSU

Subject: Follow up of projects

Date: Thursday May 8, 2008;   1:15 – 2:45 pm

Location: PMO

Summary:

- SF & TB discussed how Jenin was going very well and that Barak himself had noted that to Rice without any qualifications. Therefore, SF is optimistic that the Jenin example can be followed in other areas. TB believes there is a change in Israeli mindset after Jenin even if people don't perceive that change yet. SF stressed on the need for Israel to change its behavior and hopes that the Jenin example will help achieve that.

- Barak meeting was good in that it was frank and Barak was committal. Barak said he will look into the incident in which Israeli troops entered Jenin last week and that there will be no incursions without specific and direct threat.

- On Palestinians from Israel being allowed to come to Jenin, SF said that people, not with their own cars, will be allowed in going to happen soon but without announcements so as not to put pressure on GoI. Apparently Livni was not comfortable with the idea.

- TB is trying to get agricultural workers permission to take their cars to the Jordan valley; 150 or so to begin with and then build on that. SF said these small things help but only if they are a start for more easing of restrictions.

- Work is going ahead on the Jalame industrial estate. TB confirmed that Israel has no issues with that. He also added that the Israelis have given approval for a school in Area C in that area.

- Barak promised to freeze house demolitions but said he his mandate does not extend to Jerusalem.

- TB put forward to the Israelis a set of checkpoints to lift. Objective is not the number of checkpoints but the actual improvement of movement. He believes the Israelis are willing to approach this in a phased manner. He asked if it is fine by SF to have this as part of a package that Israel delivers. SF said that the PA will not be involved in this but encouraged TB to pursue it with Israel.

1

- TB's idea has for elements:
  1. Economic projects
  2. Projects in area C
  3. The checkpoints
  4. Jenin specifically

- On the Bethlehem conference TB cautioned that on the one hand investors should be told frankly of the challenges but on the other hand they should be encouraged to invest. Therefore, the message should be that this is a first step and that great opportunities lie ahead. Once it starts gaining momentum, TB believes Israel will internalize this fact and facilitate access and investments.

- On Gaza, SF is going to Egypt to discuss ways of easing the situation. TB mentioned that it is important that either convince Hamas of a period of calm so that West Bank gets opportunity to improve or make clear that Hamas received a reasonable offer that they turned down. SF noted that with the siege it is difficult to change the situation. Therefore, if the passages are open under PA control that will put a wedge between Hamas and the people of Gaza and will put pressure on Hamas.

2

Trilateral Meeting Minutes

Jerusalem – Inpal Hotel (Larome)
15 June 2008
16:15 – 18:15

Attendees

American side: - Condoleeza Rice
- David Walsh
- Eliot Abrams
- Jamal Hilal

Palestinian side: - Ahmad Qurei (Abu Ala)
- Dr Saeb Erekat
- Salah Ilayan

Israeli side: - Tzipi Livni
- Tal Becker
- Udi Dekel

Rice: - I thank you for this meeting. Our last trilateral meeting was very useful. These meetings are important for evaluating the negotiation process. The US wants to see what it can do to help both sides achieve progress in this process.

- I think that it possible to reach an agreement by the end of this year.
- I understood that at this time three issues must be dealt with: borders, security, refugees.
- I do not want to hear each side separately, but I want to discuss each issue together so that we can reach a decision concerning the mechanisms that we need in order to achieve progress in each issue and how to relate it to other issues.
- We start with borders, then we move on to security and refugees. Perhaps we will not be able to discuss these three issues today, but we can do that at another time, may be in Berlin.

Abu Ala': - We hope to reach an agreement by the end of this year, and therefore both sides must work seriously.

- The issues are difficult and need decisions, but there are serious clashes in the negotiations. We must see together and not separately how we can reach an agreement about each issue .
- Other difficulties that we face include the continuous settlement activities. This is a deadly point for us. Settlement activities have cornered us and if they continue they will embarrass us before Palestinian public opinion and the Arab world which is urging us to negotiate but at the same time is demanding us not to make the negotiations an umbrella for the continuation of settlement activities.

- We spoke with Olmert and Livni about settlement activities, but the activities go on. Each day bids to build settlement residential units in Jerusalem and the West Bank are announced.
- I hope that these settlement activities will stop immediately until we see what will happen at the end of this year.
- There are the other issues that are being discussed in the trilateral mechanism between Fayyad, Barak and Dayton regarding commitment to the first stage of Roadmap. We talked about this also with Olmert and Livni.
- There are C areas that surround restricted Palestinian areas where Palestinian civilians cannot expand in spite of the existence of large empty land in and around Area C. We talked with Olmert about Area C that surround Abu Dis and Ramallah, and he promised to study that. So far we have gotten no answer.
- We asked the Israelis to allow Palestinians set up tourist facilities on the Dead Sea like Jordan and Israel, but we have gotten no answer about this.
- These issues are not part of the negotiations, but they help create better ambiance for the negotiations and reinforce public opinion. We must have an Israeli response about these issues.
- As for the negotiations, we have talked about all the issues and focused on three main issues. We agreed to start drafting the Palestinian and the Israeli position regarding each issue. Then Abu Mazen, Olmert, Livni and I will sit together. We will also ask for your help to fill in gaps.
- If we started drafting, then we would move from the brainstorming stage to the practical stage.
- I will start with the land issue. If a breakthrough takes place in this issue then other issues become easier, because defining the land will determine our future.
- Our position is that the two state solution should be based on 1967 borders and this includes the West Bank, East Jerusalem, the Jordan Valley, No Man's Land, the Dead Sea and the Gaza Strip. 1967 borders are internationally recognized. Since the beginning we said we are ready to make slight amendments on the borders provided that these amendments do not undermine Palestinian rights and interests. Swap should be for the ratio of 1:1 and for the same value and area.
- The Israeli position is that there are facts on the ground and thus let us see what can be removed. This attitude creates disagreement between the two sides. Israel proposed to annex 7.3% of the total area of the West Bank according to Israeli estimation. The Israeli prime minister proposed in exchange 5% from the land of Israel in the desert area located south of Hebron and north of the Gaza Strip.
- We proposed that the ratio of swap should not exceed 1.9% from the total area of the West Bank, including East Jerusalem and the Gaza Strip, and that swapped land should be located on 1967 borders.
- As for settlements, we proposed the following: Removal of some settlements, annexation of others, and keeping others under Palestinian sovereignty.
- This last proposition could help in the swap process. We proposed that Israel annexes all settlements in Jerusalem except Jabal Abu Ghneim (Har Homa). This is the first time in history that we make such a proposition; we refused to do so n Camp David.

- We cannot accept the annexation of Ma'ale Adumim, Ariel, Giv'at Ze'ev, Ephrat and Har Homa settlements.
- There is a settlement belt around Jerusalem and work is done everyday to complete it. Only yesterday Minister of Housing Ze'ev Boim announced a plan to build 1300 residential units on land in Beit Hanina in order to connect Giv'at Ze'ev settlement in Jerusalem. This is not a way to achieve progress in the negotiations.
- We focused on our work and gave clear directives to experts; and I think we could achieve progress in the issue of borders.
- There is also the Safe Passage between the West Bank and the Gaza Strip. I think it is in the proposition presented by Olmert.

Livni: There will be a Safe Passage.

Abu Ala': If we agree on the concept, I think that in three weeks we can reach an agreement on borders and land issues.

Livni: I want to understand one thing, since you have come back to 1967 borders. At that time there was no Palestinian state. Today we want part of this land and we think that you deserve to be compensated for what we want. My question is: Do you have a problem because of the area of Ma'ale Adumim or its location?

Abu Ala': Our problem is not in the kilometers, but the settlement block Jerusalem from the East, and from the south there are Kidar and Jabal Abu Ghneim settlements that block Jerusalem. There is a settlement belt around Jerusalem.

Livni: I think I mentioned in the last meeting on borders that there is a misunderstanding and the idea we have is not to block Jerusalem completely.

Abu Ala': - We do not want to live in enclaves. We want people to live in peace and to fight against terrorism.

- Perhaps Ma'ale Adumim will remain under Palestinian sovereignty and it could be a model for cooperation and coexistence. We may also have international forces and make security arrangements for some time. It is the location of Ma'ale Adumim not its size.
- There is also Ariel settlement which was set up on the largest water basin. It was not set up simply to provide Israeli with housing units but rather to control the water basin.

Livni: - The idea behind our desire to annex Ariel settlement was not to get more water but because thousands of people live there. We want to have an answer for those who have lived there for forty years.

- Future borders will be complicated but clear. I have seen in Yugoslavia how areas can be connected. The matter is not simply giving a passport to settlers.

Abu Ala': Having Ariel under our control means also that the water basin will be under our control.

Livni: We have said that even if we agreed to have Ariel under Israeli control, we have to find a solution to the water issue.

Abu Ala': We find this hard to swallow.

Rice: - Let us put Ma'ale Adumim and Ariel aside. I am not trying to solve them here.

- Let us go back to ratios. You are not taking mere land but taking land that cannot be dealt with as ratios. Most settlements can be dealt with in terms of how much will be annexed and how much will be compensated for. But there are some locations that pose certain problems and must be dealt with creatively.
- There are settlements whose location poses a problem. But there will be a Palestinian state and Israel will annex part of the land of this state and give compensation for it.
- Let me ask Tzipi: There is part of the land that will be annexed and part that will be compensated for. We must start with the land occupied in 1967 and I believe that the basis is all the land that was occupied in 1967. Let us now leave Ma'ale Adumim and Ariel because their location is problematic.

Livni: - When we decided on the annexation, we made it clear to the Palestinians that we will not compensate them with land that is part of Israel now.

- The issue now is that the Palestinians will not accept that some locations become part of Israel.

Rice: This is exactly what I am saying.

Livni: Are you talking about two locations only?

Abu Ala': There are more than two locations. There are Ma'ale Adumim, Ariel, Ephrat, Giv'at Ze'ev, Jabal Abu Ghneim (Har Homa).

Livni: If we exclude Ma'ale Adumim and Ariel, how would the ratio be 1.9% only?

Saeb: Take it and study it.

Abu Ala': Our experts made a positive and constructive proposition that fascinated me.

Saeb: According to aerial pictures, the ratio of constructed areas is 1.2%. We suggested in our proposition the inclusion of the largest number possible of settlers. We found that most settlers live in Jerusalem settlements, Gush Itzyon and Latroun.

Abu Ala': Ariel goes for 19 kilometers into the West Bank, and this impedes geographical contiguity and enables Israel to control water resources.

Saeb: Our proposition will allow for the inclusion of 70% of settlers, that is about 310,000 settlers.

Rice: Did you see their proposition?

Livni: We looked at it. There are no Ma'ale Adumim, Ephrat, Ariel, Giv'at Ze'ev or Hara Homa (Jabal Abu Ghneim).

Saeb: Why do I not say the opposite, that there are Zakhron Ya'cov, the French Hill, Ramat Eshkol, Ramot Alon, Ramat Shlomo, Gilo, Tal Piot, and the Jewish Quarter in the old city of Jerusalem.

Rice: - It is useful to talk about ratios and swaps. It is good to say also that some areas are important because of their locations and because they have natural resources. They are also important because of geographical contiguity. The question is how to find a creative way that would meet the needs of Israel by annexing these areas, on the one hand, and your control of natural resources and geographical contiguity with Jerusalem, on the other.

- If I come back in two weeks I will ask about the mechanism that you will agree on to solve these issues.
- Did you start talk about that?

Livni: Yes, we did.

Rice: My father used to say that if I asked something of him and I wanted an answer today then the answer was 'no', but if I waited for an answer till tomorrow, then the answer would be 'maybe'.

Livni: And if you ask me today, my answer is nigh to 'no', and the means to get to 'maybe' is to go together in a filed tour on the ground.

Rice: Are you working on that?

Saeb: We want to do this, but until now we are not convinced that you need these areas. We go together to see the areas and you have to try to convince us that you need them.

Rice: I divided the problem into two parts: annexation and compensation; the rest is the state of Palestine. There are two sites that create a problem and they are Ma'ale Adumim because it prevents connection with Jerusalem, and Ariel because of the natural resources. My question is about swap, and it seems to me that it is not necessary now to know the areas for swap. But did you suggest to them the areas designated for swap?

Saeb: We did that on our part, but they have not suggested anything to us.

Livni: I think that before we talk about the areas for swap we must focus on the future of Ma'ale Adumim and Ariel.

Saeb: We presented our suggestion in full, and it includes the areas for swap because we want to prevent the market mentality of bargaining.

Livni: I believe we have gone beyond that.

Abu Ala': The problem is that if you take any settlement and its distance from 1967 borders, you will find out that the Israelis want to annex the settlement, the infrastructure and security areas around it. Therefore the easier way is to annex the settlements near the borders.

Rice: When will you go on the field tour?

Udi: We will arrange for this soon.

Saeb: All we ask from you is to present to us a logical and convincing offer. I do not wish to present to the minister the Israeli proposition made to us about the borders. This is your task.

Livni: We agreed that there will be no agreement before agreeing on everything.

Abu Ala': And not to inform the media about what is going on in the negotiations. All the issues are put for discussion, and we are working to reach a comprehensive agreement, this is our reference.

Livni: - We are not working to reach an interim agreement, and until now we have been talking about the land that you will take. 'Take' is perhaps not the right word; the land that will be the state of Palestine. You offered 1.9% and stopped there.

- As for drafting and regarding the issue of borders, all we need to write is one phrase: Borders as shown in the annexed maps.

Abu Ala': - It is not that easy. There is the issue of evacuation, withdrawal and dismantling military bases, the timetable for doing that, and the supervisory party.

- As for security, the gaps are not big, but the Israelis have put conditions which are cards for bargaining.
- The suggestion we offered in this field is that we are ready to fulfill the Israeli security demands without any exaggeration and in a manner that will reduce the Israeli presence on our land. Transparency in dealing with the Israelis in this field is more efficient than military bases and alert stations. We will also be the bridge for Israel to all countries in the region.

- The problem in Israel is with security personnel and not with politicians because they consider the current situation and build up on it. They do not look to the time after independence.
- We said that Palestine will be an independent state, with limited militarization but not limited dignity, and it will have sovereignty and full control over its land, air space and regional water.
- In order to fulfill our internal security needs, our security forces must be equipped with arms and other equipment so that they can perform their tasks and responsibilities in enforcing the rule of law, order and fight against terrorism.
- We want no more and no less than any other state that is able to protect its borders from any external threat, but Israel says that we want this to protect ourselves from her.

Livni: Yes.

Abu Ala': - We do not want an army. We want the army of a third party to help us build our security capabilities and protect us.

- Israel wants to have security areas and alert stations and control our air space and monitor crossings and borders.

Rice: Tzipi will present Israel's security needs.

Livni: We have a common interest in enforcing the rule of law and order, but we cannot accept protection from outside because we see that as a protection for you from Israel and not from Jordan and Egypt. Therefore we have disagreement about the main concept of security.

Saeb: If we find a solution to the security issue then we will be in good condition. We demand security forces to enforce the rule of law and order; one authority and legal arms. We specify the appropriate arms in order for our forces to be able to perform their tasks and duties. Abu Ala' did not talk about our need for a Palestinian army.

Abu Ala': Why not?

Saeb: - We heard ideas about preparing a 'yes' list for allowed arms and a 'no' list for disallowed arms. We said that if we do that we will be lost, and we also said that we will seriously take any Israeli worry regarding security so that their stay on our land will be shortened. A third party will monitor the implementation of the agreement, take part in its implementation, monitor our obligations in the agreement, and protect us from any external threats. We do not want borders that have Israeli forces.

- We suggested to you to present us with ideas on how to shorten your stay on our land but you never came back to us. You are following the British model in the negotiations and that is to tell us about things we cannot have. We also said that if external threats reach Jordan then they will reach us as well and that is why we asked to have US forces. The idea of a third party emanated from this.

Livni: We agreed to prepare a list including the needs of your security apparatuses to be able to enforce internal security, but you added a third party on the borders.

Rice: Let us not leave the issues and talk about potential threat. At this time there is no threat from the east because our forces are in Iraq and will stay there for a long time.

Saeb: For a very, very long time.

Rice: - The potential threat comes from terrorism and smuggling, and I think there are solutions to these threats by including other parties to these efforts and not by the model of international peace forces.

-    There is no state that can confront terror threats by itself; all countries cooperate to prevent threats.
-    Another point for you Abu Ala': There will be a Palestinian state but it will not be friends with Israel. Usually the generals that sit together in a general staff meeting do not plan for possible peace but for a war that might break out. They meet to put a good system to confront something bad that might take place. When we talk about sovereignty, the Palestinian state will have sovereignty. America is a sovereign state but there are certain procedures in our dealing with Mexico concerning the issue of borders. Germany is a sovereign country, but it committed itself to have no more than 370,000 of its forces on the borders. I am not talking about restrictions on sovereignty.

Abu Ala': What we need is a state capable of providing security for its citizens and controlling its air space and borders. We understand the Israeli worry and sensitivity for security, but it should not be that kind of security that breaches our right for sovereignty and the establishment of a truly independent state.

Rice: You air space is too small not like the American air space. How long does it take to fly from Jordan and enter into your air space?

Udi: Two minutes.

Rice: We have to identify the threats and the goals and then decide on the scenarios that fulfill the goals.

Udi: Unfortunately, at the other side they think that mere reaching an agreement will bring about peace between us and that Hamas will disappear and that we will live in peace and security.

Abu Ala': You have a stronger force.

Rice: - I try to put myself in the Israeli and Palestinian security. You have to think, after having your own state, that the situation will be different, and we will help you think of choices and different scenarios.

- Even we do not deal with our air space in the same way. I was with President Bush at the emergency center on September 11 and it was the hardest time in my life when we issued an order to drop down any airplane that enters our air space. How can I issue an order to drop down a civil airplane carrying 200 passengers. I was a bit relieved to know that our air forces did not drop down the civil plane that fell in Pennsylvania but that it fell by itself.

Livni: - I want to be able to live with the decisions that I take. I am not an expert in everything and I do not know if we are in need of alert stations. It is not our army only that decides. I supported withdrawal from the Gaza Strip.

- Hamas has missiles in the Gaza Strip because we are not there, and there are no missiles in the west Bank because we are there. We have to take into consideration the possibility of a threat that might come to the future state of Palestine; Hamas might control the situation. We have the example of Philadelphia Crossing and Lebanon. I admire Siniora and how he faced Hizbollah. But at the time that he sits as a head of government, there are arms that come to Hizbollah, and these arms are a threat to Siniora himself and to Israel.
- We have to think about what might happen if we do not reach a peace treaty. The choice is that the army is there. What will happen the next day is crucial to the decisions that I will take regarding the land and the borders because I have to live with the decisions that I will take.
- Potential threat will not come from Jordan but from Palestine. I understand your dignity but after signing a peace agreement we will face the threat of opponents to this treaty, and this is a common interest.
- In the meantime, you do not face any external threat and therefore we asked for the preparation of a list including the arms and equipment that you need to enforce the rule of law and fight terrorism. But you have added something else and that is the third part to protect you from external threats. The only external threat is Israel.

Saeb: Not true.

Livni: Now in Gaza we have the same problem, and it is not a question of fancy but a reality in which we are living. I do not want to convince myself that the Palestinian state does not constitute a threat because I do not want to reoccupy you. We want to leave and not come back. I want to trust that terrorism will not come to us from your state.

Saeb: - I respect your ideas and analysis, and I do not ask to be like Jordan or Egypt or Israel armed with thousands of warplanes and tanks. But do you agree that my air space be denied to all planes and my land is void of tanks? Do you want me to inform the Arab League, in which I am member, that the agreement forbids me to use my air space.

- What Abu Ala' means by the army of a third party is defense borders and whatever shortens your stay on our land.

Rice: We know that to confront terrorism we have to use the intelligence apparatuses.

Livni: I agree.

Rice: - We have to work to improve the performance of the intelligence. Even America cannot protect its borders without cooperation with Canada. What is the way then?

- Israel defeated some armies and we defeated others. Then armies do no pose a threat but terrorism does.

Livni: - Those who oppose an agreement in Israel want us to stay there and not to depend on Palestinians in our intelligence.

- The Palestinians have a choice either to remain under occupation or get enough independence and dignity—not through slogans. I think the latter is the better choice.
- I do not accept Palestinians who do not support Israel in what she is doing to confront our and their own common enemy, i.e. Hamas.
- When matters have to do with principles, I know how sensitive you are about the land and Jerusalem. Why then do you feel surprised at our security needs?

Rice: Technology has changed the situation. I already mentioned that sovereignty means the same for all countries, and I gave the examples of Mexico and Germany.

Saeb: All that I am asking is to shorten your stay on our land. Do you accept not to have any presence on our land?

Livni: Abu Ala', does Saeb represent you?

Rice: The most important thing in relation to borders is the customs and smuggling, and these call for enormous efforts from joint intelligence.

Abu Ala': The problem is that Israel wants to do the whole thing by herself. Since 2000 and during the Intifada, Israeli demolished all security quarters and equipment thinking that this would provide her with security; but it did not.

Livni: I remember the joint patrol in the Gaza Strip in which an Israeli soldier of Ethiopian origin was killed.

Abu Ala': I am talking about security.

Livni: There will be an interim period.

Rice: - The issue is that even if Israel has full trust in you, you are still incapable.

- I have full trust in Nouri Malki, Iraq's Prime Minister, but he is incapable. Canada has sincere desire but there came a time when Canada was incapable of controlling the borders.
- I have not heard from both sides about a defense force, but the Israelis have to be convinced that there will be no deterioration in the security situation, and you have to convince me that you will have a real state.

Abu Ala': They left the Gaza Strip and kept it under siege.

Saeb: Because this had happened unilaterally, and because I will build my capabilities gradually with the assistance of a third party, like what the Americans are currently doing in Nablus and Jenin.

Rice: Shall we try again in the next meeting.

Saeb: What do you suggest?

Rice: Berlin. I think Livni will be there.

Livni: I will consult with Rice and Abu Ala' about this.

Saeb: Let us prepare a matrix about the positions regarding the different issues.

Livni: I am worried that it will be leaked to the press. If we achieve progress in the issues of borders and security we can then start drafting. We want to agree that the ratio of 1.9% is not final.

Rice: Do you have a paper on the refugees.

Livni: - Saeb and Tal drafted 7 issues related to the refugees.

- Drafting positions and having others take part in it is against our interest. We agreed that the agreement is bilateral and that we should not have others take part in it.
- In the issue of security, we are still in the beginning.

Saeb: Ami Ayalon is a minister in your government and he made press statements about an agreement on swap land between the two parties.

Rice: - You can trust that we will have no one take part in what is happening between you.

- We will not announce Berlin meeting but we may announce about it after it takes place.

Livni: We will see what will happen between Abu Ala' and me, and then decide about the meeting.

Rice: It will be helpful to declare that the negotiations are achieving slow progress and that there are calls to convene international conferences since Annapolis has been torn apart.

Minutes of the General Plenary Meeting
Held on June 30, 2008 [5:00 PM- 7:00 PM],
King David Hotel, West Jerusalem

1   **Attendees:**

2   *Palestinian*

3   • Ahmed Qurei (AA)

4   • Dr. Saeb Erekat (SE)

5   • Salah Aleyan

6   • Rami Dajani

7   *Israeli*

8   • Tzipi Livni (TL)

9   • Udi Dekel (UD)

10   • Tal Becker (TB)

11

12   **Meeting Minutes:**

13   TL: [Discussion of internal Israeli party politics] Kadima primaries will be between

14   September 11 – 19. We will know the exact date on July 10. I said it can't be around

15   the 18th because that is when the UNGA meets, and we need to be there to show

16   achievements. The competition will start after that time [ie the primary].

17   AA: I would vote for you …

18   TL: Between Mofaz and me you don't have much of a dilemma. The question is

19   whether "he" will participate. He recently said [in Hebrew] "many will not be surprised

20   by my decision" – which can mean anything. [TL discussed previous experience with

21   Likud, particularly in 1999, with Sharon, Shitrit and Olmert]. Back to business…

22   AA: We are meeting to evaluate what we have done and discuss how to proceed.

23   TL: Do we work from the Saeb – Tal draft or by committees?

24   AA: We go over issues and repeat the positions.

1

| 1 | TB: | Do we go by committee or by issue? |

1   TB: Do we go by committee or by issue?

2   SE: By issues is best.

3   TB: Let us start the preamble and general provisions. We put aside certain

4   disagreements – in the preamble the "Jewish / Palestinian right to self-determination".

5   TL: I believe these can be solved once we get to a general agreement.

6   TB: The general provisions are not controversial. On borders, we have not drafted.

7   We have focused on the map and now the field trips.

8   TL: We know the gaps, and now we are seeing whether we can minimize them –

9   looking at the blocs and how we can relate that to swaps and also deal with the safe

10   passage from the West Bank to the Gaza Strip.

11   AA: [to TB] is this a joint document?

12   TB: It's what we have drafted.

13   TL: So, on borders, let's start with your position …

14   AA: No, we need to go back to general things. We need to state the rules we agreed:

15   nothing is agreed until everything is agreed; we will deal with all the issues and not

16   postpone anything; there will be no negotiations through the media…

17   TL: Except by your infrastructure committee head – in French.

18   SE: He didn't know … [discussion on public statements]

19   AA: We need a comprehensive agreement, not a declaration of principles, or a

20   framework, and not provisional borders. The negotiations are simultaneous with

21   meetings on the implementation of the Road Map – on both sides, we on security on

22   you on the settlement freeze.

23   TL: Yes and with the implementation itself. You are talking about things that we

24   postponed.

2

1   AA: I am speaking about what we agreed. To continue: the meetings between Olmert

2   and Abu Mazen to follow up and support the negotiations ...

3   TL: And they follow up closely ...

4   AA: Trilateral meetings with the US.

5   TL: We said whenever they want—but we never agreed that trilateral meetings were

6   part of the process.

7   AA: I don't want to embarrass you with the Americans.

8   TL: When they ask we obey but not as part of an understanding. Obama is coming at

9   the end of July [side discussion on Obama and potential meetings with both sides]

10   AA: We also agreed for both sides to start drafting.

11   TL: That they would draft what they can. As for the agreement itself, as I said in

12   Berlin, it should provide for the interests of each side – with the necessary detail that

13   this requires – in a manner that minimizes friction and problems.

14   AA: Agreement needs to be clear – we don't want to go to arbitration ... it also

15   needs timetables.

16   TL: So this is simultaneous with the Road Map implementation, and after we reach

17   agreement or treaty, then we start negotiations on implementation ...

18   SE: Mechanisms

19   UD: Arrangements

20   AA: So, for example, if there is agreement on dismantling a certain settlement, the

21   implementation will deal with withdrawal, how long, phases – all this can be discussed.

22   TL: [hands over Chart entitled "Peace Process – Time Line" to AA]

23   AA: And we have the terms of reference: international legitimacy; Security Council

24   resolutions 242, 338, resolution 194 ...

3

1   TL: Will not agree to 194 ...

2   AA: The Arab Peace Initiative; the Road Map; and international law.

3   TL: I want to ask you: we've had these discussions before Annapolis, this is taking

4   us back. We are now drafting – at the end we can go back to these.

5   AA: But you asked us to evaluate.

6   TL: But you are going back ...

7   SE: We are just citing the things we have put down.

8   TL: But it will make it look like we disagree on terms of reference.

9   AA: This applies to your approach to borders, where you said the baseline is facts on

10   the ground – you don't recognize the 67 borders.

11   TL: We are now looking at what we have and where are the gaps. Without writing

12   this down you know we are working according to 242 and 338. We are not talking

13   about giving you all of 67, but when you look at the facts on the ground and the

14   discussion on swaps, it is based on it. And we cannot accept 194.

15   AA: You know how many refugees there are? You will accept 194.

16   TB: 4 million.

17   AA: Now it's 6 million. The API is important [cites language].

18   TL: We are in the middle of negotiations ...

19   AA: I am just stating our position.

20   TL: You are taking us back to pre-Annapolis. At the end, it can be phrased in any

21   way. We are past that – I know that as part of the agreement you need the Arab Peace

22   Initiative ... to get the Arabs on board. I can understand that. This is something that can

23   be dealt with in the end. So let's go on to the next item.

4

1   AA: Territory, borders: Our position is the 1967 line – the Green Line -- the

2   occupation that started in 1967. The West Bank and Gaza and one territorial unity,

3   including Jerusalem, the Dead Sea, the Jordan Valley, and the No Man's Land. West

4   Bank and Gaza must be linked by a safe passage that is permanent, secured, and

5   without any control or intervention by Israel. So the basis of the negotiations in 67; any

6   modification must be minor and discussed as swap on the basis of equal quality and

7   quantity. We do not accept the settlement blocs, but can study the case of Jews who

8   wish to stay and live under Palestinian law.

9   TL: I have a bad feeling, because we start from the beginning. We are making a

10   mistake. Now you don't even want to say "minor" – your map, for example, 1.9%. The

11   idea is not to start with basic points. I know your position…

12   AA: I am afraid you forget.

13   TL: Believe me I want to, but I can't. This makes me want to go back to my position

14   at the beginning.

15   AA: Did you change? It is the same. 7.3% -- the same map.

16   TL: This was reached after several discussions. We did not enter the negotiation

17   with 7.3%. We discussed what is needed… My concerns, our concerns (both) are

18   internal and with the international community. We both want an agreement reached. If I

19   knew that we're close to the end of the process, and a last compromise is needed,

20   knowing it's the end of the conflict, it's different. Same with you, you could make a

21   last compromise, for example more than 1.9%. Both of us don't want to be without and

22   agreement, but having made a compromise. So don't go back to positions that we

23   passed in the understanding. The 7.3% offer by Olmert is the most generous, and will

24   be perceived by Israelis as the most fair.

5

1	AA:	Why?
2	TL:	Because it is almost equal.
3	AA:	The 5%?
4	TL:	I know it is important for you to keep the number to a minimum.
5	AA:	We have no problem with swaps, but the 7.3 position just does not allow a state
6		to survive, and it takes all around Jerusalem, and gives to the south of the West Bank
7		and next to Gaza.
8	TL:	Let's ask from TB or UD or SE to assess where we stand.
9	TB:	We did not mean to assess, but to evaluate where we stand in the committees, to
10		look at what is happening in each committee and see if there is something else we can
11		start drafting or working on.
12	AA:	[re swaps] so for an area in Sheikh Jarrah, I have to see and equivalent area.
13	TB:	This is about making progress on issues on the table …
14	TL:	[re 7.3%] This is the offer. [adding to TB] Se we know where each sides stands.
15		And for example on the safe passage, to identify a list of things – other articles in a
16		future agreement.
17	AA:	So where do we concentrate?
18	TL:	One is things we know where we stand. Two is things we need to work on. So
19		on security we know your position, international force, no Israeli presence – we need to
20		continue working.
21	AA:	On refugees…
22	TL:	We have a gap on mechanism; the wording – for you "responsibility," for us
23		"suffering"; and return.

6

1   TB: We meet on Wednesday to continue exchange of drafts. We are waiting for

2   Palestinian response to our last draft.

3   UD: Water. There will be an expert committee to investigate and come back to us.

4   SE: They will be meeting on Sunday. You have a paper from us on an experts

5   committee on water, so cut the red tape, let's move to collecting all the required data.

6   AA: Why don't they meet earlier?

7   UD: It's hard to convene people, scheduling… [Discussion on Fadel Kawash being

8   in Cyprus; discussion on security experts: Hazem Atallah away in Berlin and Amos

9   Gilad sick in hospital].

10   TL: Maybe SE and UD can sit on security. Without Hazem or Amos.

11   AA: Hazem is back.

12   SE: I am really worried about security. It is the backbone for both sides – the US has

13   three generals here…

14   TL: Maybe I should sit on it [security meeting]

15   AA: Let SE and UD meet and discuss the paper. See what is agreed and not.

16   TL: You are meeting anyway. See if Amos and Hazem can attend. Next is

17   settlements.

18   TB: We agreed that SE and I will draft something…

19   AA: This is part of territory …

20   TB: Eventually – the article refers to evacuation, time line, [unclear] "furnished or

21   not" – these are arrangements regardless where the border is. Then we have the safe

22   passage.

23   AA: Refugees?

24   TB: Waiting for response from SE.

7

1	SE:	Five issues will be decided.
2	TB:	There is the issue of the border regime and the passages – this is not just
3		security.
4	TL:	Write it down as an issue. We'll see where it will be.
5	SE:	We are one team; it doesn't matter.
6	TL:	Regardless we need to define where it will be discussed.
7	SE:	On refugees, as I said to Condoleezza Rice and to you, there is a serious
8		Jordanian concern on compensation.
9	AA:	Can they agree instead of 'compensation' to 'assistance' …
10	SE:	They won't accept.
11	TB:	That's our proposal.
12	TL:	We have a problem with the infrastructure committee.
13	SE:	Muhammad Shtayyeh and Hazai are meeting next week; after that we can bring
14		them to AA and TL.
15	AA:	Muhammad is angry because you refuse to give an answer on Qalandia airport.
16	UD:	We told him, as we see it, this is not part of the committee. It is part of the
17		passages.
18	SE:	No it's for the plenary.
19	TL:	On to environment… [SE and UD agree it is going well].
20	SE:	We can start drafting once they have more meetings [SE noted and protested the
21		lack of permits for 5 experts from Gaza to attend the workshop on environment].
22	TL:	State to state. A good meeting yesterday on health …
23	SE:	Yes. We meet again on the 8th: tourism, agriculture and health.
24	TB:	On health we can start drafting.

8

1   AA: This is a mistake – tourism should be in the economic committee. [discussion
2   on placement of issues in committees]

3   UD: On legal …

4   TL: Can you start drafting?

5   TB: Yes. The most controversial issues are going to be dealt with in other
6   committees.

7   TL: Culture of Peace is complete. Already written. Prisoners: [??] met today …

8   AA: Your prisoner release to Hizbollah and Hamas – how many Palestinians to
9   Hizbollah? Famous leaders?

10   TL: To Hizbollah – over my dead body. I fought it yesterday, and only agreed after
11   Ofer Dekel assured the Palestinians were few and not important. That was my
12   condition. [Discussion on prisoner exchange]. I raised yesterday what you [AA] said in
13   Berlin. When we need to release prisoners, we need to do it with the moderates –
14   otherwise it sends the message that only way to release prisoners is by kidnapping
15   soldiers …

16   AA: Can AM expect 1000 released?

17   TL: No. Let's see. Did AM raise it with Olmert?

18   AA: Yes.

19   SE: And I raise it now with you. This is an important issue. I just met with families
20   of prisoners, and this is very important.

21   TL: The decision is not up to the committee, Abdel Razeq and Blass – it's a political
22   decision. I am thinking … can we do something that relates to a change on the ground,
23   so it can be our "excuse" – let's invent something.

9

1   SE: You used "benchmarks" in Berlin. So let's invent something – how about we

2   are in this political process, as part of the process.

3   TL: How about a link to the situation in Jenin and Shechem [Nablus] – areas with

4   greater Palestinian security control. Can we release to those areas?

5   [Discussion on criteria for release, numbers, lists, Hamas list].

6   TL: Just throwing ideas: let's assume Hamas asked for a list – we release some to

7   them and some …

8   SE: Don't link us. It is time to release prisoners as part of the political process.

9   TL: If I give you "heavy" ones, I may then need to give Hamas "heavier" ones.

10   AA: You can release some to AM before Hamas, and some after.

11   TL: Most of the "big fishes" are on the Hamas list.

12   SE: Hamas is doing that to show they are more responsible for the people than

13   Fatah.

14   AA: [Refers to an article by ? in the Israeli press] It argued that Israel responds more

15   to terror. This is what you are doing.

16   TL: In Israeli society, there is a strong feeling about the soldier in the hands of

17   Hamas.

18   AA: There are, daily, soldiers everywhere in the West Bank that can be kidnapped…

19   you don't want that to change.

20   TL: This is perceived as a weakness by some in the Arab World, but we Israelis act

21   like a big family – some perceive it as responding only to terror.

22   AA: Due to the continuous requests of AM, and to move the process forward, and

23   since we are now enforcing security and the rule of law, you must release a certain

24   number of prisoners.

10

1   TL: I am trying to think of an "event".

2   SE: Suggestion: I know the complexity of the lists, and the price will be the price.

3   But if you want to tell Palestinians that is not the only way you function, look at the list

4   of pre-Oslo prisoners. After the date of Shalit [release] we can have an event.

5   TL: I prefer to release for the peace process than on a holiday.

6   SE: This is a lose-lose situation – while Gaza looks 'protected' by Hamas, there are

7   Israeli raids in Ramallah. What is the balance of having us irrelevant? If you want to

8   sign an agreement – you want to make us weak… Now Manar TV is broadcasting your

9   own reports with subtitles about how Israel was humiliated. The prisoner issue –

10   Barghouti -- was raised by AM in every meeting with Olmert. So instead of Hamas

11   releasing Marwan Barghouthi, have AM do it – the same with the pre 93 prisoners.

12   Like AA's idea: before and after.

13   TL: I understand that the Tahdi'a weakens you – and we agreed with Egypt that

14   Rafah crossing will open only with PA.

15   AA: There are reports that Hamas is involved.

16   TL: No. Maybe we can connect Gilad Shalit, as we have done to Rafah, and as

17   opening Rafah is connected to you – you get credit. That way you get credit for release

18   of prisoners.

19   AA: We ask for prisoner release and area C…

20   TL: I wrote a letter to Barak on the issue in Abu Dis and he understands it's serious.

21   AA: We have a lot of people wanting to invest – we have the labour force. So if we

22   have areas we an offer to investors that we be a great help [discussion on investors and

23   lack of space in Abu Dis, Ramallah] If there are places that can be agreed on, give them

24   the facility to work.

11

THE PAGES

---

1   TL: This is something that Tony Blair has raised. [UD made a reference to

2   Tarqumia].

3   SE: Back to Shalit and Rafah Crossing: Do not link Shalit to Rafah. If I am

4   negotiating opening Rafah and saying Hamas has nothing to do with the arrangement –

5   think of the consequences of linking it to Shalit. Zahhar goes on Al-Jazeera and says if

6   I send a letter to Egypt the crossing will be open. [Further discussion on area C – Abu

7   Dis and industrial estate in Jericho]

8   TL: There is another issue … "this city", and then we can talk about

9   implementation, and what we called "steps toward the establishment of a Palestinian

10   state."

11   AA: I want to put to you our position on Jerusalem.

12   TL: Since I cannot refer to it I wont say anything. I am going to just listen. [TL

13   receives message that bill got preliminary approval in Knesset that would require

14   referendum on giving up territory annexed by Israel].

15   AA: Will the Israeli pubic vote in favour of returning the Golan?

16   TL: No. Even though the Golan is not part of what we call the "Land of Israel" the

17   majority of Israelis will not give it back to Syria. This law applies also to Jerusalem.

18   AA: Jerusalem is part of the territory occupied in 67. We can discuss and agree on

19   many issues relating to Jerusalem: religious places, infrastructure, municipal function,

20   economic issues, security, settlements. However, the municipal borders for us are 67.

21   This is the basis, and this is where we can start.

22   [Silence]

23   TL: Houston, we have a problem.

24   AA: Silence is agreement …

12

1   SE: It is no secret that on our map we proposed we are offering you the biggest

2   Yerushalayim in history. But we must talk about the concept of Al-Quds.

3   TL: Do you have a concept?

4   SE: Yes. We have a detailed concept – but we will only discuss with a partner. And

5   it's doable.

6   TL: No, I can't.

7   TB: On process, we will continue drafting on settlements, refugees, end of claims,

8   and culture of peace. The next topics we will start drafting are legal, environment and

9   state to state – health. Water will meet on Sunday and perhaps we can start soon.

10   TL: Next meeting? [Discussion – dates proposed are either Thursday July 3 in the

11   morning, or Wednesday July 9).

12   [END]

13

Minutes of Security Meeting
Held on July 2, 2008 [4:00 PM- 6:00 PM],
King David Hotel, West Jerusalem

1 **Attendees:**

2 *Palestinian*

3   •   Dr. Saeb Erekat (SE)

4   •   Rami Dajani (RD)

5 *Israeli*

6   •   Udi Dekel (UD)

7   •   Kamil Abu-Rukon (KAR)

8

9 **Meeting Minutes: (Highlights -- Not verbatim)**

10 [Discussion on bulldozer attack in West Jerusalem earlier the same day]

11 UD: I want to clarify at the beginning that the MoD, that is Amos Gilad, is

12 responsible for the security committee. We are here to review the issues and see how

13 things are proceeding.

14 [Discussion on the tours of settlement areas: places visited; upcoming tour to Ariel; UD

15 asserted that the tour to Maale Adumim showed that it was not closing the areas around

16 and that there was space available]

17 UD: Why does your side keep mentioning Jerusalem in every meeting – isn't there

18 an understanding on this between the leaders…

19 SE: We are offering you a complete security concept – no need to wait for Amos

20 Gilad to discuss things seriously with Hazem. The MoD is simply not interested in an

21 agreement. Barak told John Kerry there will be no agreement by end of the year. I will

22 present to the concept that we have introduced to your side, which is also what we gave

23 General Jones. [Asks RD for copy of the Jones letter].

24 RD: It would be good to exchange our responses to Jones.

1

1   SE: If you give us your paper to Jones we can share ours with you.

2   UD: I don't have anything. It's the MoD that deals with this.

3   SE: So let me summarize [starting presenting Palestinian position on security forces

4   structure, functions, one authority – one gun; rule of law; capacity building up to

5   international standards, ongoing process] …

6   UD: [interrupting] What is international standard? There is no such thing in security.

7   You cannot tell me what this standard is.

8   SE: This is the objective set for us by the international community. I did not invent

9   anything. It's the work that the US, General Dayton, and the Europeans, EU COPPS,

10   are doing. They are the ones who use the term "international standards". There are

11   objective things relating to rule of law, one authority one gun, professional work.

12   RD: And for example standards relating to chain of command …

13   SE: So we've said, instead of talking about lists of restrictions at the beginning, let's

14   start by identifying the needs – the responsibilities and function of the security forces:

15   to fight crime and terrorism; to maintain law and order and carry out law enforcement;

16   to protect the borders from smuggling and infiltration; and to maintain overall national

17   security.

18   UD: This does not tell me anything. I need to know in detail how you will be able to

19   stop terrorism [continued talking about terrorist threats and how the Israelis know how

20   to deal with them; the Palestinians do not].

21   SE: Another element in our security concept is the third party role. We propose a

22   long term international presence …

23   UD: [interrupt] What is long term? That doesn't mean anything.

2

1	SE: It depends, could be around 10 years. The international presence we propose
2	will carry out a number of functions [SE presents the functions: capacity building;
3	assist in management and security of crossings; monitor implementation of agreement;
4	assist with border security; and carry out any function required by Israel in place of
5	Israeli military]
6	UD: We reject the idea of international force instead of our presence.
7	SE: You tell me your concerns, and I will ensure they are met by the third party –
8	anything short of your military's presence on my territory. For example, if you need
9	early warning stations – you tell me where to put them, what specifications they should
10	have; you don't even pay for them. But they will be run by others, not you. This way I
11	am meeting your concerns, not undermining them. Anything short of an Israeli soldier
12	on Palestinian territory.
13	UD: We insist on some Israeli 'stuff'; but maybe we can talk about hiding it or other
14	ways …
15	SE: No. In that case we prefer the occupation.
16	UD: Why are you going from one extreme to the other. Maybe we can hide it.
17	SE: When there is a Palestinian state, your occupation will be over. Your only
18	presence will be civilian – doctors, technicians … no soldiers. We will not accept
19	limited sovereignty.
20	UD: I don't understand why you say it's limited sovereignty. You can agree to it.
21	RD: In all cases of arms limitations, the country demanding the limitation is not the
22	one to maintain a military presence. That would essentially make us your protectorate.
23	UD: When you say third party, it is not so simple. There are many scenarios where
24	they cannot be useful. For example in the airspace you need the planes all the time in

3

189

1   the airspace to deal with any risk – things always show up on the radar, sometimes

2   flocks of birds or even clouds. You need to react to any possible threat right away.

3   SE: Let me finish [presenting the concept]

4   UD: I don't want to be rude, but this is not useful. We need to discuss details and

5   scenarios. This is too general. I know that you think when there is peace there will be

6   security. We can't and don't think that way. For us, in order to have peace, we need

7   security first.

8   SE: As I said, we start by agreeing the needs and responsibilities, and then discuss

9   what weapons they will have. We look to international standards – what Dayton and

10   EU COPPS are doing. This is an ongoing process, the building of our security forces

11   up to international standards – happening now and will continue even after the creation

12   of the state. We are serious. We know it is a big responsibility. We are doing all the

13   training and capacity building now in full coordination with you. You can ask the MoD.

14   You can ask Dayton about the success and positive results.

15   UD: On the internationals, the problem is that they don't live here. They don't know

16   what the results are. I would like to be happy with the 'results' [mocking] but it is

17   important to say, again, the reason there is no terror from the West Bank is because of

18   our ability to control it. We learned from our past mistakes. There is no terror now

19   because of us 'cutting the grass'. To fight terror you need determination … [UD goes

20   on discussing terrorism, and describes Jordan as a great example of how to build the

21   security system to fight terrorism]. So based on what I see, there is a big gap between

22   us on security.

23   SE: Let me continue [presenting concept]. The international presence will be at the

24   crossings, they will help with capacity, monitor implementation, and perform all

4

1   needed Israeli requirements. They will help with the transition. We also propose full

2   cooperation and coordination through operation centres: trilateral with each of Jordan

3   and Egypt; and multilateral with all five sides. It can function 24 hours per day and

4   respond immediately to any emergency.

5   UD: This does not work. We need to respond immediately. Even if something shows

6   on the radar and it's a flock of birds. Our fighters need to be able to intercept.

7   SE: As Nietzsche said, the devil is in the details. So we can discuss what is needed

8   in the operation rooms for them to work. We can discuss modalities, mandate, functions

9   etc in detail. Regarding military planes, [according to] the model we have proposed, no

10   military aircraft uses Palestinian airspace – not us, you, or third parties. The same for

11   our territory and territorial waters – no armies, irrespective of nationality. We want to

12   have this special status, and will go to the Arab League and others and request this.

13   This is our concept.

14   UD: Your vision. I think you have good will and are trying to solve the problem. But

15   I feel you don't understand our security needs. We understand the end answer and

16   response to security challenges, and your concept is not enough. It does not address

17   specific scenarios – it is a good cover but does not respond to the details. What the

18   experts need to discuss is: first the challenges, then the objectives, and finally the

19   missions. [mentions Philadelphi as example]

20   SE: So you want to be in the Jordan Valley?

21   UD: We have the experience of Philadelphi.

22   SE: What about Jordan on the other side? Can't they continue to maintain total

23   control and security like they do now on their side? If you insist on a presence in the

24   Jordan Valley, let's not waste time. I have done everything to meet your needs and

5

1   concerns. I said put the early warning stations and connect it to the operations room in

2   Tel Aviv. Anything short of your presence. Give me a concept short of your presence,

3   that insures your interests. You can be creative. I have given you so many openings.

4   UD: Frankly, I don't imagine the US or Europe will deploy forces –even with our

5   agreement. They cannot be effective.

6   SE: The US has the best military in the world. Its fleet is right here in the

7   Mediterranean, its forces are all around.

8   UD: Let me say some words about the international force. Until now, the Israeli

9   position is that we do not support this. But it is one of the things we can discuss. As a

10   host country you can invite them and ask them to go away. It's your business. But third

11   party simply cannot carry out the functions we need [UD mentioned there are 9

12   functions]. If we discuss the scenarios then we can show you how it does not work.

13   SE: Your presence is a non-starter. Question: Can you propose anything short of

14   your presence?

15   UD: What makes you think the third party will not be seen as occupation? What is

16   the difference?

17   SE: We have the TIPH example and model. [SE explains role and status of TIPH

18   among Palestinians in Hebron. RD mentions EU BAM and effectiveness of mission,

19   good relations with the public even under difficult conditions.]

20   SE: If you have an Israeli base in the Jordan Valley, the kids will be looking for

21   ways to attack it. If we have a British base, they will be looking for jobs there. The

22   Palestinians want to end the occupation. They will not see third party as occupier, but

23   as helpers.

6

1   UD: Look at UNIFIL, it is proof that the internationals will change their entire

2   mission and its implementation when it came to one terror attack. They just changed

3   their way of doing business. They don't have the determination. It is not the foreigner

4   that will protect people in Tel Aviv.

5   SE: In this case we will need an army. I would like you to come to a tour with me to

6   the Jordan Valley. I will show you things you will be ashamed of as an Israeli [SE

7   discusses several Israeli policies and measures suffocating Palestinian life in the Jordan

8   Valley]. It is the most exploitative colonial system – it is not security. I will show you

9   the meaning of security in the Jordan Valley.

10   [Discussion on having the tour in the coming week. Parties agreed that technical

11   meeting should take place as soon as possible now that Hazem Atallah is back and

12   Amos Gilad has recovered].

13   END

7

Minutes from Bilateral US-PAL Session
Post Annapolis
Wednesday, 16th July 2008, 11h00am to 1h00pm
State Department, Washington, DC

Attendees:
Palestinian
- Ahmed Querei (AA)
- Dr. Saeb Erekat (SE)
- Zeinah Salahi (ZS)

United States
- Secretary of State Condoleezza Rice (CR)
- David Welsh (DW)
- Jake Walles (JW)
- Jonathan Shwartz (JS)

Meeting Summary (*not verbatim*):

CR:
- I'd like to first hear where you are, then push through and try to find a way to get this done.
- We see this in two phases – first before the UNGA in September. Something that shows substantial progress to hold the international community's attention.
- Then the UNGA to the end of the year.
- At the end of the meeting we can discuss – how do you see the product that would be reached by the UNGA, and that at the end of the year?

AA:
- Will you come to the region?

CR:
- First there will be a trilateral – you and TL will come here around the 30th. I will go around the 15th of August.

AA:
- Can you postpone a week or so?

CR:
- It will be hard. [Explains travel schedule.]

AA:
- I talked to TL in Paris, she can come for one day. I thought it would be good to postpone to give us a little more time to prepare… But whatever you decide we will work out.

1

DW:
- First meeting will be on the 30th. Then a second meeting on the 19th or the 20th.

AA:
- If it is in August there is more time to make progress. I told her [TL] that we need to start to write. She is reluctant but…

CR:
- My view is that we can do all of those.

AA:
- I want to explain the details and where we are.
- 1. After Annapolis – where are we? We agreed on two things – the first phase of the Roadmap, and the Peace process.
- On the first phase – nothing has happened. There are daily violations. [AA notes recent announcements regarding housing. Also notes the extreme detrimental impact of the prisoner release to Hizbollah. Later in the meeting hands CR an article on factories being built in Ariel, and the last monthly report. She notes she has already gotten the monthly report.] Everyone is saying look at what they get from violence, etc. Even Yaser Abd Rabbo – who is one of us -- is saying we need to stop negotiations. Please – we need your help on settlements [i.e. freeze] and the other phase one obligations – roadblocks, outposts, etc.
- I tried at the last meeting to discuss the terms of reference. TL responded that you are taking us back to pre-Annapolis. She doesn't want to discuss. It is different for a permanent status agreement. 242, 338, Roadmap, Bush vision, Arab Peace Initiative…
- We repeat – no issues to be excluded or postponed. [i.e. Jerusalem]
- We agree on everything or nothing.
- We agreed that [we are reaching] a whole agreement – not a state with provisional borders, or another interim.
- We are talking about a comprehensive agreement. We don't want to go to arbitration a week after [like Egypt had to with Taba]. The agreement must include all of the dates and timelines for implementation. Otherwise it will be another shelf agreement.
- AM is committed – he hopes as much as possible to have an agreement by the end of the year. And we will continue under all circumstances. We are talking about an independent sovereign state – with all the sovereignty like states everywhere else in the world. What we are talking about is [with respect to] all the issues. [If we talk about full sovereignty, we mean if there is water in Jericho it is Palestinian water.]
- We start from the 1967 border. Any modifications in or out, we can talk about. Israel starts from the status quo. Jerusalem with their annexation, the settlements. I think without this understanding we will not be able to get any agreement. We consider the 1967 border is already the biggest concession we made in our history. Modifications, etc. on a swap basis we are willing to discuss. If the 1967

2

is approved as the basis for the discussions, we can move forward. [If they insist on starting from] the status quo – we can't go anywhere.

- 242, 338, the Roadmap – all make it clear. If you, or the Security Council, can make it clearer that would be great.
- Olmert offered 7.3 – where, why he needs 7.3… we don't know. 5 or 7.3 – we can't accept it. It will turn the Palestinian state into cantons. [Discusses the negative impact of Ariel on Palestine.]
- We offered 1.9%. It is reasonable. We included the settlements inside Jerusalem – Psgat Zeev, etc. It's the first time!
- The territory we are talking about is the West Bank, Gaza, Jerusalem, the Jordan Valley, the Dead Sea. The No Man's Land – they don't have the right to take it without negotiations. Just like the safe passage connecting the West Bank and the Gaza Strip – when we talk about a comprehensive agreement, need to take all these things into consideration. On a one to one basis. The gap is not about the difference in percentages, it is not about comparing the maps. The question is how to reach an agreement? What is the basis that we are negotiating on? This is the problem.
- Jerusalem – the last meeting we had we talked about it. She couldn't respond. [AA notes the distinction between sovereignty arrangements, and cooperation/modalities in Jerusalem.] East Jerusalem is part of the 1967 border. Anything [discussed] there should be part of the swap.
- Unfortunately, what we heard from Olmert is that he can't stop building because it is Jerusalem.
- Water – it should be easier if the other issues are agreed.
- Refugees – On responsibility – TL refused. It is important for Israel to recognize its responsibility. On the right of return – the API says a just and agreed upon solution in accordance with 194. This means that the Arab League authorized the PLO to negotiate. Therefore if we talk about the number of refugees over the number of years, that would be good.
- There are many other issues – the host countries. I know your position regarding the precedents.
- The Fund – the Absentee Property Fund – this is a good basis for compensation. I know that TL and Shlomo Ben Ami both say not one single dollar exists in the fund. I cannot accept it. Therefore it is important when we talk about the international fund, that this be the basis of that fund.
- Security – the third party will be under the UN or NATO, and will help with the borders, training Palestinian security forces, etc. [The key is no Israeli presence.]
- The problem is that Israel thinks about the situation as it is today when they think about the day after.
- Demilitarization versus limited arms – we say limited arms. We can discuss what kinds of things might be excluded.
- Prisoners – Olmert in Paris said to AM that 120 will be released. We said that this not enough. They need to be pre-Oslo prisoners. There are 364 pre-Oslo prisoners. If there is a release for Hamas, they need to release for AM both before and after.

3

THE PAPERS

CR:

- I completely agree with you on that.

AA:

- The other issues are going well. Between now and the UNGA if you can solve the issue of territory, including Jerusalem…

CR:

- As I see it, the role we can play is 1. to step back and say what we think is possible. 2. try to bridge the gaps. This is why I want to see you alone. So I can tell you what I think of your positions, without hurting my role as the "honest broker". The same with the Israelis.
- On security and borders – they need to come to you. But on borders you need to move too.
- First on the ToRs and the Basis.
- On the ToR – just say it is based on Annapolis. I worked hard, and David worked hard, to get the ToR at Annapolis. Israel didn't like it, but they came. [i.e. they agreed to it by coming since that is what Annapolis was based on.]
- The starting point for what is determining the borders – to create a state, a new state, starting from the occupation that began in 1967. I don't think it matters much if you start from the status quo, or 1967. What matters is where the borders end up. They made an offer – it's not good, but it's not bad. 7.3 – 5 is 2.3, which leaves 97.7 percent of the West Bank and Gaza Strip, and the safe passage. AM said he'd be prepared to count the safe passage.
- Ariel is a problem, I told them – it protrudes down far into the Palestinian state.

AA:

- And for water too.

CR:

- We need to deal with the aquifer. Also – it would be difficult for Israel to protect Ariel without a large perimeter.
- But are you really going to stop a Palestinian state on a few percentages?
- '67 is the point of reference. [We all know it.]

AA:

- Just like Ariel, Maale Addumim is a problem. Jerusalem is out if they take Maale Addumim. [AA notes the impact on the surrounding villagers who get squeezed out by the settlements around Jerusalem.]

CR:

- No – Jerusalem is not out! Everyone understands that what is Jewish is Israeli and what is Arab is Palestinian.

AA:

- But we don't want to fly to Jerusalem by helicopter!

4

CR:
- I don't think that any Israeli leader is going to cede Maale Addumim.

AA:
- Or any Palestinian leader.

CR:
- Then you won't have a state!

AA:
- It's like the refugees – they can live under Palestinian law.

CR:
- Both states will be ugly. They will not be easily connected. What we need to do is that instead of [arguing over base points] you are going to have to end up in a discussion.
- I asked TL – are you talking about all the land within 1967? She said yes. You won this argument! [Discussion continues.]
- I think when we write this down we'll find a way to reference 1967.
- They were created – they do have some land that belongs to Israel.
- I don't think that 7.3 is the number. But 1.9 or 2.3 is not.
- Yaser told me that one concern is Gaza – that it needs to expand because of long term growth.
- Maale Addumim can't look like LA! [i.e. sprawling]
- I'd like to see you talk about how to make the connection to Maale Addumim useful.

[SE shows the map of Israel's proposed swaps.]

SE:
- It's not LA it's California!!!
- If you get them to clarify that we are talking about all of 1967…

CR:
- I will make it clear that the US is working on the assumption that it is all the territory occupied in 1967. That their 7.3 is based on that. 7.3 and 5.

AA:
- On the swap – it needs to be one to one. Equal and equitable. Not Jerusalem for Gaza.

CR:
- There are different ways to discuss value. There is no place to build around Jerusalem. You can't even move in Jerusalem!

5

AA:
- We have areas outlined. [Noting that Palestinians have looked at areas they'd like to see swapped back.]

[SE hands CR the map with the 1.9% and the swaps. CR hands to Jonathan who keeps it.]

CR:
- I believe that the assumptions should be, the US will [secure this]. Any swaps will be in reference to the area occupied in 1967. When they talk about 7.3 they are talking about this. You say one to one in quality and quantity. I would say you need to think more about what quality means. [She alludes to their proposal to build up the agricultural value of areas to be swapped, but doesn't reference it explicitly.]

DW:
- We don't want to get into theology. But there needs to be a common reference. We have good computer mapping on this. We can use this as the basis. [I.e. US would present a map depicting the positions on a common base map.]

CR:
- I think that you will have to find an answer to Maale Addumim. And we will need to find an answer to Ariel.

SE:
- Your approach on the maps is good. We are using some of your satellite imagery already.
- The agreement is that we are going to reach an agreement but not a treaty by UNGA. [CR notes that she has received our timeline diagram.]
- The Treaty is the agreement plus all the annexes. The trilateral needs to be guided by this assumption. So we need dates, timelines, etc.

CR:
- I agree.

SE:
- Second, for example on security. We said anything short of an Israeli presence. Olmert implied that he appreciated [our flexibility on this]. For example, in the Jordan Valley – if there are any stations there can the Germans staff them?

CR:
- They need to come to you on security. I think Jones – we need the help. There are some good ideas in the security paper you gave us. The US will have to play a role. Security is more than just strategic depth. It is borders, [capacities], etc.

6

To talk about airspace is amazing to me. In the time it takes me to walk to the conference room, your airspace would be covered.

SE:
- [Notes that if there is a presence of Israelis, it will be the basis of hostility from the Palestinian population. If it is foreigners, Palestinians will look for jobs there.]

CR:
- I need affirmation of – you are defining a demilitarized state or non-militarized – where principally you are looking at internal security, and you are defining the responsibilities?   [And then we can talk about what they need for those responsibilities?]

DW:
- You had a good presentation on roles and responsibilities – but you didn't answer one question – is the third party on the Palestinian-Israeli border?

SE:
- The third party will help with compliance, passages, the operations room with Israel, Palestinian, Jordan, Egypt and third party, and regional issues and counter terrorism.

AA:
- [Could be, could not, we can discuss.]

CR:
- They are afraid that the third party and Israel will clash. But we hear you saying that the relations between you and Israel will be non-military and peaceful. There will be common threats against you both, and some of them will be in Palestinian. You will need a common response.

SE:
- Anything short of Palestinian forces going into Israel, and Israeli forces going into Palestine.

AA:
- [Notes recent Nablus example of Israel coming in and taking matters into their own hands, including stealing a computer.] This cannot be for the future.

CR:
- No one thinks that that will be the future.

AA:
- [Notes prisoner issue again.]

CR:

7

- You see your forces – with limited arms, primarily internal? The roles and missions and arms are to be agreed? The third party is not an interpositional force – you can write the agreement in such a way as to make clear that the incursions are not welcome. No country will agree to be an interpositional force.

AA:

- [Notes importance of regional cooperation.]

CR:

- [Notes that there will necessarily be a transitional period, for withdrawal and capacity building. The total withdrawal to no Israeli presence will not be the day after the agreement.]

SE:

- [Returns to the issue of refugees. Notes that Jonathan needs to be briefed by NSU.]

CR:

- On refugees: I read your side by side matrix. It seems that the closest is on refugees – although it requires some decisions.

AA:

- What if we postpone until after the UNGA?

CR:

- No – we need to discuss it.
- I will come to the trilateral with some initial ideas on the mechanism.
- [SE: we will be able to review and comment before you present anything right? We don't want to be surprised! CR/US team: yes of course.]
- By the way I did talk to the Jordanians at a very high level. They didn't press the issue. I told them that international law will not help you because all the compensation is to the individual refugees. There are no precedents where states get compensation.
- 1. You need to decide soon that you will offer all Palestinians citizenship wherever they are.

AA:

- This I think will be done.

CR:

- 2. Rehabilitation, relocation, help for families going forward. I saw hints of this in both your positions. [ZS notes that this is not a controversial issue.]
- I think that when you say that all Palestinians are citizens, the Lebanese will relax that it will not impact their confessional balance.

SE:

8

- For the Lebanese, but for the Jordanians – they will need to decide not to allow dual citizenship.

CR:

- I think that they may.
- For individuals who have lost property, they have a right to claim. [With Germany, all they had to do was show up with a picture of the house and we allowed them to claim.]
- Two things that are hard are:
- 4. non- material damages. There is no precedents anywhere else for this. It will be a hard sell. [ZS argued that no other place has 50 years of dispossession supported by consistent and extensive state actions. CR responded Albania, and US with respect to the Native Americans.]
- 5. responsibility.

AA:

- I accept what Yossi Belin said in his book. [US: what's that?] That it is Israel's responsibility.

CR:

- If you want to talk about responsibility it is the responsibility of the international community, not Israel. They created Israel. [ZS argues that Israeli actions post-statehood are clearly their responsibility. This is dismissed by CR.]

SE:

- It is a nation interrupted!

CR:

- That is true – a nation's development is interrupted. You should [look to a solution that describes the conditions and tries to work from there.] Responsibility is a loaded term.
- [Notes the example of reparations for slavery in the US.] I've always objected to it. It's not forward looking. Would I personally be better off? I don't know. But I do support affirmative action. [ZS argues that this is the same point – it's as if we are trying to restore Palestinians to a status, similar to the post-civil rights movement. Except unlike in the US, Palestinians options are far more limited as we are not talking about unlimited return to Israel, and there is 50 years of suffering. In other words many of the elements of "moving forward" (such as affirmative actions programs) are missing in the solution here. Key, in order for Palestinians to be able to compromise on implementation points, is that there be a recognition of responsibility. This also is part and parcel of the non-material damages point.]
- [Bad things happen to people all around the world all the time. You need to look forward.]
- The first compensation is a state [describes state].

9

- Second is that the world and Israel accept that the Palestinians need help to get back on their feet. [i.e. as evidenced by participation in the mechanism]
- Israel had to put away some of their aspirations – like taking all of "Judea and Samaria".

AA:

- Do you think that the Israelis can implement an agreement?

CR:

- Yes. No one will run right of Ariel Sharon. But it needs to be sellable to the Israeli people, just like to the Palestinians.

DW:

- You said you don't want to be blamed, like post-Camp David. That will not happen. Failure is also not an option. But we need to have some irreversibility to this process.

CR:

- Israel needs to move on security. You need to move on borders.
- On the reference point – it will be easier if you nail that down.
- On the refugee mechanism, we will come with ideas.
- On the narrative – you need to move to try to imply responsibility without using that word/saying it directly.

SE:

- Five points I need to go through fast.
- 1. What AA said now – we keep talking, but when we start writing is when we see movement. On the refugees, to help with this, we need Jonathan to come our way for two days to discuss.
- 2. Irreversibility – [we don't want to create a situation where we keep climbing and are so close and then crash down the mountain like at Camp David.]
- 3. Prisoners – [reiterates through an analogy that prisoner releases support Hanieh, and stresses the importance of releasing pre-1993 prisoners to AM].

CR:

- Pre-Annapolis Israel said that they couldn't release prisoners with blood on their hands. This guy they released today has more blood than anyone! I am very sympathetic to you on the prisoner issue.

SE:

- Jerusalem – the East Jerusalem consulate should remain open.

CR:

10

- I wouldn't worry about what people say in their campaigns. Bush said he would immediately start the process of moving the embassy to Jerusalem. He is still "starting the process…"

SE:
- 5. We have a major problem of visas to Palestinian officials. [Discussion of Mahmoud Darwish case.]

[Side discussion of Syria and Iran.]

CR:
- I would like you [before the 30th] to keep – not to present to the Israelis – language on responsibility without using the word "responsibility". Forward looking.
- I will work on the basis for the map.
- They need to work on Ariel.
- You need to work on Maale Addumim.
- On security – I think we'll be ok.
- July 30th a trilateral (DC). I will try to make clear the basis. I would hope that you would start to discuss the refugee issue. And Ariel and Maale Addumim.
- August 20th another trilateral (Jerusalem). [DW notes that all these will follow the same format. Separate bilaterals with each side, and then the trilateral.]
- September, pre-UNGA trilateral (Jerusalem).

11

Summary of the meetings on Refugees

Held on August 14, 2008 [4 PM-5:30 PM], King David Hotel, Jerusalem

<u>Attendees:</u>

Palestinians: Dr Saeb Erekat (SE); Zeinah Salahi (ZS); Ziyad Clot (ZC)

Israeli: Tal Becker (TB); Daniel Taub (DT), Israeli lawyer (blond girl)

<u>Summary (not verbatim):</u>

- SE indicated that this was not a negotiation session. The purpose of the meeting was to present the Palestinian proposal on the international mechanism ("IM") for refugees.
- ZC delivered the standard presentation on the international mechanism which will be in charge of the implementation of Palestinian refugees' rights. The participants showed interest, took notes and asked questions during and after the presentation. The main questions are set out below:

  - ➢ *TB: Why is rehabilitation not a 3rd program in the structure of the IM? Why is it part of the return program?*
  - ➢ *TB: What do you mean by compensation criteria?*
  - ➢ *TB: What is a displacement claim?*
  - ➢ *TB: What precedents did you rely on to design the IM?*
  - ➢ *TB: Have you find precedents that involved such a long period of time (between the creation of the problem and its resolution)?*
  - ➢ *TB: To what extent your work on the IM is connected to the I&P document we are currently negotiating with Saeb?*

  - ➢ *SE: Should the compensation for Host States be part of the mechanism?*
  - ➢ *SE: Why can't the US lead the IM?*

  - ➢ *DT: What do you mean by comprehensive agreement? What should be the parties to such agreement?*
  - ➢ *DT: From your experience in the work shops, do you have an idea of refugees' expectations? How do they react to your work on the IM?*

Summary of the meetings on Refugees

Held on August, 2008 [PM- PM], Hotel, Jerusalem

Attendees:

Palestinian: Dr Saeb Erekat (SE); Ziyad Clot (ZC)

Israeli: Tal Becker (TB),

Summary (not verbatim):

SE briefs TB on his secret plan which he shared with the French (if no agreement by the end of the year, a matrix of the positions will be given to the US and the French to enable the possible continuation of the process). TB seems to agree but insist that this should remain secret.

TB: I hear rumors: - there seem to be some back channels
- Rice is apparently under great pressure. She will probably force a deal.

SE: I don't have any information whatsoever on these.

TB: But you are represented in some track 2 channels and seem to want to upgrade them.

SE: No, Rajoub requested that we participate to a meeting. We did it just once. We will not participate anymore.

[TB passes State to State document to SE. ZC will give to ZS]

TB: Anyways, C. Rice is now busy with Georgia. What do you think of J. Bodin?

SE: He has been my friend for 20 years. He's the best thing that could happen to us. His experience in the region is unmarked.

[TB begins to discuss the I&P document. SE asks that we begin with his comments on the Palestinian proposal on the mechanism, as previously agreed].

TB: I will only make some general comments at this stage on the model you presented.

On the mechanism, what struck us is your capacity to expose simply an issue that is extremely complicated. I have to say however that some of the programs/issues you presented are problematic: our disagreement on substance is reflected in your vision on the mechanism. For example, restitution is totally unrealistic in the Palestinian case.

Generally speaking, the international mechanism raises some tensions on our side. I also feel that there is a tendency on the Palestinian side to insist on individual justice. You put too much focus on the individual. A balance will have to be found between effectiveness and legitimacy. Your model is too individually-based. It is not feasible. Some people will not be happy with the solution on refugees. The

2

Israelis and the Palestinians will have to get prepared for that. We cannot create expectations which will not be able to meet.

These are my personal feelings. This is not the Israeli position on this: it is not defined at this stage. Again, you try to make this issue simple. But it is incredibly complex. In this file, the Palestinians are making the demands and the Israelis have to define what could be given.

According to the Palestinians, the refugees would be several millions. How could this mechanism work? We also understand that the compensation should come primarily from Israel. For me, your claim for NMD is not acceptable. We have to focus on providing rehabilitation assistance to refugees. You can think about the best way to market it.

ZC answers on 4 points essentially:

- No one minimizes the complexity of the Palestinian refugee issue. However, relying on international best practice is the best way to prepare for the resolution as long as the specifics of then Palestinian case are not overlooked. This is our approach. In Irak, the UNCC processed 2.7 millions claims in 10 years. It was a long and difficult process, but the initial goal was reached.

- It is no surprise that the discussion on the mechanism raises the same tensions usually generated by this file since this model is meant to be an implementation mechanism. The comprehensive model presented is adaptable to the parties' policy decisions. For instance, it remains pertinent irrespective of what will be the parties' decisions on return and restitution.

- The focus on individual justice is totally assumed. As you pointed out, the problem has been ongoing for 60 years. To be frank, a Palestinian refugee from Lebanon, a Palestinian refugee in Jordan may not feel represented by the PLO because they have been living in a foreign environment for so many years. Therefore, the only way to facilitate a "buy in" of the various refugee communities is to put the emphasis on individual justice: to the best extent possible, each refugee will have to feel that his/her personal experience is acknowledged.

- Palestinian rights for NMD is a right according to international law. It has been recognized in mass claims program. Practically, if it is not recognized, there is a chance that a large proportion of the Palestinian refugee population will be left without any form of compensation.

[Discussion moves to an animated discussion the 1948 narrative]

SE: Recognition of responsibility is a bilateral issue. I don't want the Americans to be involved in this. These are my bargaining chips.

TB: Our respective narratives cannot be reconciled. You think you are the victims. We think we are the victims.

SE: How can you seriously think you are the victims of the Israeli-Palestinian conflict?

TB: We were invaded by the Arab armies. The Arabs never accepted the partition plan. You problem Saeb, and the problem of the Palestinian people and of the Arab countries is that you still don't recognize us, as a people, the Jewish people. Judaism is not only a religion. First, we are a people.

3

[Discussion goes on the narratives without progress. AC stops functioning]

ZC: Let's consider for one second that our narratives of what happened in 1947-48 cannot be reconciled with our –which I don't believe. I have two comments:

- The first one is that there are two dimensions in the issue of responsibility regarding refugees: first, the refugees left their homes (let's try to put the reasons which caused the exile on the side, for the moment); secondly, Palestinian were prevented from returning. Can Israel reasonably challenge that it has taken concrete and legal measures to prevent their return after 1948? There are different laws of the Knesset which legally recognized and enforced the confiscation of refugee lands; the State of Israel refused to provide Palestinian refugees with Israeli citizenships… These laws were passed after the war and are still in force. These statutes are in complete contradiction with international law. Can Israel reasonably deny these facts?

- Secondly, one could argue that the international community also has some kind of responsibility in the creation and absence of resolution of the refugee matter. Do you think that Israel could envision a recognition of shared responsibility with the international community? Would this facilitate the terms of our discussion?

[TB does not answer]

[discussion gets back to the mechanism]

TB: I understand that there is an assumption on your side that a new mechanism should be created. Why? Do you need something new because you think the refugees will prefer it or because it will be more efficient or because it will be more efficient?

ZC: Both. The conviction of the necessity of a new mechanism is the result of a reality: no organization or institution is adequately equipped to resolve this complex issue. This doesn't mean that existing structure will not have to be associated to the implementation of the solution –on the contrary- but there is a need for the creation of a new structure. Refugees will have to have one main interlocutor. In addition, the creation of a new mechanism will generate the belief that the specificity of their experience is properly addressed.

TB: To say it simply, I think that your vision is unrealistic. My view is that the work on the mechanism should be driven by the following factors:

- What can be sold, to the Israelis & to the Palestinians;

- What can be supported by the international community;

- What will work in practice.

Israel will not agree to participate in a mechanism where it would take the risk of facing the veto of other countries (Syria for instance).

ZC: the participation of host countries in the mechanism is necessary since decisions touching to their sovereignty will be at stake.

[SE requests to review the I&P together]

TB: In article 6.6 (the international fund), I think the reference to the [P: two] programs is not necessary, especially since the international fund may also serve to finance other programs of the

4

mechanism which are note stipulated in article 6.5. We could say instead "to finance the programs, including as set out in Article 6.5".

In 6.8, the reference to the Treaty should replace the other suggested reference (Article, Agreement). The Treaty would be defined in a footnote.

[SE asks ZC to note down the proposals and indicate to TB that the Palestinian side will examine them]

TB: In 6.4, let me explain the motives behind my *[I: in respect of claims out of the refugee issue]*: We are ready to recognize refugees' rights for compensation. However, we are opposed to the Palestinian claim for compensation for occupation. This article has to clearly refer to refugee claims only.

ZC: I understand your concern and agree that some clarification is needed. This being said, the reference to "the refugee issue" does not resolve the problem. Unless of course we agree on the definition of "refugee" and "refugee issue". In the absence of such definition at this stage, I would suggest rather referring to the "claims arising out of the forced displacement and dispossession" or something along these terms.

TB: No, I don't like it. It touches our narrative.

ZC: it doesn't. It just describes the reality of the problem we are trying to solve. We can discuss the wording.

SE: We will consider your suggestion.

TB: in 6.5., for the mechanism, I need a "mail box". This is what I mean when I suggest the US leadership.

SE: what about the UN?

TB: we don't trust the UN.

ZC: The US leadership raises a lot of questions and concerns. First, we would to clarify what we are exactly talking about. Second, the parties have to keep in mind that the success of the resolution will highly depend on our capacity to market a resolution proposal to refugees' communities and host states. Selling a "US led" proposal might be quite a challenge in the region these days. The US is of course our partner in this process and the ally of both sides. It may also have some leverage to impose a solution on Jordan. But what about Lebanon? Syria? Can we take the risk to alienate these countries? It is also not in both parties' interests to give ammunitions to Hezbollah or Hamás.

TB: If you allow me, I would like to ask a question which is intentionally a bit provocative. Rather than establishing a complex mechanism, wouldn't it be simpler to agree on a lump sum that would given to the PA or the PLO? The Palestinian Government would be then in charge of distributing the money to refugees.

SE: No. It is not feasible. The resolution process on refugees needs to be transparent.

TB: Do you mean that your people don't trust you?

SE: In a way, yes. The risk exists. We don't want to give people the impression that peace will be made on refugee's back

TB: that's interesting.

5

TB: On 6.3. I am confident that you will accept our "I": the Palestinian refugees should be entitled to Palestinian citizenship in accordance to Palestinian law. When I discussed with my Israeli friends, it is clear to everybody that the Palestinian refugees will become Palestinian citizens.

In 6.4, I cannot agree to [full] compensation. Do we need this adjective at this stage? Cannot we just postpone the discussion over the extent of compensation?

SE: What about restitution?

TB: it is of course not acceptable. I didn't even mentioned it

ZC: these are the only legal requirement that applies here: when restitution is not possible, refugees should be compensated in full. No, no compromise or postponement possible here. There are the individual rights of refugees.

TB: So, let's summarize. We have made good progress: the Israelis are ready to accept the structure of the Article you have offered. I think we can accept to replace the word "options" by "choices" in 6.3. We need to remain aware of the risk to create expectations which may not be met, but I think that this modification is acceptable.

For our next meeting, we will try to see if we can find draft that will be acceptable by both sides on article 6.5 and discuss further the points mentioned today. I also think we agree on the reference to Treaty in 6.8.

[Parties agree to meet on Thursday at 6pm]

[to be completed]

6

THE PAPERS

Summary of Olmert's "Package" Offer to Abu Mazen[1]
(Made on 31 August 2008)

General
- The preamble will state that the agreement represents the implementation of UNSC Res. 242 and 338, as well as fulfillment of the API (no mention of UNGA Res. 194).

Territory[2]
- Israel would annex 6.8% of the West Bank,[3] including the four main settlement "blocs" of Gush 'Etzion (with Efrata), Ma'ale Adumim, Giv'at Ze'ev and Ariel), as well as all of the settlements in East Jerusalem (with Har Homa), in exchange for the equivalent of 5.5% from Israeli territory.
- The "safe passage" (i.e., territorial link) between Gaza and the West Bank would be under Israeli sovereignty with Palestinian control, and is not included in the above percentages.
- There will be a special road connecting Bethlehem with Ramallah, thus by-passing East Jerusalem (most likely the same road currently planned around Adumim).
- East Jerusalem would be divided territorially along the lines of the Clinton Parameters, with the exception of the "Holy Basin", whose sovereignty would be delayed to a later stage (see Jerusalem below).
- There was no mention of the Jordan Valley.

Jerusalem
- Sovereignty over the "Holy Basin", which Olmert said comprises 0.04% of the West Bank (approximately 2.2 km^2), would be delayed to a later stage.
- The issue would continue to be negotiated bilaterally between Israel and Palestine with the involvement of the United States, Saudi Arabia, Jordan and Egypt, but without the ability of these third parties to force an agreement on the parties.

Refugees
- Israel would acknowledge the *suffering* of – but not responsibility for – Palestinian refugees (language is in the preamble). In parallel, there must also be a mention of Israeli (or Jewish) suffering.
- Israel would take in 1,000 refugees per year for a period of 5 years on "humanitarian" grounds. In addition, programs of "family reunification" would continue.
- Israel would contribute to the compensation of the refugees through the mechanism and based on suffering.
- Not clear what the heads of damage for compensation would be, just that there would be no acknowledgement of responsibility for the refugees, and that compensation, and not restitution or return (apart from the 5,000), would be the only remedy.

Security
- The "package" apparently made no mention of security.

---

[1] Summary is based on information provided by Dr. Erakat on 9 September 2008.
[2] A map was presented to Abu Mazen but he was not allowed to keep it. See revised NSU map projections (*jersep08P.pdf* and *wbgazasep08P.pdf*).
[3] Percentages are based on Israeli calculations for the West Bank (*i.e.*, excluding the NML and East Jerusalem).

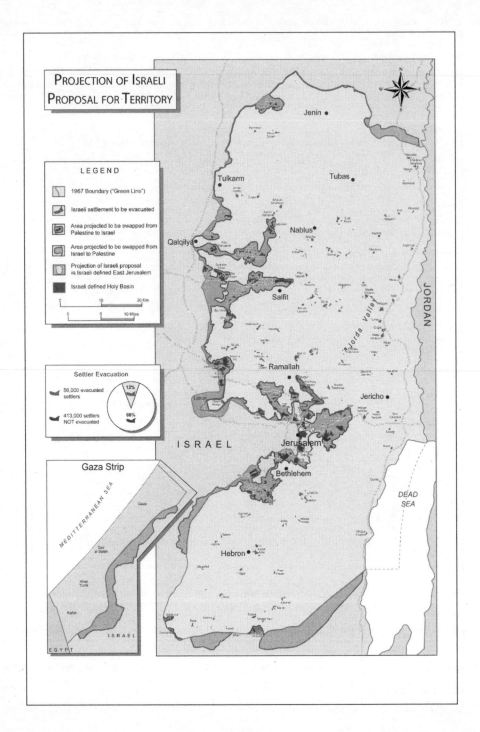

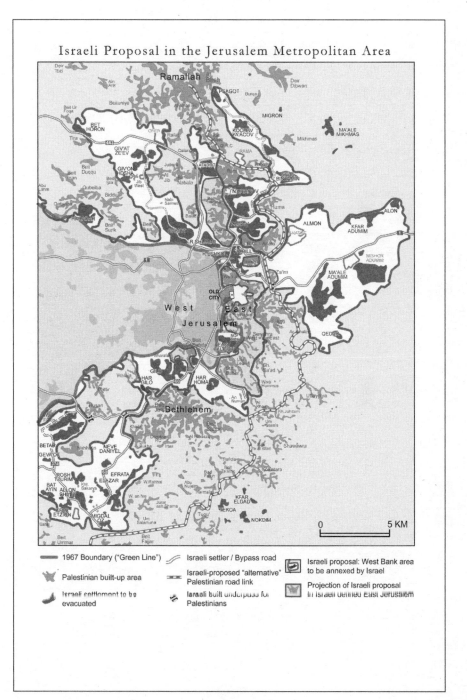

Israeli Proposal in the Jerusalem Metropolitan Area

<u>Talking Points and Questions</u>
<u>September 16 2008</u>

- Regardless of what happens in Israel, you are my partner until your last hour in office. I hope that we will remain in touch afterwards.

- We have come a long way since Annapolis – I reassure you that the negotiations will continue between us uninterrupted.

- I have carefully considered the proposals you made to me in our last meeting. Despite the fact that I was not given the map you showed me, I have several questions to help me understand what you have in mind.

- I cannot fully assess your proposal without the map and a [detailed] explanation [in writing] addressing the questions I am asking you today.

<u>Territory</u>

- Does the proposal you showed me on the map include the Dead Sea, Jordan Valley, and East Jerusalem within the territory of the Palestinian state? Is that the baseline from which you calculated the swap percentages? If not, please explain in detail how you came up with these percentages.

- The sum total of the built-up areas of all the settlements in the West Bank is around 70 km^2 (or 1.2% of the West Bank), yet you are seeking to annex around 500 km^2 (what you presented as 6.8%).
  - What is the basis of this demand?
  - What interests are you trying to achieve?
  - How do you see it addressing our interests, especially as Ariel, Maale Adumim, Givat Zeev, Har Homa and Efrat clearly prejudice contiguity, water aquifers, and the viability of Palestine?

- You suggested giving us territory from Israel equivalent to what you calculate as being 5.5% of the West Bank
  - How much is that in square kilometres? 300 km^2?

    o How do you see the specific areas that you suggested to swap from Israel to Palestine addressing our interest of swapping territory equal in size and value?

    o What is valuable to us, in your opinion, in these specific areas?

- I understood that you propose to divide the No Man's Land equally between us. Is this correct?

Safe Passage / Territorial Link

- If you are proposing a territorial link,
  - o under whose sovereignty would it fall?
  - o Under whose control?
  - o What would be included in it (just a road, or will it include other infrastructure?)
  - o More specifically, regarding sovereignty / control, what actual powers do you seek – would you have power to decide who uses it and when? Would you have the power to close it down?

Refugees

- What does it mean to acknowledge the suffering of refugees, without reference to responsibility? How is that different from acknowledging the suffering of people as a result of, say, a natural disaster? How do you propose to deal with the issue of responsibility?

- If you recognise suffering, why do you refuse to deal with compensation for non-material damages?

- Why is the suffering of Israelis relevant to the refugee issue?

- Regarding the 1000 annually for 5 years: while we agree to negotiate the number of returnees in consideration of Israel's capacity of absorption, this offer is not serious and cannot be accepted. Nonetheless, are you proposing this will be under the right of return, or on humanitarian grounds under your discretion? Given this distinction, who decides, and

2

what would be the criteria for deciding who is included among the returnees?

- What does it mean to continue family reunification, and how is this linked to the refugees?

- How do you propose to deal with restitution? How do you offer to deal with the assets of the "Absentees"?

- How do you envisage your participation and contribution to the international mechanism?

"Ramallah-Bethlehem Link"

- Isn't the assumption that East Jerusalem will be part of the state of Palestine? If so, why are you proposing a special link between Ramallah and Bethlehem? Where would it run?

Jerusalem

- We agreed in Annapolis to negotiate all core issues. Why are you delaying Jerusalem? How do you envisage East Jerusalem? Do you propose to divide it based on Arab/Jewish neighbourhoods? Will there be a hard or soft border? one or two municipalities?

- What do you mean by "Holy Basin" and what do you propose regarding:
  - o Who administers it in the proposed "interim"?
  - o Who (which parties) negotiate the final status?
  - o What is the deadline for the negotiation?
  - o What happens if there is no agreement by the deadline?
  - o In the proposed "interim", what will happen to the current Israeli policies, such as access, excavations and demolitions?

UNSC 242 / 338

- How does the proposal constitute implementation of the resolutions if it postpones the issue of Jerusalem and the "holy basin"?

3

General Questions

- Under the proposal, will there be a full withdrawal (including evacuation of all settlers, and redeployment of all military and security personnel) to the agreed border? If not, what specific exceptions do you have in mind?

- We have proposed, on security, the presence of a third party and no Israeli presence. Do you agree on both?

- Since the proposal makes no reference to water, are we correct in assuming then that the agreement for allocation of water will be based on international law?

- Since the proposal makes no reference to compensation, can I assume that compensation for occupation will be resolved in accordance with the principles of international law?

- Do you agree that all prisoners will be released upon the signing of the agreement?

Concluding remarks

- As I said, even though I saw the map briefly, I did not see the details, and I certainly did not memorize it. So I hope you will submit to us the full proposal, including the map and answers [in writing] to the questions I asked you today.

- I reiterate to you my commitment to continue our negotiations uninterrupted, regardless of the internal situation on either side.

- However, settlement expansion, particularly in and around East Jerusalem, is making our task much more difficult. Therefore I ask you to comply with your commitments and immediately freeze all settlement activity for the mutual benefit of both our peoples.

[Other issues: Ahmed Hilles, Cars, Deportees, Chamber of Commerce (East Jerusalem)]

4

Meeting Minutes
Erekat – Welch
Washington, D.C.
Tuesday December 2, 2008 12:00pm – 1:30pm

Attendance:

Palestinians:

Dr Saeb Erekat (SE)
Rami Dajani

US:

David Welch (DW)
Jonathan Schwartz (JS)
Gemal Hilal (GH)
Payton Knopf

SE: Good meeting in Cairo.

DW: Good that you attended and gave the presentation. Otherwise Amr Moussa predominates.

SE: I told Amr Moussa to behave well. I told him there are millions of dollars turned around from Gaza in the past, and the people are starving there, if you want me to tell Al-jazeera. So he decided to behave well. Abul Gheit gave an excellent presentation on the dialogue with Hamas. I said we don't want the blame game, and explained what the president did with the Quartet at Sharm, and that there is no secret agreement. Regarding Hamas, no one questions they won the elections -- that they are a political party – but they should have acted as a responsible government. When they were elected I congratulated Haniye as the prime minister of all Palestinians. They should have acted as the government and not as Hamas the movement. It was not democracy that failed, it was Hamas that failed. [SE gave examples of successor states accepting previous obligations, including Khomeini in Iran].

The Syrians (Muallem), Sudan, and Qatar objected that it was unfair that Hamas was not present at the meeting to give the other side. [SE made references to Islamic history]. The next time Sudan is discussed maybe the Darfur rebels should be invited [similar example of Yemen was given]. I told them Palestine will not be a card. I have the statement and you should vote on it. It was 11 hours and 40 minutes to pass the statement as introduced by Abul Gheit, condemning that the dialogue did not take place as scheduled on Nov 10, that Abu Mazen should continue in office until elections are held in accordance with the Basic Law.

DW: How were the Saudis?

SE: They were good. Saud al-Faisal interrupted the Sudanese complaint about the absence of Hamas; he said that Saeb Erekat spoke like a statesman. Bahrain and Oman were tough too.

DW: Do you expect the dialogue to resume?

SE: Yes, but not soon. Egypt was slapped, so it won't restart easily.

DW: The situation with the *hujjaj* in Gaza, is it because of the tougher position by Saudi? ...

SE: They are waiting. There are people who think Barak Obama was elected to the Iranian parliament! They don't realize that US policy won't change; that it is not made by one person.

DW: They're in for a big surprise. What do you think of Olmert's presentations?

SE: [Hands DW paper with questions submitted to Olmert in the past]. There was no proposal – there was nothing in writing. We asked Olmert to respond to the questions and explain in writing what he is proposing but he didn't respond. I asked him again on November 16 – there was no response, no map.

So we proposed: basically on territory we know it is the 67 border in general, with modifications ... [SE described briefly the Palestinian proposal]. Instead he wants 6.5% (not clear of what) ... the settlement blocs, Ariel, Maale Adumim, Gush Etzion. We offered 2% swap that would allow 70% of settlers to remain. We had no answer.

DW: You know he said to Abu Mazem he has a three page document.

SE: I did not receive it. He declined [?]. He said how about meeting with Shalom and his team.

DW: map experts...

SE: I don't know who Shalom will bring. They are nervous. Tal called twice since I got here. The committees continue to meet. Four committees met last week with Udi Dekel and Tal Becker, others were postponed because of this trip. Things that are agreed, are agreed. We have Is and Ps, things that require decision. We have the matrix. They don't want this because of the elections. They are afraid of leaks. If Olmert doesn't trust us, they can give their [paper] to you. We can also give you our position, and what we offer on each issue. This way you can preserve irreversibility of the process – by getting something from them in writing. Of course it won't be the 11th 'commandment' for the next government, but since we said "irreversible" we will know where we reached.

DW: Regarding Olmert's presentations, how does Livni see them?

SE: They [Livni and Becker] think we agreed to the approach of confidentiality, 'nothing is agreed until everything is agreed', that we won't have partial agreements, or declarations, and that the process is irreversible. We said this at Sharm with Condi, and we should honour it.

DW: On irreversibility Olmert has some proposals that …

SE: So give them to us. We have not received it. We don't know what it means. This is unfair. We need something writing with such sensitive issues. Otherwise how can you say we have an offer?

DW: In the absence of that is there any "common view" on the status of the negotiations even though there is no agreement.

SE: I've been asking them about this since August. Olmert wants to lock in that Palestinians agreed to his proposal. But what this proposal is we don't know. If they are worried that any of this can be used against them in the elections, I told them that two of us (Tal and I) can come to Washington to work on it. To protect the process, we are willing to engage on a joint progress report, a matrix that shows that positions.

DW: Their answer?

SE: She's worried about leakage.

DW: So she wants it confidential …

SE: Yes, we too. This is like a bypass surgery – can look messy.

DW: But what value can it have if it's confidential other than handing over the process to the new administration?

SE: It will explain to the next administration – this is where we are.

DW: But we already know that. We need to preserve, but also build. If it's not confidential then you have an opportunity.

SE: I can give you my positions on paper. It's up to you to do with it what you want.

DW: How do you assess the Arab understanding of all of this?

SE: Jordan and Egypt are fully briefed on all issues and are fully on board. The Saudis (through Saud al-Faisal) are fully aware. We have a channel with Syria, and they are somewhat aware (through the president and Muhammad Naseef). We are trying to set up a channel with Lebanon, particularly as they are affected by refugees, security and water. [discussion on approach to briefing Lebanon]. \

SE: Saud al-Faisal is very supportive, and wants an agreement. He sent, or will be sending, a letter to Obama on the Arab Peace Initiative (API).

DW: From Saudi Arabia?

SE: As Head of the Arab Council of Ministers. I asked them to be proactive. He is committed to the two state solution. They [the council] will do it.

DW: Do you think it's useful to gather this support and express further support to the negotiations, if there's enough value in the process for you to want it to be irreversible?

SE: Saudi's main concern is Jerusalem – not swaps and neighbourhoods. To them Jerusalem is the Haram.

DW: So they want to know who will "own" it?

SE: The status. I told them: I cannot tell you. What defines this "holy basin," what it includes … I don't know. [Reference to the difficulties on getting Jerusalem addressed, Shas, and the Annapolis statement on the core issues]. To Livni's credit, she did not become prime minister because she refused to say that Jerusalem was not on the table. We said at the beginning: no partial agreements, no fragmentation, no declarations. Why is Olmert now saying 3 pages?

GH: How does Livni want to proceed, if she wants to be elected?

SE: She believes negotiations should go on. I can appear with her as an academic in public events to demonstrate we have something since Annapolis. We are arranging for Abu Mazen to see her. We are worried about what Olmert is telling us.

Winning elections is about math, not what she says or does with us. Kadima can win only if the centre-left is organized [SE discussed internal party dynamics in Israel]. This is the only way to block Netanyahu.

GH: Would Livni support the idea of a matrix?

SE: She is cautious – walking in a minefield. Tal called me last night at 2am Tel Aviv time and he usually sleeps at 10.

JS: The Barack Obama team: do you plan to confide in them before or after he takes office?

SE: Before Obama's visit to Ramallah and the campaign I was put in touch with Dr Susan Rice …

GH: Let me add: when Obama spoke to Abu Mazen, he told him "I won't wait till January 20th. I will choose someone from us to be in touch, to start working with Palestinians and Israelis".

SE: To be honest, I don't know. Biden and Jones are my friends, I sent them an email to congratulate them…

GH: There is one president at a time …

SE: I am not meeting with anyone else. The only other meeting I have is with Dan Abraham. Olmert was calling him every hour. I will tell him to drop it.

JS: The secretary wants to personally brief the incoming team. She will take the decisions on what to share. If she offers her opinions, the Obama people can check, or the two sides can take the initiative to brief them. There are many ways of doing this.

DW: The president wants to ensure a smooth transition. [Discussion on upcoming meeting between Abu Mazen and Bush – Dec 17, 18 being tentative dates]

JS: During the transition the secretary will "educate" the successor. Since we have one president at a time, you should not be briefing the next team before they are in office.

SE: Regarding the new team, neither we nor the Israelis will deal with them without your suggestion or approval. … We will deal with you till Jan 20. Any recommendations from you will be respected regarding how to deal with the next administration. We are not rushing. You should help us get answers to these questions [to Olmert] in writing. You cannot leave it to speculation as to what Olmert said or didn't say. You can bring me and Tal off the radar. We can walk you through it – provided we preserve 'nothing is agreed until everything is agreed'.

DW: There are two different conceptual exercises: One is the status of the negotiations. You were personally involved, and your teams. We have a good understanding of them. We were also involved in some of that (the trilaterals).

SE: There were 261 meetings – you are fully briefed.

DW: We have that, and your views, and we have been in the trilateral. So we have our summary – internal and confidential. We can use that to brief the successors.

But the question is the second exercise, what to do with Olmert's proposals? While they are not clear, or in writing, they represent something. Since you want irreversibility, how can we use this?

SE: Ask for it in writing.

DW: I asked Shalom. He said proposals are not put in writing.

SE: Shalom will not tell you it's a proposal. In other matters we have put things in writing. I will not deviate from the rules we put in the Quartet statement.

END

Meeting Minutes
February 27, 2009
US Consulate General, Jerusalem

Attendance:

US: Sen. George Mitchell (GM)
        Amb. David Hale
        CG Jacob Walles
        Gemal Hilal
        Peter Evans
        Payton Knopf
        Mara Rudman
        Unidentified person

Palestinian: Dr. Saeb Erekat (SE)
               Rami Dajani

SE: How were your meetings with the Israelis?

GM: Good.

SE: It seems they are moving towards a government with 65 seats. Livni told Netanyahu her conditions for coalition: two states and political negotiations. AM cannot demand less than Livni. We want to continue the political process and negotiations. We are committed to that. But if Israel doesn't recognize the two-state solution and continues settlements, it will be the last nail in AM's coffin if we send him to negotiate. He is setting conditions internally and the international community demands them. But when the Israeli government comes in, nothing! We can't have these double standards. We will lose big. So, your policies are important. I understand your constraints and US politics – I know I don't stand a chance against them. But the stakes are great.

Regarding Netanyahu, I know him and his team. They will say that they strive for peace with the Palestinians. You are in a strong position. There's the Road Map. The Palestinians accepted it. We recognized Israel. Israel must accept a Palestinian state that is viable. We have our commitments regarding one authority, one gun, and terrorism – they have their commitments on settlements.

If Netanyahu forms a government with a party that has 15 seats, with an official platform of ethnic cleansing and expulsion of Muslims and Christians who are Israeli citizens … if Barack Obama wants a policy of reconciliation with the Muslim and Arab world … with your kids dying all over the region. You do not win the battle with marines – so stop treating

1

Israel as a country above the laws of man. We recognized Israel on 78% of historic Palestine in exchange for a state on the remaining 22%. In exchange we have our credibility destroyed with the settlements and the wall …

You have a choice. There is no need to reinvent the wheel. You have either the cost-free way: pressure us to negotiate, which means AM negotiating with Netanyahu under continuing settlement and without recognition – this would be the last nail in AM's coffin, or you have another choice: take the Annapolis statement: two states, and negotiations over all core issues. If the Israeli government doesn't include in its mandate the two-states and negotiating on all issues including Jerusalem … [hands GM paper submitted to the EU via the Czechs] We are committed to peace and negotiations for two states, but we won't engage without this.

Netanyahu will go to President Obama and tell him "Iran." He will say he is committed. Then he will build settlements in E1 and elsewhere – like he did in Har Homa. You cannot be expected to demand less of Netanyahu than what Livni demanded.

Last time we met, I gave you a matrix detailing the progress on the permanent status negotiations. If you look at it carefully, you'll see that the negotiations have exhausted themselves. What is left are the needed tradeoffs. When Olmert spoke of 6.5% in exchange for 5.8, and AM agreed to swaps in East Jerusalem, this is significant. Same with security. We recognize that Palestine will not have an army, navy and air force, but will have no limitation on dignity, and will require a third party to help us. On refugees, there were discussions on numbers that will return to Israel over a number of years. The deal is there. With it you can develop the 'Obama plan' with your associates in Europe. AM can call for an emergency Arab / Islamic summit and submit to them the offer, and tell them: 'you decide with me.' I think they will go with it, like with the API (which now nobody can talk about). The matrix we gave you is the most accurate account of the discussion in all 10 committees. With AM and Olmert, the most significant were two or three sessions: if Olmert had offered AM in writing, things would be different. Instead he refused to hand him the map. We prepared questions for Olmert to clarify what he was offering [SE discussed several examples of the questions, notably on Jerusalem and the so-called 'holy basin'].

On security we sat with General Jones and worked with him on many occasions. We accept 'no navy, air force, army' but need internal security based on our responsibilities. What we can't do, we can have internationals carry it out – not Israelis. [SE gave examples of AWACS, bases, and early warning stations].

On Jerusalem we discussed the issues including having a joint body to administer the city. We have looked at all details of the day after. Now it's about decisions. I cannot negotiate on percentages and numbers of refugees any longer. The choice is yours now. It's time for a decision. The two states are inevitable.

During these negotiations we learned our lesson: after each session we went to Jordan to coordinate. We want Jordan to be prosperous and strong. We did the same with Egypt, Saudi Arabia, even Syria.

2

Now we can't have permanent status negotiations without: recognition of two state solution, stopping settlement, and respecting signed agreements. This does not impact security cooperation. We are happy you are opening your office here. [SE briefed on the reconciliation talks in Cairo and the committees formed to follow up on discussions]. It is premature to judge the outcome at this stage. Fatah needs to look good, it must not derail discussions, but when it comes to the details, there are enormous problems. Israel is being blunt. They require explicit acceptance of conditions by a national unity government. So I say you have to do the same, which is only fair.

GM: How do they respond to that?

SE: I tell them to convey it to their leadership. You should discuss this with AM tonight. Fair is fair. The Quartet cannot impose conditions on one side and play with 'constructive ambiguity' on the other.

GM: Thank you for coming here, and thank you for your usual candour and clarity. I understand what you said and will do my best. The US is committed to the two state solution. I am not interested in process, but results. We also understand the need for comprehensive approach. I relayed to President Obama explicitly what your side told me and how you want to proceed. I was happy to hear that you and all others on your side urged the Syria track to proceed. This is different from 2001. I will do my best to move the process forward the best I can. We're trying to work out mechanisms to make the upcoming conference a success. Again, we will do our very best to make all this possible. I will be meeting Salam Fayyad now, then dinner with AM. Tomorrow we head to Jordan, then Abu Dhabi, then to Sharm.

END

3

Meeting Minutes
Dr. Saeb Erakat Meeting with the Negotiations Support Unit
June 2, 2009

Attendance: Dr. Saeb Erekat (SE); NSU.

SE: The purpose of this meeting is to brief you on our meetings in Washington. Much of what I say to you today is just between us. The Washington I went to last week isn't the Washington I knew before. I went twice in preparation before Obama meeting. We met with Biden, Jones, Clinton, Mitchell, and the Joint Chiefs of Staff. Admiral Mullen and Abu Mazen (AM) met for 30 minutes. Mullen said he has 230,000 troops in Iraq and Afghanistan. Every week he has 10 troops coming home in wheelchairs and body bags. He is going to get them out politically, not militarily. He told AM, "you are the most important man in the Middle East." He said the Palestinian state that will happen will not be a failed state and that we should focus on our obligations – authority, lawlessness, 'one authority, one gun' – and that eventually Israel will realize it has to live up to its obligations. This argument was endorsed by the NSC, Jim Jones, and recently I read General Petraeus saying the same thing in an interview in Al-Hayat.

There is a growing sense in the U.S. that something must be done soon. Washington is very concerned about the state of the Middle East. Palestine is an issue on the minds of Arabs and Muslims everywhere. Washington is speaking with one voice, from the White House to the Congress. So what do we do to build on this? We have to do something that speaks in the language of their interests.

I went to Syria and met with real people. Several Arab countries are saying 'get rid of AM, Hamas is the card that will deliver. I don't care if they have Mish'al and others. These are cards that Syria can play and they know that. I advised AM to go to Tehran. To solve our problems, we must work with Tehran and Syria and break the ice between Mubarak and Assad. We can't do anything with the Iranians until the elections, but we must do something.

Palestinians are speaking with 2,000 voices just when we need to be speaking with one.

Netanyahu is going to burn the West Bank. He will give the green light in Gaza, let Hamas run loose, while burning the West Bank to show that AM can't deliver. Netanyahu is capable of anything.

We are hearing new language from Washington on Iran. They are referring to Iran as a "growing threat" instead of a "threat." This is a big difference. They are saying that they hope Iran will seize this historic opportunity, signaling that they are working on something big. My analysis is that Washington may offer to move the Iran file from the SC to the IAEA so that Iran, in turn, will allow inspection of their nuclear facilities. I talked with El Baradei, he said Iran is 12 years away from making a nuclear bomb.

1

Abu Mazen did a fantastic job in Washington. He gave a very comprehensive, focused presentation to Obama and to the Americans. There were two meetings. In the closed door meeting (Obama, AM, and notetakers) AM said, "I have one question: are you serious about the two-state solution? If you are, I cannot comprehend that you would allow a single settlement housing unit to be built in the West Bank. If Israel refuses to stop settlements, what is the alternative? A) 1 state or B) chaos, extremism, violence. You have the choice. You can take the cost free road, applying double standards, which would shoot me and other moderates in the head and make this Bin Laden's region. Or say we are not against Israel but against Israel's actions. If you cannot make Israel stop settlements and resume permanent status negotiations, who can?

Obama responded that the "the establishment of the Palestinian state is a must for me personally. In an expeditious manner, we will get to the two-state solution" Obama said he appreciated the formation of the new government, and said it was courageous of AM. He asked AM to continue reforms and institution building and asked when Fatah would convene its conference. He said he spoke to Netanyahu in a tough, candid, and focused manner and that what was seen in public is what was said in private. Obama told him that if the Israeli gov't coalition can't deliver, that's their problem. The U.S. needs an answer by July 1st. Shapiro, Hale, and Mitchell will be the team to get the answers from their counterparts, Meridor, Arad, and Malcha. Obama said "I cannot report anything to you, what we heard from the Israelis doesn't deserve your time."

Rami Dajani (RD): Why July 1st?

SE: Obama is going to Moscow on July 6th for US-Russia Summit. He wants results to be able to declare – in terms of a timeline and an endgame. If there is going to be a Moscow conference, they don't want a photo-op only, like at Annapolis.

Obama said that Netanyahu is not ready to resume negotiations so we should stop saying that we have preconditions for negotiations.

Ehud Barak is going to DC to present on road blocks, settlements, and outposts, but what he will really be talking about is the restrictions of his coalition.

Abu Mazen told Obama that he will shoulder all of his commitments (1 authority 1 gun, Dayton security, EU-BAM, etc.), will continue reforms, will hold the Fatah Conference no later than July, and prepare for elections.

Obama said he supports talks between Fatah and Hamas but that we should not surprise him with a unity government that doesn't recognize the two-state solution, and accept Quartet conditions

Abu Mazen told Obama that Israeli obligations don't just include settlements. They also include going back to the Sept. 28 lines, allowing EJ institutions to function, ending the siege on Gaza.

2

Then we said "thank you for everything, now we want to give you something": the Regional Road Map (RRM). You will make our life a lot easier if you let our people know the endgame. With respect to the issues of settlement building, East Jerusalem, etc., the endgame is an end to the occupation. We came a long way with Olmert, we do not need to start from scratch. The RRM already has approval from many countries [SE noted states that have been consulted and have approved the RRM]. Abbas told Obama that once the borders are defined then borders, Jerusalem, settlements and water will be settled. On security, we have the work done by Gen. Jones. On refugees, AM said we need a credible number, not 5 million but not 1,000. Abu Mazen said "I am ready for the endgame. I know there are lots of painful decisions to make, but I am ready to make them. I hope I have a partner in Israel.'

Then Obama brought up incitement. We told him that in the Wye River Agreement an incitement committee was established. We should revive it. We should prepare for them a file on who is actually inciting. The demand to recognize Israel as a Jewish state is incitement. [To the NSU] Look very carefully at incitement. Bring as much evidence as possible on Israeli incitement against us, including legislation, speeches, books …

Gabriel Fahel (GF): Do we want to entertain this distraction?

SE: We want to isolate this issue and take away pretexts

Abu Mazen told Obama, "I will do security, reform, institution building, Fatah convention, and win the elections. But Israel needs to agree to two-state solution, stop settlement, including "natural growth." Natural growth in Ma'ale Adumim is building on my roof in Jericho. What you need is a matrix of interests and responsibilities. You also need to help me pay salaries. When we resume negotiations we want to resume from Dec. 2008.
We can't ask less of the Israeli government than Livni does: discuss all core issues without exception and accept the two-state solution.

Obama was impressed with AM. He said there needs to be Fatah reforms. If you run on the treadmill and don't sweat you don't get rid of the poison.

US wants steps from Arab countries. I warned them against this. It is unfair of the U.S. to pressure Arab countries to make concessions vis-à-vis Israel without pressuring Israel as well.

Obama said he got Israel to commit to stop construction in E1 but nothing yet on home demolitions.

Andrew Kuhn (AK): We could help with monitoring on E1.

SE: Yes, and we'll send the reports to Jones and share with Selva and Mitchell.

[To NSU] Also, give me a one page summary of RM obligations for both Palestinians and Israelis and their status (by 10:00 am June 3rd)

3

Clinton said the next 5 weeks leading up to Obama's visit to Moscow will be a crucial period. Mitchell said Obama was very tough with Bibi, Clinton said the same. The meeting with the Israelis did not produce anything besides the commitment to stop E1 construction, but that is secret.

Our strategy is that we want to see real steps on the ground from the U.S., Israel, and the Arabs and we will focus on our obligations. Abu Mazen's presidency is the most important thing in the region

RD: Was there any mention of the June 4th speech?

SE: It will not be a plan. It will be a rapprochement with the Arabs and Muslims. They like what is being done with Cairo University.

Hala Rashed (HR): If Obama said Netanyahu is not ready for negotiations and will focus on a settlement freeze, but he is not ready to use sticks, what is he expecting?

SE: I wouldn't go that far. When I sat with several congressmen they are all bringing Obama's message – "Bibi must stop settlements." The U.S. knows very well how to deal with Israel. How and what? I don't know.

HR: Is there concern about pressuring Arab states to offer carrots?

SE: We told Obama not to make Arab states give carrots without Israeli action. We need to focus on the bigger picture. I told Solana to come here and get his act together. He should confirm and commit to the U.S. that Europe will be the needed third party.

Arab states have different agendas when they go to Washington, they don't like when Palestine dominates the agenda. They are worried about the billions they receive. But in the media they beg us to praise their leaders.

RD: Building on Hala's question, what are the scenarios if Netanyahu doesn't meet his obligations?

SE: That's none of my business. We didn't talk about it. We want Israel to meet its obligations. If an Israeli Prime Minister fights with almost any world leader, Israelis will side with their Prime Minister. If an Israeli Prime Minister fights with a U.S. leader, they will side with the U.S. I've been watching closely what leading Israeli journalists like Akiva Eldar and Nahum Barnea are saying.

AK: In the Israeli press, they are saying that the understandings between Bush and Sharon have been taken off of the table. Is this true?

SE: No. When bush reached that agreement we were very tough with the U.S. and told them it is none of their business. But we don't know what they did with it.

4

Fouad Hallak (FH): Do you have any comment on the recent statements in the press about the issue of Islamic sovereignty in Jerusalem?

SE: That was very stupid of Abdel Qader. If it wasn't for the difficulties in Fatah, I would have taken this issue up with him. The issue is about sovereignty and occupation, not about churches or mosques. [To NSU] Ask Fayyad be tough with them. It is selling out Jerusalem. I haven't visited the PM's office in ages because these people are so sensitive. Spend time with Abdel Qader, tell him this is very dangerous.

AK: What about Abu Rudeina's comments on two states for two peoples?

SE: I haven't heard them. I'll talk to Nabil.

HR: Alstom has won a bid from Saudi Arabia to build a railway, and are now bidding on a second one. This violates the Arab League resolution and international law. We should pressure Arab states to not do business with these companies and to respect the Arab League resolution. We have also heard that people in the PA are thinking of entering into a contract with Veolia.

SE: Who should I talk to about this? Tell Fayyad to get his act together.

RD: we can prepare a brief memo outlining the issues.

SE: Prepare it. Identify Arab countries.

HR: There may also be potential dealings by the PA with these companies.

SE: Please make sure with Fayyad no one in the PA does this.

Bader Rock (BR): There is a problem regarding asking Israel to expropriate land in Area C for industrial construction...

SE: You have a lot of assignments Hala. Take the case of Jiftlik. I cannot ask Israel to confiscate land, it would mean any land confiscated is legal. The government needs to pursue these sensitive issues with our help.

HR: My direct contact with the PM has been diminished

SE: I will ask him about this. We help when asked – we cannot force ourselves on him.

BR: Can we say it is the policy of the PLO not to ask Israel to expropriate land?

SE: Absolutely. Use the Jiftlik letter.

5

RD: [Handing SE Israeli military order] There is an issue of Israel revising the population registry, treating the WB and Gaza as separate entities. This is a fundamental breach of Oslo and an attempt to divide the WB and Gaza, and is illegal under international law.

SE: Hamas is the sword around my neck. What should I do? Prepare a letter to Amos Gilad on this issue and I will sign it. (Possibly a press release as well)

Sharif Hamadeh (SH): There are conflicting reports about what Abu Mazen and Olmert discussed re: refugees. Can you clarify?

SE: Olmert said 1,000 refugees over 10 years. Abu Mazen said "are you joking."

SH: Was it Right of Return or Family reunification?

SE: I don't know. But, if that is being reported, it's good to say that Olmert agreed to the principle of Right of Return.

SH: AM used the figure 5 million refugees? This is not what we use. We will prepare a memo on terms and methodology for counting refugees so we can coordinate.

Tarek Hamam (TH): Could you shed light on why the issue of refugee arrangements is being discussed in public in the media?

SE: I cannot stand guard on the lips of every Palestinian.

Michael Talhami (MT): Obama opened the door with comments on lack of clean water in Gaza. Was there any further discussion on water?

SE: Abu Mazen said this issue will be solved if we figured out borders. We said the basis for water negotiations is international law.

MT: Water is the only issue that is win-win. Should we align it with the RRM and API framework?

SE: Why not? Make an internal document. I like to read all of your ideas.

Enas Abu Laban (EA): Do you think that when negotiations resume they will have the same structure as Annapolis?

SE: I don't know. This time will be easier. I will head the delegation. Abu Alaa won't be involved. I don't even know if we will have negotiations. But you should be prepared.

EA: Regarding telecom, the situation is bad. We have a meeting tomorrow with the international community. It is a critical time for Israel to release the frequencies.

6

SE: I made a mistake in giving up this issue. I have no evidence, but I'm sure some Palestinians businessmen are making deals with Israel. We must find a way not to include businessmen in politics. Israel is making jokes about these big shots.

EA: We should request that the donors put pressure on Israel to release the frequencies

AK: Gabe and Azem met with John Murray to put together lessons learned on Annapolis. We will send you the recommendations. And I'm sure John will want to meet with you.

SE: Sure but make sure to send me the recommendations before the meeting.

RD: Will you be briefing Heads of Missions soon? We've been hearing many are interested.

SE: Yes I need you prepare packets for that – like the ones we gave out in Washington.

RD: [Summary of the Tasks]

7

Meeting Summary
Dr. Saeb Erekat – LTG Keith Dayton
NAD Ramallah June 24, 2009

Attendance:

US: LTG Keith Dayton (KD)
              Col. Stephen Moniz (SM)
              Dov. Schwartz
              Major Lawrence Martin

Palestinians: Dr Saeb Erekat (SE)
              Rami Dajani (RD)

SE: I want to share with you some materials we gave to Senator Mitchell (GM) during his last trip, one paper on security and another on judicial reform.

KD: Thank you for this. I would really appreciate sharing your discussions with GM because we're not necessarily getting this information from him.

SE: I have some questions for you today. First, about the Mitchell mission, and how you plan to work together.

KD: When GM first came out to the region, he made the rounds. We explained to him what we're doing, and recommended he take the USSC as part of his effort. So he agreed that I would be his deputy for security. GM went around and came back and said "I accept your offer". He said he will use my staff, who are based here and are engaged on the ground. His condition was that I extend my mandate to December 2010 – I was planning to leave after this summer. Now, nothing is simple in Washington. The State Department is still looking for some Presidential authorization for this to be formal. I now have a memorandum of agreement stating that I work primarily for GM. However, I continue to coordinate and work through Jake in Jerusalem and Cunningham in Tel Aviv, and Feltman in DC.

GM rewrote my job description: essentially more of the same and more quickly. He has also helped with my budget. You recall our work together two years ago -- back then I had no funding whatsoever. Now we have Congress allocating over $80 M in FY 2009. Some of that is still available for spending. We are looking at over $100M in FY 2010. So there's a lot more money coming in from Congress and the Administration.

GM wants me to get into other areas of security assistance and coordination. So far we've been working mainly on the NSF and the PG. He wants me to take a bigger role on police, working with the Europeans. Hazem is excellent, but there are many needs – and structural issues.

- 1 -

He wants us to work on justice sector and corrections (prisons). So we started working with the Europeans on this. Also, border and crossings management. We have a budget line of $10M so there is a lot of potential there – the Canadians have expressed a commitment to this work. They have made an assessment – it's too bad they didn't meet with you when they were here.

RD: You mean Denis Lefebvre's assessment?

KD: Yes.

RD: He did meet with the NSU and we discussed the various possibilities for work on crossings with him.

SE: That's good. If he meets with the NSU it's like meeting with me.

KD: There is a draft master-plan that they're working on. It is hard to figure out who in the PA is responsible. It seems like there are three addresses.

SE: You have to meet with the NSU. Rami is your contact.

RD: We are happy to review anything on borders or crossings for implications on permanent status positions and issues …

SE: Work with the NSU and get back to me so we can see how to deal with it. My view is that this needs to be done through the Ministry of Interior.

KD: The next area I'll be working on is counter-terrorism. I've talked to the Israelis – they had no push back on the concept. Their military officers think it's now time. They also acknowledged the PA's needs for special equipment. The question is who should have this equipment: Hazem Atallah, Abu Fatah, the PG? Jordan is also willing to help.

SE: I seem to recall there was a decision by the president on this issue. I remember translating it for him to English. I believe it was an anti-terrorism unit in the PG. I will check and get back to you on that.

KD: Next is civil defence. This has been much neglected. We are planning new facilities and training in Jordan. I saw Gen. Atiani in Jordan and we are happy with his response.

[SE briefed on contacts with Jordan and recent openings with Syria, and the broader Arab and regional context]

KD: I am glad to hear all this from you because GM is not telling me anything. He says he doesn't need to tell me as long as I am doing what I need to be doing. What is clear is that the administration is really serious about creating a Palestinian state.

- 2 -

[SE briefed on AM meetings in DC, and the commitment shown by the US administration on this issue]

SE: A lot of this is a result of your help that we have made so much progress on security.

KD: It's hard to believe but even the Israelis are giving me credit.

SE: It is really rare that Palestinians and Israelis agree on anything. Whenever I see that happen I study it really carefully.

KD: Co-operation is also good now…

SE: I have your speech you know. [Brief discussion of KD's WINEP speech]

KD: Because of all this we now have broad congressional support.

SE: Yes – I met with several congressmen recently (Berman, Levin …). This is true.

KD: You are talking to the right people….We are now the surest thing ….

SE: Now to some contentious points. You know I work off the radar, I examine and assess the situation – for example in Qalqilya recently. This time things are right as far as security is concerned. I want to know: is that your assessment? I am seeing Amos Gilad tonight – even he tells me things are different. He used to tell me "big zero" but not anymore.

KD: He's now a supporter of our mission.

SE: I want an assessment from you for the president. We hear from Hazem and the MoI, but we need to hear from you.

KD: They have come a long way, but I worry about some things. In the great tradition of the US Army, I will ask my colonel to go first, then I'll comment on it!

SE: I really need to know what you really think. I predicted what would happen in Gaza contrary to all the assessment and intelligence information. I wrote a paper for the president in 2005 and predicted the "Mogadishu Syndrome" in Gaza – the social structure and fabric etc… I don't want to repeat those mistakes in the West Bank. This is for me and my family – I don't want to run away across the bridge.

SM: First, with regard to capabilities, we assess the situation by governorate; the environment in each is different. In some, the PASF are ready to take over full security responsibilities (for example in Bethlehem). There you have good coordination, full force presence and no settler problem. Hebron, in contrast, is problematic because of the settlers. Still we are developing another battalion to improve force level. Some of the people originally trained in Jordan and now training the ones who weren't.

- 3 -

Regarding chain of command, the assessment is very good. The senior officers course has been useful and has established greater visibility for them. There are some outstanding problems mainly at the company and battalion level. For example, Abu Fatah is a good man – he commands a lot of respect, but there are some issues.

KD: On Hebron – the problem is the presence of settlers – guys who will provoke. There is also a strong Hamas presence and the clan issues. Jenin / Toubas is different: no settlers, Islamic Jihad rather than Hamas – the area commander is really good. Overall Bethlehem is the strongest area commander. Tulkarem is somewhere in between. In Nablus it's close as well: the relation between the occupying force and the PASF is very good. Qalqilya is not so good.

I can say that the security forces have done what AM has asked them: one authority, one gun. The problem now is political – that is, Hamas. I don't think they have that fully under control. We will continue working – with just three battalions this is just the beginning. We are looking at a goal of ten trained NSF battalions [*RD note: this is a force of approximately 5000*].

The experience in Qalqilya is instructive – in that it was not done well. The police didn't do what they were supposed to do in support of the NSF, like blocking off streets and keeping people out. Yet the result was positive.

SE: We lost three kids. It's unfortunate.

KD: That's true. Phase 2 was resolved when the Jordan-trained platoon came over from Tulkarem. They showed a disciplined chain of command. They completed the operation in one hour – which might have taken 15 otherwise.

What worries me is organization. You need to organize them. We can't do that for you. The rivalry is still there. The president or the MoI has not addressed this.

SE: I understand the security file is with the PM. What's SF's role in this?

KD: He gave it to the MoI. But the MoI does not do anything. The NSF still considers that it works for the president.

SE: But the president gave it to SF!

KD: The same problems with the intelligence units. The PSO reports to the MoI, but the GI reports to the president. The police: HA works on his own – like he has his own MoI. I've said "good for him" – at least he's doing things that need to be done.

SE: Hazem is great. I told the president to promote him. I nominated him to take on the security file in the permanent status negotiations. I think he should be MoI. I supported him on that. But I can see how he is working on his own.

- 4 -

KD: By the way, the intelligence guys are good. The Israelis like them. They say they are giving as much as they are taking from them – but they are causing some problems for international donors because they are torturing people. Hamas does it …

SE: That is not an excuse.

KD: I've only started working on this very recently. I don't need to tell you who was working with them before … As for Abu Fatah, he is respected and strong, but he does not even recognize the authority of the MoI. I go to the minister and he says go ask Abu Fatah. I want to empower the minister, but I need something to work with.

SE: You should meet the president. When was the last time you met him?

KD: I've been trying to meet him for the last year.

SE: I will set it up for you – next week.

KD: I will be in Washington, back July 7.

SE: We'll have it when you get back. You should prepare a few points to raise with him: what is good and what is deficient. He needs to hear this. We need to work on institutions. I know HA is great, but this way he is working on his own.

KD: I want to say that Civil Defence is well run. Military intelligence is also well run. Raji Faraj is great.

SE: I met him recently and was really impressed. He has a strategic outlook. I found the conversation with him going into real strategic issues.

KD: My president is really serious about a Palestinian state. I know SF has a two year plan. So we have no time to waste. We really need to work on the institutions – GM wants me to deliver on overall structure. For that we need to get at the "autonomy" of certain institutions. I need to be able to count on your president.

SE: You can count on him. I want to raise an important concern: You know I teach a course on hostage negotiations in Jericho. One thing I notice dealing with the kids there is the impact of Israeli military actions on them. We need to find a way to stop these incursions. This is the main factor of doubt about what we are doing. Israel tells me KD is not worried about this.

KD: I am not indifferent about the incursions. I want them to stop completely during daytime. At night, they should be limited to cases where the PA does not respond to an Israeli warning, and the occupying force needs to act. You know some governorates have no more curfews now – where area A is 24hrs under PA control.

- 5 -

SE: You need to have a mechanism that allows these guys to maintain the stature and dignity. This is the most important thing – more important than weapons or training. You have to give them a chance. For example, that they have 6 hours to act …

KD: One way to work on this is to have a "right of first refusal" – PA forces have for example 2 hours to act (6 hours is too long for dealing with a threat).

SE: You should develop a mechanism.

KD: Qalqilya proved useful for that – in dealing with armed groups. I repeat: I am not indifferent to incursions.

SE: This has a demoralizing effect on them. Dignity, pride, and conviction are the most important things. I see it in the course in Jericho.

KD: I don't disagree and am not indifferent. But if there is a serious target and the Palestinians don't do something about it, the Israelis will act. One thing that would help is if you have a general commander – if not the MoI. Bottom line is you can't have autonomous security apparatuses is you're aiming to build a state.

SE: You work on a low profile. This is important. That is how you command respect. This time we should not mess around and we cannot afford mistakes.

KD: We need to work on these things because in two years you might find yourself with a state.

SE: I don't want it to be a failed state.

KD: Do you know what this 100 day plan is?

SE: Plans are good. Everybody needs plans. SF needs to improve his image. For example, everything I get from the Israelis I ask him to announce it. He is the one to "cut the ribbons". He needs this for his image. Like you I work with a low profile. Sometimes that means people like us have unfair reputations.

KD: I'm really happy with my reputation. Apparently I run the PA!

SE: Even the Saudis think we're arms smugglers …

KD: That was just an excuse. What do you want from me on Gaza?

SE: You will have an answer when you get back. By then we'll know more about the Cairo talks. The Syrians are interested in playing a constructive role. You know from your work in Iraq. They want a US ambassador in Damascus. For them Hamas is a card: one item one price. So we are hopeful there will be a rapprochement which will help us in Gaza. Let's wait and talk when you get back.

- 6 -

Meeting Minutes
Saeb Erakat – David Hale
September 16 2009 9:00am
NAD – Jericho

Palestinian:

      Dr Saeb Erakat (SE)
      Issa Kassissieh (IK)
      Rami Dajani (RD)

US:

      David Hale (DH)
      Mara Rudman (MR)

DH: Mitchell (along with Dan Shapiro) is now meeting with BN. Jonathan Schwartz couldn't come today. We're here to discuss the trilateral meeting to relaunch negotiations on the 2 state outcome. That session will not be long. Afterwards the president will make a statement. Today we should discuss issues to enable the meeting to take place. The package is essential – I am well aware you have misgivings regarding the quality of the package with Israel, but we will not be able to meet all expectations of all parties. In the aggregate, however, it's a good package. Our understanding is there will be language on Jerusalem in the president's statement, and a reference to 67 territory.

SE: What is the US understanding of a settlement freeze – as stated in the Road Map. Your Road Map.

DH: A freeze is a flexible concept – every Israeli official has a different concept of it. For the President it means an end to all settlement activity – and he will say this. His position is that the settlements are illegitimate, and we've been working to bring an end to construction that is credible and that the Israelis are willing to do.

SE: [notes the exclusions as stated by BN] For your information this will mean more settlement construction in 2009 than in 2008. This is the biggest gaem of deceit since 67. I am not saying this to undermine you – I am satisfied with your answer that a freeze means the end to all construction. You know BN stated these exclusions at the very beginning. I am not here to score points, just to explain my position. So I want to ask you questions to clarify your position in order to decide about the trilateral.

DH: You are prejudging the package based on what you hear in the Israeli media.

SE: Not media. Based on what Israeli officials are saying, and what BN said in the Knesset. I told the Arabs that it is not a US position, but Israel's. But, if this is in fact a deal … it took us 4 years to rebuild our image – we will not allow him to destroy us, like he did in 96 to 99 – do you remember?

1

MR: I was working for the administration then.

SE: I simply can't ask less of BN than Livni did [SE discusses Kadima position and forming a coalition that excludes Jerusalem]. If this is the package, it's a no go. It's about credibility. You had three options: you convince BN, he convinces you, or you maintain a disagreement – it seems he convinced you.

DH: You're reacting to something that does not yet exist. Many things get said in the media. We intend to have a freeze – an end to activity. This is significant; no other president has invested so much and done so much on that before. If there is no meeting, there will be no freeze, so all our work will be wasted. And all the other elements will not be there. No one will get what they want. We said an explicit reference to Jerusalem and 67 territory. Will these change the equation?

SE: I need to clarify things first. What do you mean by "public construction"?

DH: We've discussed every angle, but there is no agreement yet.

MR: You're relying on public statements …

SE: Last night GM told AM this is the best he could get. After several months of meetings with the Israelis. You need to give me a report. Instead you say a meeting on the 22nd – next Wednesday. You never discussed with me.

DH: We have not reached an agreement so there is nothing I can tell you.

SE: When can I find out? If it turns out these are the exclusions, it's a no go.

DH: Regardless of other elements?

SE: You spent 8 months with the Israelis – no time with me. We at least need to spend some time to build a political framework. You don't know what the framework will be. Maybe you don't have a plan. If you do you have to lay it out. I have to answer to Fatah and the PLO executive committees about this today. The Arabs are calling, asking about the press reports. I was on the phone till 2am with them. I said GM did not say anything – that these are Israeli positions. The meeting you propose is on the 22nd. In the past we would have a statement ready.

DH: This is a different president and a different approach – we won't negotiate letters of invitation or ToRs …

SE: But he will make a statement … ? on settlement freeze, if it's not a total freeze, it's a no-go. I know Israel. They will offer a state with provisional borders on 42% of the WB. Peres is trying to convince BN to make it 55%.. Do you think Uzi Arad will sit with me and discuss Jerusalem?! I've been through this –Rice threw me out of her office once.

2

We had Frazier and monitoring – and it was the same as always. This time let me make myself clear: We will not compromise on our people. We held the Fatah conference, we've carried out security reform – one authority one gun, rule of law – we've rebuilt the PA. This is the time for clarity. If BO cannot stop BN for 9 months while we negotiate, why would we negotiate 67 or Jerusalem?

DH: Our whole approach is based on the freeze …

SE: Once they present it in the Knesset it is reliable …

DH: I don't agree.

SE: Do you deny the statements in the Knesset?

MR: We're not done yet.

SE: These are statements not comments. I need information from you in order to make decisions. Information is the basis of our decisions.

DH: The package will not be 100% of what you want or we want. But we did what is required.

MR: Also you haven't done a 100% …

SE: We have carried out our obligations. Ask your generals and the Israelis.

MR: There's the issue of incitement.

SE: We have asked for the convening of the trilateral committee on incitement. We have done our work – there are many things we would like to ask the Israelis about.

MR: But it's not complete.

SE: When will we know about the package? Before the 22nd? Is today the last meeting with BN?

DH: It's the last scheduled meeting. We can't predict.

SE: The package was submitted to the Knesset by BN yesterday. I told the Arabs it's Israel's package not the US. It's in Haaretz. Some of them believe me, others don't. I have more questions: regarding the trilateral, what is the agenda? The outcome? Why not have bilaterals instead?

DH: There are some important issues that need to be discussed prior to the 22nd, but there are others that do not. They can be discussed between the 22nd and mid-October. The outcome is that the president will emerge from the meeting with the two leaders and

3

he will make comments to the press (alone but in their presence). It will be straightforward and simple, it won't break new ground, it will state key pertinent aspects and to the extent necessary previous agreements. He will announce a package that enables us to relaunch negotiations to end the conflict. He will also announce the intention to meet in Egypt towards the end of October. He will say a "contiguous, viable, democratic state of Palestine living side by side – you know the formula – with the Jewish state of Israel.

RD: You said "Jewish"?

DH: Yes.

SE: Will he mention the core issues?

DH: To compensate for less than 100% freeze, maybe he will mention the core issues.

SE: We told Mitchell, we need recognition by the US of Palestinian state on 67 borders. You have the meeting with Rice on July 30 2008. She told me she wrote an 11 page memo on this. So what we need is consistency in the statement of Obama, according to the Road Map – ending the occupation that started in 67 – so recognition of Palestinian state on 67 border with swaps agreed between the parties and incremental steps, third party. We said this to Mitchell. He said he will use Road Map language.

MR: In the Annapolis statement you didn't get the core issues, so this is giving you more. We would like to be able to mention all core issues …

DH: There will be reference to 2 states, a reference to West Bank territory – will that satisfy or compensate for the gaps?

SE: How can I? I am just asking you to state your own position – US policy and international law!

RD: [explains that reference to "territory" is not an acceptable alternative to "border" and illustrates with reference to state with provisional borders]

DH: we are trying to make a distinction between describing the principal goals (67 territory) and defining the outcome of negotiations. We want to say it in such a way that it doesn't impose an outcome.

MR: We can look at previous language for ToRs.

RD: The ToRs and the end game in Annapolis were not clearly defined which led to open-ended negotiations and stalling by Israel. Defining the ToRs is not imposing an outcome and it needs to be done at the outset for negotiations to be meaningful.

4

SE: I know BN and how he works. You're saying the outcome is more or less the Road Map. The formula I need is 1967 borders with agreed swaps, third party and incremental steps. Anything less is meaningless after all the way we have come. After the Cairo speech, Obama comes and says what Bush said! How do you sell that? I need to stay the course with my people.

DH: Let me elaborate: in addition to mentioning PS issues, 242, 338, the territory formula, lasting peace, mutual recognition, freedom from incitement and terror, respect for the principle of not prejudging outcome – that unilateral actions will not prejudice the outcome – the President will make clear that the US will have an active and sustained role ...

SE: At the level of Mitchell?

DH: Yes but he won't say that in the speech. The US will be involved actively but may not be there in the room at all times.

MR: On Gaza, he will make an overall reference to the challenges facing all parties as a result of what happened. He will allude to the Quartet principles and Hamas in the manner he did in the Cairo speech. He will refer to the problem of smuggling and he will mention Shalit.

SE: What about Palestinian prisoners? 9000 and their families? To balance Shalit. Believe me I want Shalit to go home, but as balance and humanitarian issue.

DH: He won't address that. He will talk about comprehensive peace- the regional initiative. He will mention the API and say it has constructive elements.

RD: So short of endorsing it?

DH: He will not endorse it. He will make a brief reference to the multilaterals – since it's premature. We will wait once there is traction in the bilateral. He will say "relaunch" negotiations ...

SE: Why not "resume negotiations from where the parties left off"?

DH: We prefer "relaunch" since there was no agreement – nothing is agreed until everything is agreed.

SE: There is a detailed record of our negotiations. The US administration kept it – it is perhaps our only achievement with the Bush administration. And so much for Obama and rapprochement ... there is not a new word! Give me something at least to save face!
DH: There is a lot of new stuff. The settlement freeze – new language; it is not the old formulas... we can use the period leading to October meeting to prepare

5

SE: We should not go into this thing leading to October without knowing what we will negotiate about. When can you tell me about the package?

DH: Hopefully soon.

SE: What about incentives on Jerusalem? Just mentioning it? It's already in Oslo. So now I need to pay a price to have it mentioned!? What about real incentives. There are families sleeping on the street, kicked out of their homes, there are institutions closed, Iftar dinners shut down … fulfilling their obligations! That is what I mean by incentives!

DH: These elements are part of the preliminary package.

IK: Is the wall part of it?

DH: It is not on the agenda. For Israel there are five substantive elements: Settlements, Jerusalem, outposts, access and movement, and E1. We are also discussing monitoring. On the Arab side it's investment, support for PA and bilateral negotiations, and regional initiative. For the PA it's continued effort on security and anti-incitement. The president will speak generally. Mitchell will speak in more detail later.

SE: What do you include in what you consider settlements – what types of settlement activities are you including? What about guarantees, and result of violations, monitoring?

DH: We've reached an understanding with BN of the US monitoring role and access to information, and how we would respond if there is a violation.

RD: One of the lessons from Annapolis is the need for a real monitoring and enforcement mechanism. What we have now is a confidential report made by Selva to the State Department that is not even shared with the Quartet. What measures are you considering in case there is a violation?

DH: The strength of the monitoring is being discussed. Regarding types of settlements: all housing …

RD: infrastructure, roads …?

DH: It's being discussed in the package.

RD: But you don't consider the wall as part of the settlements?

DH: No.

SE: We need a fallback position – we need to make sure there is no finger pointing. We need to sit down and agree and political framework that needs to be established before negotiations. I can sit with Arad or Molho. Do you know if they are prepared? Do they have team? What about committees?

6

DH: This can be done as a practical matter after the 22nd.

SE: Regardless if there isn't a meeting on the 22nd. It shouldn't be all doom and gloom.

DH: If there is no meeting on the 22nd then there will be no freeze and everything we have accomplished will unravel. You will have nothing.

RD: If there is no freeze before or after what is there to unravel?

MR: Depends on how you define the freeze.

RD: It's objective.

SE: Let's not talk hypothetically. I have more questions: Will you define the end game? Incremental steps, third party, and timeframes? I would also like to hear your position on state with provisional borders. For us it is not an option, and we have informed everyone about this. Looking at the regional picture it is very dangerous [discussion of regional repercussions of US policy going in this direction]

DH: On the end game and 67 I will get back to you. On State with provisional borders I understand what you said. The US position is that we want negotiations to succeed regardless of approach. Our initial view is that state with provisional borders is not the best approach, and not likely to have success, but we won't dictate anything to the parties. On phased withdrawal and timeframes, that's just a creative way for you to get us to deal with the borders. As I said we will look into it. Regarding third party, I would like you to elaborate what you mean.

SE: *[Discusses PS implementation scenarios, work done with General Jones in 2008 and the security role for third parties following a PS agreement,. SE asked RD to provide the Mitchell mission with the materials submitted to Gen. Jones by the PLO on these issues].*

Have you asked BN about his seriousness and willingness to enter negotiations? Have you considered the lessons learned from Camp David – failure to prepare properly can lead to explosion? What about the rest of the Road Map phase I obligations? And

DH: Regarding BN's willingness to enter into negotiations, I'm not a mind reader, but he has told us he is willing to enter meetings for the "two state outcome". On Camp David – you know there are positive and negative lessons from all previous rounds. This time it's different from Camp David. It is not a "summit" and will not lead to collapsed expectations. Rather we are looking at launching a process. You asked about Road Map obligations: we've touched on all of them; they've been on the agenda with Israel since April – based on our discussion with you back in April. East Jerusalem institutions are not part of the package. However, access and movement is part. On Gaza, the

7

humanitarian situation needs to be addressed. Regarding your question about other interested parties: we've had contacts at multiple levels, but have not shared the elements of the package the same we did not share with you. The sense is they are generally supportive.

SE: Do you consider the credibility of the US, after Obama's speech in Cairo, when you are discussing this package?

DH: We do consider the credibility of the US. The Cairo speech shows that the President understands the consequences and the need to rebuild US image. This is the foundation of his approach. We need the help of friends like you.

SE: I hope this so. His success is my survival.

MR: You will not have a better president or a better moment in this presidency.

SE: I have no quarrel with Obama or the US administration. My quarrel is with the Israeli government. BN wants to undo everything we have achieved.

DH: Regarding the Arab states, there is a spectrum of support ranging from the meaningful to the rhetorical. But no other administration has put the regional dimension as centrally – embracing the API and working toward support from the Arabs – for example financial support like the president did with Saudi Arabia. Without Obama you would not have received it.

SE: Thank you for that.

DH: You are right about the importance of the regional dynamics, and we understand that you are being judged with the Fatah conference – that there are higher expectations...

SE: More limitations.

DH: But you are in a position to bring peace- this is what distinguished you and your leadership from the others. So yes we need certain principles, and we need something tangible soon. That is the point of New York ... something you can deliver. I understand the freeze possible is a little less than what you wanted, but if there is no New York, we lose everything and you have nothing to show for ...

SE: I hope we will not be put in this position: accept, or else – like previous US administrations. It's not that we don't want to – we can't. So please don't put us in this position. To allow us to help you, you need to help us.

[Parties agreed to meet again the following day (Sept 17) to continue discussion]

8

Meeting Minutes
Saeb Erakat – David Hale
September 17 2009 9:00am
NAD – Jericho

Palestinian:

      Dr Saeb Erakat (SE)
      Issa Kassissieh
      Rami Dajani

US:

      David Hale (DH)
      Daniel Rubenstein (DR)
      Dan Shapiro (DS)
      Mara Rudman (MR)
      Jonathan Schwartz

[SE, DH and DR meet in private. They are then joined by IK and RD]

DH: Senator Mitchell will be meeting with AM tomorrow at 9:45.

SE: From the Israeli view the deal is what BN spoke about in the Knesset: 2500 housing units under construction – notice it's units not buildings; 450 tenders; exclusion of Jerusalem; exclusion of public buildings.

DH: It is understandable that for political reasons BN talks only about part of the package, not all. What he said it's not the totality and it's his spin. The point about the package is that there is no new construction – nothing new begins.

SE: That's not true based on what BN is saying. If you think that he is putting you on.

DH: Construction will stop – all new activities.

SE: I know you did your best, and it's not the outcome you wanted. For the last decades you have been dealing with Israeli governments based on what is possible – what is it that Israel can live with. I've been saying you should pursue what is needed – what is in your interests. Instead this is the best you can get. With this deal Bibi will say settlements will continue, and they will continue – there will be more settlements in 2010 than in 2009 or 2008. Plus I don't have a framework: you will not recognize the 1967 border, or the resumption of negotiations from where we left off. Instead you give me

1

Shalit, the tunnels and the Jewish state. If Jerusalem is excluded, no Muslim or Arab will engage.

DH: Who said Jerusalem is excluded?

SE: BN did …

DH: There are still issues under negotiation. The duration – and the public buildings will be limited.

SE: I know Bibi is preparing to announce a package of construction – Pisgat Zeev, Har Homa …

DH: I know we wanted more but there are political constraints. Restraint on settlements is better than unrestricted growth everywhere.

SE: As far as I'm concerned settlements will continue everywhere. There is a difference this time from the past. We've had General Dayton, the EU COPPS and others. We have had to kill Palestinians to establish one authority one gun and the rule of law. We continue to perform our obligations. We held the Fatah conference – our country remains divided. With this in mind BN begins the process of destroying AM and SF and the PA institutions. We are back to 1996 – 1999 again. If the US government now tailors its policy to BN, not just the Palestinians, but the whole region will go down.

DR: The package includes no new tenders, no new confiscation …

SE: I'm not coming from Mars! 40% of the West Bank is already confiscated. They can keep building for years without new tenders!

[MR, DS and JS join the meeting]

 DH: Regarding the statement, if it includes a reference to Jerusalem – if we can achieve that – that would be a substantial concession from the Israelis. Regarding reference to 67, we've had a long discussion with Israelis yesterday. We are working on language to state in some fashion regarding territory a reference to 67. If we achieve these along with elements of the package, will that enable you to overlook the imperfections – with an end to new settlement activity – and start a political process?

SE: I need to see a text – I would need to work with you on it. Anything short of 2 states on the 1967 border is meaningless. We've had language formulas in the past, in Oslo, in the Road Map. Now after the last negotiations with Olmert, the US needs to state this position regarding the borders. So we can work on the statement …

DH: Let's go over it again. There are two levels of text: first, what President Obama will say, the goals and principles; second, Mitchell will speak in more detail to the press as a background brief and explain the package and what each side, Israel, Palestinians

2

and Arabs have committed to. Regarding the president's statement, we want to make sure neither side is surprised.

DS: We are developing building blocks for the speech. We hope to be able to reach and understanding on the concepts. Then the White House speechwriting machine would take it and turn it into actual words. So we cannot go over the speech but can ensure there are absolutely no surprises.

DH: The statement will be general. We will have time after the 22nd to work on details before the next meeting, we hope in October. We also will want to make sure we don't close any doors.

SE: When talking with the Israelis, did you ask them if they are willing to resume negotiations from where we left off?

DH: We like to say "relaunch" and state the objective. That's our position on this.

SE: So let's say we do this. We go the trilateral and then to Sharm and then we sit in a room with the Israelis and Mitchell. I bring a map of Jerusalem – how would the Israelis react?

DH: We will look at these issue – sequencing etc. but we will be mentioning Jerusalem in the statement.

DS: If the president states Jerusalem clearly then it is an issue …

SE: It is! Of course, but for now we can't talk about it … problems with the coalition, Shas, Lieberman … I know how this works.

DS: Clearly we can't give you guarantees on what Israel will negotiate – we can only speak on our position.

MR: Sequencing is always an issue.

SE: So what do I discuss with them – state with provisional borders? Let me be candid: you made a great effort to get a settlement freeze and you did not succeed. You did not get what was required from BN in order to relaunch PS negotiations. What Israel will tell me and everyone is: no Jerusalem, thousands of housing units, public buildings, 9 months – by the way they will agree to the 9 months – that is their bottom line. Then they will renegotiate it with you. Therefore: no settlement freeze at all – not for 1 hour! More construction in 2010 than 2009. [Speaking to DR] You know this. You team has the numbers.

On substance, from day one BN said: Jerusalem the eternal undivided capital of Israel, demilitarized state without control over borders or airspace, no refugees. Once you agree to this we can negotiate a piece of paper and an anthem. We have invested time and effort

3

and even killed our own people to maintain order and the rule of law. The PM is doing everything possible to build the institutions. We are not a country yet, but we are the only ones in the Arab world who control the Zakat and the sermons in the mosques. We are getting our act together. Now we have BN back again like in 96. Back then Israeli Palestinian relations were at their best. No attacks or violence. He consistently undermined this- and I believe he has begun that same process again. You know I tried to have meetings with the Israelis – with Arad and Molho. They adamantly rejected. Arad cancelled three times.

So there are three options: 1. we go to NY to the trilateral under this formula. This is a non-starter. It is not an option for us. 2. We don't go and declare failure – doom and gloom. This will lead to an explosion and strengthen Hamas and others. 3. we have bilateral meetings and continue talking about a package with much more clarity. Maybe you can recognize a Palestinian state on the 67 borders. Don't underestimate the Palestinian public and its expectations, and what you have helped us build. When Bibi talks about excluding Jerusalem it is to make sure we can't attend, because he doesn't want to.

DS: So by not going aren't you playing into his hand?

SE: You put me in this position! It's like having a gun to my head – damned if you do and damned if you don't. I thought at the very least you would have a moratorium and not surprise me with this.

DR: Put aside Bibi's statements. Your achievements are real – the future Palestine is in the making, and we will continue to support it. But you can't make that vision a reality without a negotiation process. So this point is a transition – a pivotal point.

SE: I've been doing this for 16 years. This is the last shot. I will only go into it with an end game. Preparations must be there. In the meantime, we continue to build and will continue security cooperation regardless because it is in our interest. This time there should be careful preparation for political negotiations.

DH: So what would you do instead of what we are proposing?

SE: I will sit with the Israelis and probe them to see if there is anything we can discuss. So if they want a state with provisional borders, we can discuss 3rd further redeployment instead. I need to see what they have to offer. What I don't want is the US to acquiesce to settlements and take me on a ride. We don't need to reinvent the wheel or eat the apple from the start – we've been through these discussions with the Israelis in detail – including arrangements for example for the cemetery next to the 7 Arches Hotel that would become the Israeli embassy. So I can ask the Israelis directly- what can you do with me? And remember Israel is not only BN and Molho and Arad. Many in Israel don't want to be crowned king of Israel for years to come. Many want to bring him down. This is politics – It's fair game.

4

Today we Palestinians speak with one voice on these matter. We have learned from previous mistakes. We are a young nation and lacked experience. But we have learned now from dealing with previous administrations.

DS: The President has demonstrated a personal and real commitment to you. What you are saying indicates that you tend to discount the President's commitment. It strikes me that it doesn't seem to be worth a lot to you.

SE: This is not about personalities or conscience. Bush did not wake up one day and his conscience told him "two state solution". It's about interests. We have waited a painful 17 years in this process, to take our fate in our own hands. We cannot allow this to be undermined.

DH: This will be undermined if you don't pursue the two state outcome.

SE: BN will not give 2 states. If the US government, over several months cannot get him to do what Senator Mitchell himself wrote – before the Road Map, in the Mitchell Report …

DH: We cannot force a sovereign government. We can use persuasion and negotiations and shared interests.

SE: Of course you could if you wanted. How do you think this will reflect on the credibility of the US, if you can't get this done?

DS: We make the call on our own credibility…

[DH asks for a one on one meeting with SE]

5

Meeting Minutes
Dr Saeb Erekat – Sen. George Mitchell
United States Mission to the United Nations
Thursday Sept 24 2009

Attendance (not all were present throughout the meeting)

Palestine: Dr Saeb Erekat (SE)
              Akram Haniyeh (AH)
              Rami Dajani (RD)

US: Sen. George Mitchell (GM)
              David Hale (DH)
              Dan Shapiro (DS)
              Daniel Rubenstein (DR)
              Mara Rudman (MR)
              Jonathan Schwartz (JS)

DH: Apologies for GM's getting delayed. He is meeting with the Kuwaitis. Part of it is about getting aid to be more cash assistance.

AH: AM met with the foreign minister and discussed these issues.

DH: GM should be here in half an hour. We've met with Molho and Herzog, and now with you we want to discuss the way forward.

SE: And GM also say Ehud Barak …

DH: This morning.

AH: Did he ask him about the new settlements he announced?

DH: I don't know. They met alone. Our intention is to move quickly to relaunch negotiations. We are wrapping up an agreement on a package with Israel, and including other parties. So we want to get the right context – and the formula to resume negotiations.. President Obama's speech at the UN yesterday is our starting point for the ToRs. We want to know if you think this is a good starting point. Regarding Palestinian steps, you know there is incitement, and demonstrable efforts on security and institution building. Our intention is to meet with both sides in the second half of next week. Based on the outcome of that, either we will be ready, or there will be one more trip by the senator.

SE: Are your negotiations still ongoing with Israel on the package?

DH: Yes – but agreement is within reach – hopefully by the end of next week in DC.

AH: Are the components the same that have been discussed? For example, is Jerusalem excluded?

DH: Jerusalem is not yet agreed. You know from the beginning we've treated Jerusalem and settlements as separate issues. So there will be something on Jerusalem in the package other than settlements.

SE: When the US president says settlements are "illegitimate", what are the consequences of that? Will anything change?

DH: In the interest of reaching a solution we need to reach a package. We need to move forward and get the parties to take steps – for example that lead to reduction – no new construction …

SE: When we began I asked you about the package, because it is unfair if we are not told what it is before we are asked to respond. Until then we keep asking the same questions.

DH: But GM told you the other day about the elements. A couple of issues remain to be resolved: the time it starts, the duration, and the Jerusalem element – which I doubt we will reach agreement on.

SE: From the beginning we were clear and did not hide our position. If Jerusalem is not part of the moratorium, it's a non starter. You know what destroyed Camp David? It was Jerusalem. The US underestimated the importance of Jerusalem. Your colleagues did that and it led to the collapse. In the Trilateral on Tuesday, when President Obama said that Jerusalem will be in the negotiations, Netanyahu told him "you know my position" …

DH: But these are two separate issues [meaning the freeze and ToRs].

SE: No. For me Jerusalem is the same as the rest of West Bank. No one, including your government says it's not occupied territory! So by allowing them this to take place we will be acquiescing to it. We cannot allow it. Again, I appreciate your efforts, but Israel is the occupier, not the US, so it is not enough for Obama to merely say the word Jerusalem. That's why I asked if you have anything new to tell me. For me this is about international law, legitimacy and principles, not making these deals. With this, you're better off without a deal than with one. The mere fact that Jerusalem is not part of the moratorium will mean the Arabs won't accept it. It's a victory for Netanyahu and he can continue to rule for years, and I will continue to live under occupation. I've stated this to you every time we met – wherever and whenever: Anything that takes Jerusalem out will be a non-starter.

DH: Our reaction is that obviously it is no surprise you are unhappy if the settlement package has imperfections (in this case Jerusalem) – but if you want a perfect settlements package you just won't get it. Even if partial, this package will be meaningful, it will restrain the activity – there will be less of it. Otherwise we can all just go home.

2

SE: OK. That's your call. What I know is what Bibi announced in the Knesset. With that he can have more settlements in 2010 than in 2009.

DH: I disagree. [Hands a chart depicting lower rates of settlement construction over time]. The only construction allowed will be completion of building under construction.

MR: As you see, as building is completed, there is nothing started, so it goes down.

SE: Let's go back to the Roadmap. It is US language. You knew what you were writing. What we have is ethnic cleansing in Jerusalem …

DR: You are looking at words, not the numbers. There will be less signs of construction – visible signs because no new construction.

AH: So Jerusalem is over for you? You know the Arabs and Palestinians will not come to the table if that is the case.

DH: The package combined with the statement.

AH: So the issue is settled on Jerusalem?

DH: I don't believe we can reach a package on Jerusalem. But the statement from the US president that they are illegitimate … a difference of opinion on Jerusalem. Maybe we can help if we can get them not to take provocative measures.

AH: The mere fact that you are agreeing to it gives Netanyahu the green light.

MR: No.

SE: You know Bibi! I've heard this before and I've been there before. I simply cannot afford to go into a process that is bound to fail. I am trying to defend my existence and way of life. You know I asked to meet with the Israelis several times- they refused because they told want to answer my questions. And then he says I am a "wild beast of a man" – you know the reference to Ishmael … what a disgrace. I would shake hands with Lieberman and tell him "Shana Tovah" instead of this incitement. You talked about incitement – we have taken significant steps, the sermons in the mosques are under control …

DH: Getting back to the significance of the package in terms of restraint …

SE: It's a non-starter.

DH: So you would rather OK them building more …

SE: They're the occupying power. They can do anything they want. I am not agreeing to anything.

3

DS: If the moratorium that lacks Jerusalem is very difficult for Palestinian to accept, is it preferable to have no moratorium? Would you be prepared to enter PS negotiations?

SE: That's a good question. When BO says settlements are illegitimate in front of the whole world, Israel continues, despite this and despite all of international law – the Fourth Geneva Convention, the Hague Convention, Security Council resolutions. Why then did you reach the position that there needs to be a freeze, including natural growth? This was your language. And why did you then change your mind? Why is it now changed to "restraint"?

DS: My question to you was not rhetorical.

SE: You want to restart negotiations we have to do that from where we left off with Olmert. We have the maps, the matrix ... So in order to be able to answer your question, we need to define these negotiations. For example, let's say we start negotiations and they say Jerusalem can wait, that borders can wait. Then it's acquiescence. Bibi is a non-negotiator. I told him this to his face. You have the example of Wye River, the Hebron Agreement. Even when he signs an agreement, he does not implement it. Now we have restored the PA, we have the rule of law, no corruption, we are building institutions. So I need the US to say: a state on the 67 border, third party role, and incremental steps to withdraw. Why can't you do it? I understand Bibi won't do it ...

DH: You ask why? How would it help you if we state something so specific and then not be able to deliver?

SE: With the Israeli public, they will side with their leaders against any foreign country. But when their prime minister differs with the US, people differ with the prime minister. And I need you to state these things to bolster the PA and Fayyad's government.

DH: But that's unilateral – we want to have negotiations.

MR: You're saying we should pick this issue, and not others? You want us to state something on refugees?

SE: Look at the matrix. We have offers and counteroffers on refugees. As I told you, Netanyahu will not move with me. He wants nothing to do with the 2 state solution. Maybe I should go on Israeli TV – channel 10 and announce that he has agreed to Jerusalem being on the table!

JS: Are you willing to look at the President's UNGA speech to be the ToR?

SE: No ...

AH: He said the Jewish state.

RD: Which is indirectly taking a position on refugees.

4

DS: That's our position.

SE: But not the 67 border?

JS: But when you did Annapolis you didn't refer to it...

[Break – both sides confer separately. Meeting resumes with GM, DH and DR only on the US side]

GM: Sorry I couldn't be here for the full meeting. I was with the Kuwaitis. We were talking about you. Afterward I have to head out for the Quartet meeting. DH and DR have filled me in on the discussion so far, but I want to hear from you. Undoubtedly you've perceived the sense of urgency of the President. He attitude was consistent: we need to proceed to negotiations; delay will not be beneficial to anyone. DH mentioned the issue you raised – that the package will apply only to the West Bank and not East Jerusalem. We will continue to include Jerusalem in our messages and to make clear our difference. So whatever the package ends up being, it will include a reference to Jerusalem but not in the manner that you (or we) would have liked. Regardless of the package with the Israelis , we are not asking you to agree to it. So there is no risk of acquiescence. And, if there is no deal, this will unleash a new wave of new settlements that they haven't yet approved. I want to hear how you came up with the statement you made to the President about construction increasing under the package.

SE: I will bring detailed information next time.

GM: I want to bring discussion to a conclusion. This can't go on indefinitely. The President is strongly committed to supporting AM and his government. I've devoted half my time over the last several months to things like getting you support (for example with Kuwait) – not just financial. We will stay the course on this. There will be setbacks. I hope you will join us by taking steps.

SE: There are diverse points of view in the Palestinian leadership but no one has any doubts about President Obama's or your commitment. So when he invited us to the meeting we issued a public statement noting his personal commitment. So we have no problem with the President. Our problem is with the occupying power. We've had these experiences before and don't want to repeat them. When you came up with the Roadmap, you knew what you were doing. You said "settlement freeze including natural growth". The logic was for Israel to do this, and for the Palestinian to get their act together. When the Palestinians began to deliver on our ongoing obligations – and we said we are doing it in our own interest; to defend our actions, for example in Qalqilya, it can only be to prevent those who are obstructing the national aspirations of the Palestinian people. So we are doing our part. Dayton and the US Consulate can submit a report on our behalf. So let be clear now: in Camp David, I told your negotiator Dennis Ross "you personally belittled and undermined the importance of Jerusalem. This led to the collapse of negotiations".

AH: Dennis Ross told me how he underestimated the importance of Jerusalem.

5

SE: So anything without Jerusalem is a non-starter.

GM: So we can have years of argument.

SE: On settlements I will present to you a chart and figures. What I heard was the package announced in the Knesset. If you couldn't deliver on this why did you say that at the beginning? Why didn't you say "limitations" instead of "freeze"? Now BO is saying "restraints". [Hands GM Roadmap Phase I chart showing each side's obligations and status of performance]. Look at Israel's obligations – minus the elections – what did they do? They are not freezing Palestinian life in Jerusalem. They are destroying it. I am not refusing negotiations. I wanted negotiations to start 6 months ago. That is not the issue. During the last negotiations, we had maps. Can I put it to Molcho [shows GM a map], can I put it on the table?

GM: You can put maps but they are not bound by them.

SE: Nations need to be responsible. We had an Israeli government that accepted the 67 line with Sec. Rice present.

GM: But that was part of the principle "nothing is agreed until everything is agreed". You agreed to this principle.

SE: You know there are tradeoffs within and between issues. That's what the principle is about. So if we have agreement on something, it is a card that I won't announce until the other issue is announced.

GM: I know something about negotiations. When you say "nothing is agreed until everything is agreed" these are not empty words.

SE: How come you've abandoned the approach you took in Northern Ireland? I've been studying it – how you prepared before bringing the parties to the table, and the single text.

GM: That was not the approach in negotiations to get an agreement – those negotiations culminated in the 98 Good Friday Agreement. Then in 99 there was a collapse. So we went back . Because there was so much mistrust we had to negotiate a series of steps … so it was not for an agreement.

I have to go to the Quartet meeting, so let me conclude. I know it is hard on everyone. I faced this every day as leader of the Senate – the choice between 'bad' and 'worse'. All I can say is there is a moment in time – you don't like the PM in Israel, but you like the President of the US…

SE: I know the waiting game kills us.

GM: Then you've got to move forward.

6

SE: We need to have clarity.

GM: But the only way to get an agreement is with negotiations. You won't get it from us.

SE: So why does Obama say "Jewish state" but refuses to say 67 borders?

GM: Look at things another way: What Obama will tell Netanyahu on Jerusalem. Proclaim victory once in a while, rather than react to Netanyahu all the time. Set your objectives positively – don't always be reacting. I personally think this is the best moment. You can't negotiate detailed ToRs, so you need to say something positive. The only way to get it done is to get into negotiations. I wasn't involved in Annapolis, but one thing that guaranteed it would fail from the beginning was to keep it bilateral and keep the US out. I guarantee I will play an active role – me and DH. We want to help; to get good results.

SE: We do not doubt you at all. We are advising you about who you're dealing with.

GM: Regarding coming to DC next week – you should come next Friday.

SE: That does not give us enough time to go back and consult… You should raise it in your meeting with AM tomorrow morning.

END

7

Meeting Summary
Dr. Saeb Erekat – Senator George Mitchell
State Department
October 1 2009

Attendance (not all present throughout):

Palestinians: Dr Saeb Erekat (SE)
                Maen Areikat (MA)
                Khaled Elgindy (KE)
                Rami Dajani (RD)

US: Sen. George Mitchell (GM)
                David Hale (DH)
                Dan Shapiro (DS)
                Mara Rudman (MR)
                Jonathan Schwartz (JS)
                Alon Sakar ?
                Moira Connelly

GM asked questions based on discussion with the Israelis:

- If we can get an agreement on the ToRs leading to relaunching of negotiations, there needs to be some time before we actually relaunch – in order to discuss bilaterally and trilaterally and organize for a good start. We've proposed 2 to 4 weeks. The Israelis think a longer time may be needed.

- How formal would the launch be? The US position is something like a meeting in Sharm; Israel prefers a "crawling start". You begin with bilateral meetings then involve us. We will have an active role.

GM noted another issue: would you follow the "nothing is agreed until everything is agreed" principle? SE replied yes, but a lot depends on how you interpret it. GM said you would need clarity on that. SE explained the logic behind the rule (to allow parties to discuss scenarios linked to tradeoffs without being committed) and noted that the Israelis, including Molcho, understand this.

SE explained that the ToRs should specify the point of beginning, the end game, the structure, and described the Annapolis committees and structures as an example. In response GM asked about the time needed to relaunch negotiations. SE replied that it depends on the agreement you get – what kind of relaunching?

GM inquired about the Palestinian position on the points SE made (re ToRs). SE said decisions are needed: A Palestinian state on the 67 border with agreed swaps. He described the status of negotiations with Olmert (1.9% Palestinian offer / 6.5% Israeli offer).

GM asked how to reach the point of having that discussion. SE cautioned about the current Israeli government. It has not engaged with the Palestinian side because what it has to offer would be a shock: starting from areas A and B, 39 to 45% of the West Bank. If this is part of the 3rd further redeployment, we already have that obligation, including in the Wye River Memorandum, but it is not a starting point for PS negotiations.

GM emphasized the risk of spending months discussing ToRs in detail, and not getting to the point where you have actual negotiations. SE reiterated the need to establish the end game (state on the 67 border ...) and cut the story short in order to get to meaningful negotiations. He noted the risk of entering into negotiations with Netanyahu under current conditions: the Israelis will insist on Jerusalem as the eternal capital of Israel, and reject refugee rights. In this case Palestinian leadership can only respond by insisting on full exercise of right of return. This will increase the anger, in an environment where people live and breath the conflict, he warned, contrasting the situation with that of Northern Ireland. GM agreed that the situation was unique. SE said that Palestinians are making serious efforts; the worst would be to return us to point zero. Approach should be based on what is needed (despite the pain and the risks), not what is merely possible.

GM discussed the reference to 67 borders, and expressed understanding for the Palestinian position, but noted Israeli rejection of it. He said the ToRs will mention all permanent status issues. SE reminded that these ToRs (naming PS issues) can be found in the Oslo Agreements, and are not new. GM reassured that Jerusalem will be mentioned.

SE reiterated the need to restart negotiations from where they left off. GM argued that because of the "nothing agreed" rule nothing was binding on the parties. A discussion ensued on the interpretation of this rule and whether the current administration is bound by the position stated by Sec Rice during the Annapolis negotiations with respect to the 67 line. GM proposed to say that the negotiations will be "guided by" previous discussions. SE noted that is it a shame to lose all that was done in previous negotiations.

GM went on with the ToRs: timeframe for negotiations of 24 months; US role "active and sustained" ... SE asked whether there would be parallel committees or sequenced approach. GM said there can be sequence or concentration on borders, based on his talk with AM. He said the Israelis are willing to speak about borders. SE questioned which borders – areas A and B? a state with many provisional borders? He rejected a return to the Oslo approach.

SE asked about the 2 to 4 week period: what is to be discussed? He noted that the most important thing is to get an understanding at the outset as to what is being relaunched. Is it two states on the 67 border with agreed swaps? Then it's worth it. He cautioned against the risk of creating the incentive for the "blame game". GM replied that his concern was a delay of another 6 months, and was trying hard on the 67 border with the Israelis.

SE discussed the need for clear structures and rules for negotiations and said he would provide the US side with the structure worked out with Tal Becker in the Annapolis round as an example.

GM talked about the announcement for relaunching negotiations:

- Structured regional track – "multilateral": won't be immediate but parallel soon after bilateral
- Mention of Gaza: need to face the challenge in a manner to allow for needs of population and taking into account Israel's legitimate security concerns
- Reference to 2 state solution: building on previous agreements and obligations. SE objected that it should build on previous negotiations – that agreements and obligations are binding and should be enforced.

SE said technicalities are secondary in the absence of defining the overall approach. He questioned GM's impression that president Abbas has backed a borders first approach, noting that AM stated that many of the issues can be dealt with through the recognition of the 67 border as the baseline. He further asked whether the US has asked the Israelis about these issues – structure and parallel committees. GM said he did not.

SE cautioned that if the US announced negotiations and there is no agreement on these issues, there will be a disaster. GM replied that the alternative was months without any progress. SE disagreed, suggesting that the discussion to reach ToRs and structures need not be open ended- the US can set a limit. He noted past lessons in this regard. GM expressed skepticism that taking two weeks to discuss these issues will result in 6 more months negotiating over every detail. SE replied that the Palestinians don't even know the US offer on the package or the ToRs yet.

GM said half the time with the Israelis has been spent discussing the 67 border, that it was an overwhelming effort. He expressed personal reservations about the situation: the attitude being contentious and full of mistrust – the only way to get going is through relaunching negotiations.

SE replied that the risks of going into negotiations without preparation will be much more devastating than no negotiations at all.

DH summarized the US position on the ToRs as follows (reading from a paper):

1. Bilateral Track
2. Multilateral Track
3. Character of Negotiations
   a. Lasting peace – need for involvement of all parties to re-energize efforts; enduring commitment
   b. Mutual recognition
   c. Freedom from violence, incitement and terror
   d. Socialization for peace
   e. 2 state solution
   f. Building on previous agreements and obligations
   g. Avoiding actions that prejudice outcome

4. Goals of Negotiations
   a. End of conflict / claims
   b. Satisfaction of territorial and security issues addressed by 242 and 338
   c. Enduring arrangements based on the above
   d. 2 states living side by side … Israel with secure and recognized borders .. independent, territorially and economically viable Pal state
   e. Re 67: trying to find the right formula

SE noted that it was time for the US to upgrade its position and explicitly endorse the 67 border, as Sec Rice had done during Annapolis – it was agreed then, it is consistent with US policy regarding the occupied territory. GM replied that this means taking a new position. SE said this is a new administration that should state what others have tacitly agreed in the past.

GM noted that difficulties with the Israelis on this and other issues, that they would not agree to any mention of 67 whatsoever and that strongly objected to Obama's UNGA speech. He said he will continue to pursue the issue next week. SE suggested the following language: "two states along the 67 border with agreed swaps". He stressed the importance of parallel negotiations of all PS issues.

KE started a brief presentation on the Israeli partial freeze proposal. Discussion took place over various aspects of the presentation.

With respect to monitoring, GM said the US will be taking photographs and recording the exact location of every unit under construction at the beginning of the moratorium. If there is any indication of construction other than that he will personally inform Netanyahu, give him the opportunity to investigate, and if there is failure to comply, GM will go public that Israel is violating its undertaking.

KE briefed on how a Jerusalem exemption can be more harmful than not reaching any deal.

GM said he agreed about the importance of Jerusalem, but the Israelis will not go for it. He said you have to deal with the world as it is, not as you would like it – for that reason the best he can get is "restraint". SE interjected that this means they can accelerate Jerusalem construction, while you expect us to go ahead with negotiations. GM replied the same will happen in the absence of negotiations: Israel announces new construction, we criticize, over and over again. With negotiations, we will have more leverage, and there will be less settlement activity. To compensate, he added, the US will explicitly repeat its position on Jerusalem (non-recognition of Israeli annexation and related actions; demolitions, evictions etc.) In such a situation, with negotiations going on, if they make a provocative announcement, the US has the leverage to state that this undermines the process, and that Israel is acting in bad faith in the negotiations.

SE reiterated that the problem remains the exclusion of Jerusalem. This is not acceptable by Palestinian as well as Arab leaders. A discussion ensued on the position of the Arab states.

GM asked SE to explain his statement to President Obama that there will be more settlements in 2010 than 2009 under the package. SE said he counts East Jerusalem construction which is bound to accelerate.

GM explained his view on the limited duration of the moratorium, recognizing that an Israeli renewal of activity after the initial period would spell the end of negotiations. He further defended the approach taken in the package by arguing that under the moratorium no construction will be started. He said the Palestinians may be assuming the worst, which may be justified given the history, but we don't know what things will be like in 12 months.

SE explained that the concern over East Jerusalem is ultimately political. If we turn a blind eye to such an arrangement, this will have devastating consequences on the PA and Palestinian leadership. He reiterated the central position of Jerusalem in the conflict, noting that failures in the past were due to underestimating the importance of it for Palestinians. There has to be a way to address our concerns over Jerusalem, he concluded.

GM replied that with regard to construction there is no way, even if we engage with the Israelis till doomsday …

SE asked for a paper in writing setting out proposed terms for the ToRs. GM agreed to have a part of it ready the next morning, including language on the 67 border. He also agreed to arrange a meeting with Sec. Clinton the next day.

SE reiterated that the US should not put the Palestinians in a position of rejecting negotiations, affirming that peace through negotiations is a strategic choice – our whole future depends on it, and we are counting on the US to help us. The only option at this time is to have successful negotiations – another failure will be devastating. That is why we need the 67 border with swaps. If we don't prepare we will have the same result as Camp David.

KE concluded the presentation on settlements and there was an open discussion on Jerusalem, in particular the implications of its exclusion from the package on the ability to carry out negotiations.

Meeting Minutes
Dr. Saeb Erekat – Sen. George Mitchell
State Department
October 2 2009

Attendance:

Palestinian: Dr. Saeb Erekat (SE)
                  Amb. Maen Areikat (MA)
                  Khaled Elgindy (RD)
                  Rami Dajani (RD)

US: Sen. George Mitchell (GM)
                  David Hale (DH)
                  Mara Rudman (MR)
                  Jonathan Schwartz (JS)

SE: The president is seeing Mubarak regarding the Egyptian text on reconciliation – AM won't say no to whatever the Egyptians present to him in Amman on Oct 5.

GM: Can we be helpful?

SE: You should call them and make sure that whatever they put in the paper won't result in return of the siege. We don't want any surprises.

GM: You know the content of the paper?

SE: No but given past experience we can't take any risks. Whatever they offer AM he will have to say yes – yes to any agreement that does not bring back the siege.

GM: I talked to Omar Suleiman last week. We discussed two issues: one, the right to call elections belongs to AM, it does not require Hamas agreement; two, whatever is agreed on security forces restructuring …

SE: Yes – it has to be consistent with the PA Basic Law.

GM: We made the argument more directly: the PA has done an outstanding job in the WB. We are strongly opposed to a situation that gives control over it to Hamas.

SE: Just make sure that you see the material before they present it. You know Meshal has been working hard in Cairo.

GM: A hypothetical: what if the paper says you participate in the Gaza force but they don't in the WB.

SE: Fine. As long as it doesn't violate the Basic Law: you cannot have factions, militias –
it's one authority, one gun.

GM: Our argument is directly on the merits: it is unacceptable to the US, after the
financing and training we've carried out – this defeats the purpose.

SE: By Oct 25 AM will announce the elections. Time doesn't have to be Jan – can be
later. We are flexible on monitoring by Arab League and others. Whatever we do we cannot
undermine the legitimacy of the Salam Fayyad government. If we need to reach an
accommodation with some security forces, fine, but they can't be back in the WB. You know
very well how Washington is about these things, so make sure to see the paper.

GM: I will try to get a copy as soon as possible and will call Omar Suleiman, even if we
don't get the paper. I will ask him and tell him what we discussed. Is there an issue other than
the security forces?

SE: I don't know, but I don't want surprises. Any agreement as long as it does not re-
impose the siege.

GM: We have reviewed in complete details the Annapolis discussions. Jonathan has all his
notes. So the words we used [in the paper handed to the Palestinian side on "Goals" on the
1967 issue] are taken verbatim from Annapolis. They were repeated several times by Sec
Rice.

SE: Is this from the July 30 meeting – the minutes? Or from the letter from Sec Rice to
the new administration?

JS: I have my notes and Sec Rice used this language several times [goes over meeting
notes].

SE: [reads from minutes of July 30 meeting] On territory …

GM: We are looking at Annapolis because that is what you said is important, and the
discussion was on territory, not border.

SE: Why can't we use Rice's language?

JS: She said many things at different times. She said things about swaps and that Gaza-
WB connection would affect the final outcome on swaps … so if you prefer a different
formulation …

SE: Back then I told my assistant Zeinah Salahi to take down verbatim account of what
the secretary said.

RD: Reference to "67 border" is different from "territory" – saying the discussion is on
land occupied in 67 means that this negotiations are restricted to only that. So what about the

swaps? And what is the baseline to determine the swaps? The PLO made the compromise in 1988 to establish a state on 22% of mandate Palestine. This is the 1967 border. Now you are saying that the topic of negotiation is land occupied in 67 – as the starting point. This is not the same thing.

GM: I don't agree with this analysis as a lawyer or a judge. It is obvious that swaps would have to be on the Israeli side – I won't condone an Israeli proposal that precludes swaps on the Israeli side. Anything else?

RD: In a normal context of a courtroom perhaps. But our experience with the Israelis is a pattern of attempts to erode the terms of reference. The 67 line is the basis of the two state solution for us.

SE: The Israelis always exploit our weakness. They will go over every word we have agreed to. We have to agree to these terms and whenever we don't we are attacked – while Israel does not implement anything and gets away with it.

GM: Anything else on the language?

RD: Reference to "land" should at least be "territory" and linked to sovereignty – ie a sovereign state – so that it is clear that we are talking about land, airspace, resources, territorial waters … Also, at least it should say "the entire territory" or "all the territory".

SE: Another thing is the sentence on 242 and 338. It says "territorial and security". Why? Is it to exclude refugees?

GM: We are not excluding refugees. It states refugees as one of the issues in the next paragraph.

SE: Why this language?

JS: There are other elements in 242… "just resolution to the refugee issue"

GM: How about "including, but not limited to territorial and security" …

SE: We need to be clear. Israel exploits vagueness given our weakness – they will make sure that this serves them.

MA: Just leave it as 242 and 338.

SE: Regarding 67 why not just take it verbatim from Rice's statement. [Repeats the paragraph] On record: the base is entire territory that was occupied in 67 including the Dead Sea, East Jerusalem and No Man's Land [recounts discussion with Tal Becker on splitting NML equally]

JS: She was referring to the base of discussion in the territory negotiation …

GM: Not the substance.

SE: With respect – it is substance.

RD: Regardless, there needs to be a baseline for negotiation over territory, and the only baseline we have that is recognized in international law and that the international community considers as the line separating Israel from occupied territory, is the 67 line.

SE: Why is there no reference to the Roadmap? The parties obligations?

DH: Why do you need that? The president used the language from the RM in his speech.

SE: In PS negotiations I won't abandon RM phase I obligations.

GM: I want to remind you that we need language that both sides can agree to. If something is not clear it does not mean they can force it on you. That's what negotiation is about.

SE: They will [impose]! Before the Gaza disengagement I told Shalom Turjeman you are my masters – you can do what you want. But let's cooperate on the disengagement – otherwise we're doomed. Instead they said SE does not want Israel to withdraw and brought in Dahlan. And the result is Hamas.

GM: Why would you engage at all then with them if that's how you think they will act?

SE: I want to negotiate – yesterday and today to reach peace, but not under these terms and conditions.

GM: I know what you've said about us, your characterization of US politics – a phone call from Malcolm Honlein and all that. I reject your characterization regarding me and the president.

SE: No – that is not what I said. I want your administration to be different.

GM: The reality is: No negotiation is not in your interest. So we are trying to come up with a statement to give you a ladder to climb down on this issue – just like you asked a week ago. Now you are arguing over the colour of the ladder. And you are drawing unfounded inferences.

SE: I remember Obama telling all of us – the Arab and Muslim world in his speech in Cairo – about a full settlement freeze.

GM: You guys are now trying to come up with a history that Obama somehow invented the freeze. You and the Arabs have been calling for a freeze long before Obama. He did not pull it out of the air and impose it!

SE: You wrote it in your report.

GM: You established it as a precondition. We tried very hard, and we know what you think of us because we failed. Fine. So you can look back 10, 20, 60 years from now without negotiations or we can try to move forward.

SE: I have my BATNA, Senator. People keep telling me the consequences of this, and the consequences of that ... We have ongoing discussion in the PLO and Fatah Central Committee. If this is what we have, then we will no longer be talking about two states, but one state. I did not come here to complain, but to try to help move forward. Many people strongly objected to AM going to NYC and me coming to Washington. As AM's representative, a man of honesty and dignity – I am here to tell you what he tells the executive committee. I am not the decision maker. The ladder is 2 states on the 67 border with agreed swaps. I am saying agreed – so Israel has a veto. I need something to take back as the end game. I remind you that my 'ticket' as a partner in the peace process was to recognize Israel on the 67 border – remember Baker's words ... standing shoulder to shoulder ... now you're asking me to negotiate which part of 67 will be in the state? Israel violates all aspects of international law and the Geneva Conventions over decades – so I resort to swaps – a new idea – for the sake of peace and the two state solution. Maybe after I join the Zionist movement, recognize the Jewish state and agree to a state on 40% they will agree. That will not happen.

GM: What you just said is the best argument for taking up this text. President Obama is not like previous administrations. In US politics there never was and there never will be a president as determined to resolve this conflict. So you can argue over words and delay indefinitely, so you lose the most important thing – this opportunity: the presence of a US president completely committed to achieving the objective you want. However, as MR has said, the solution has to be agreed between the two parties. If you think Obama will force the option you've described, you are seriously misreading him. I am begging you to take this opportunity.

SE: I don't disagree with anything you said. But, what am I asking? Am I asking you to say Jerusalem as capital for two states? Refugees right of return? Equal swaps? solution based on water rights? Third party role in security? Not to support more interim periods or state with provisional borders? I am not asking you to state any of that! All I ask is to say two states on 67 border with agreed modifications. This protects me against Israeli greed and land grab – it allows Israel to keep some realities on the ground. I am avoiding stating any outcomes in the ToRs – I am just protecting the end game! When you say "discuss" about the "land occupied in 67" – discuss is meaningless – it doesn't say anything about the end game. The Bush administration agreed ...

GM: Again I tell you that President Obama does not accept prior decisions by Bush. Don't use this because it can hurt you. Countries are bound by agreements – not discussions or statements.

SE: But this was an agreement with Sec Rice.

JS: It is not legally binding – not an agreement.

SE: For God's sake, she said to put it on the record. It was the basis for the maps.

GM: When you enter negotiations and say "Nothing is Agreed Till Everything is Agreed" then there is nothing unless you have an agreement on everything.

SE: In that case there will be nothing but parallel discussions on all issues. I told you before why we had this rule – in order to discuss everything without fear of impact on trade offs. There are other examples – like what we did with General Jones – I said we will have demilitarized state – without an army. So all that is gone. We have to start from scratch.

GM: You have to decide whether you want a nothing agreed rule before you start negotiation. Personally I think it's a sensible approach. The rule means what it says – words have plain meaning – you can't cherry pick parts of the discussion.

SE: So you spent earlier this week discussing these issues with the Israelis. 8 hours? This was subject of discussion…

GM: That's why it's in brackets [the 67 language]. They didn't agree to it. We thought it gave you what you wanted. We had a similar discussion with them. They will not agree to it. We told them they will have to agree.

SE: Senator, I said I will convey to the leadership. I am trying to see what I can do to make it more passable. So I will take what I hear and report it verbatim – not in a negative way.

GM: I would like you to be positive.

SE: I told you we have nothing but you and Obama …

GM: It's Obama, not me …

SE: It's also you. 295,000 Americans would want your job, don't be humble.

GM: Reminds me of Churchill's remark about Atlee: "He is a humble man, with much to be humble about". This is a long and difficult road. It is frustrating for all. The interests of the Palestinian people are a state in two years as you are planning. Our objective is to get that done. We believe it's in everyone's interest.

SE: [reiterates AM's strategic vision and the regional dimension] We were happy with Obama's election and your appointment. We have been looking at the bigger picture and analyzing the situation. So please understand where we are coming from. We find ourselves in the eye of the storm. We want to discuss peacemaking. We pray every day that Israel will come to the point where they realize that a Palestinian state on the 67 border is in their interest. They're not there yet – even though the majority (70%) of the people both on the

Palestinian and Israeli side believe in the two state solution. That's why we are frustrated. We want to help the Israelis.

GM: Any other comments on the paper?

SE: There are many. I will take it back to the president and will respond. For example, there is no reference to the RM and 1515. If Israel is hesitating about a reference to the RM...

GM: We didn't include the RM – you said before you didn't want the language from the RM.

SE: It's the obligations, not the wording ["end the occupation the started in 67"] Is what you gave us the full text? Where is the full text?

DH: I can go over the rest of the text line by line – on the steps required from each side. Afterwards I can read out to RD the text on Goals and Character of negotiations. So the structure is:

- Steps by all sides
- Monitoring
- Palestinian steps:
  - Security related (these you have been and continue to carry out)
  - Institution building (we have some ideas on that)
  - Incitement

The Israeli paper is mainly on the moratorium. There is a commitment to take meaningful steps to create a positive context for negotiations. We know neither side will be satisfied with the other side's steps. We will monitor all steps by all sides. On the settlement moratorium – it's not complete yet. We have not agreed on the start date and the duration, but hope to agree soon. The duration will probably be 9 to 12 months, and we want it to start soon. Settlement outposts will be removed (specific ones) ...

SE: So not the RM obligation. This is a new RM!

DH: ... within a specific time frame. The Israelis will remove additional road blocks and take steps to improve access and movement. MR has been devoting a lot of efforts on this.

SE: Will we have an input on this or do we sit and wait for Israel's generosity? You know I worked out with General Dayton the 16 or 17 most important checkpoints that need to be removed...

MR: We've been working from that – high impact checkpoints.

SE: Regarding movement and access, the important issue is the time it takes to move a product between, say, Jenin and Hebron – it's not about individual checkpoints. It should be

1.5 hours. If it is 3 or 6 or more then it may not be feasible for a farmer or a trader to move the product at all. So without removing the 16 major checkpoints it is just a PR and media story. Like when Frasier said he removed 2 road blocks.

GM: Our team in Jerusalem is working on this, with MR.

SE: You know there is an Agreement on Movement and Access – the AMA. Is that off the table? Is the new Israeli government not recognizing it?

GM: The AMA is not part of this.

MR: We are also working on other elements of trade facilitation.

[US side hands over paper on Palestinian Steps]

SE: Regarding not taking steps in international forums, I cannot accept this. I want my obligations under the RM – this is what we have been basing our work on. You are now doing this exercise over again. A new RM! Is it because Molcho and others want to avoid the RM? You know we've learned from the past. This time no one can say we didn't do it. Unlike the previous time with the Intifada nonsense. We are committed to rule of law, one authority, and full security cooperation regardless of political process …

GM: Other issues we are working on are things like Wataniya, Rawabi.

SE: [Explains Wataniya issue] I can't even get the 4.8 minimum frequency. Next we will be sued in Qatar … You don't know what it is like to live 24 hours a day under occupation. I had to come here on short notice so I flew from Tel Aviv. I was humiliated at the entrance, outside the airport …

GM: I understand the frustrations.

SE: There are limits. What's in it for the Palestinian people? So this is a new RM. The Israelis managed to get rid of the RM of 2003.

GM: What's in it is a Palestinian state in 2 years and an end to what you described. On E1 the commitment is to maintain the status quo. [side discussion on the Bedouin camps in the area – Jahaleen, and the scope of the "status quo"]

SE: Why are you giving us fragments of the paper – why not the whole package?

GM: It's still a draft. The real problem is if it gets in the newspapers the next day.

SE: Since 93 our record is clean. We never leaked.

GM: I don't want to give you a draft that is not yet final.

SE: What else is there?

DH: Meeting, 24 months, multilaterals, character … I will read it out to RD after the meeting.

SE: And he will read to you our draft ToR.

GM: Based on the discussion today I have come to two observations: 1. Jerusalem is an absolutely critical issue. Actions on the ground could have adverse effect on the ability to reach an agreement. 2. The only way is to get into negotiations to get leverage to urge and insist on restraint and to get a permanent status agreement.

For 60 years, the choices open to the Palestinian people have become less and less attractive. The circumstance under which they live worse and worse. There is not a shred of evidence that delay is going to provide better choices or improve daily life – and this is true with or without Barack Obama. But with Obama, it is absolutely clear that this is the last time. And believe me it is the best time.

SE: It is the last time for the two states. My option, the BATNA, if all this goes down, is the one state.

GM: That is your decision. But the fact is that you have a president committed to this issue. All that points to the need to begin negotiations as fast as possible. We won't have a perfect ToR, or perfect negotiations, or a perfect outcome. That's life. I understand the frustration and the burden of history but please don't let this opportunity slip by.

SE: For 60 years we have suffered. For 42 years our existence was denied. I had to exist as part of the Jordanian delegation. It took a long time for the Israelis to realize that to deny that we exist does not mean we don't exist. We have a long history of the peace process. We have the ToRs from 93. We have the RM. I know how much the Israelis hate the RM, but you should not let them off the hook.

MR: The RM continues to apply.

SE: So my obligations are "upgraded" and theirs are "downgraded".

MR: It continues and we will continue to monitor.

[GM and SE agree to continue discussion. GM will be in the region the coming week]

US Non-Paper, October 2nd 2009

[Introduction / Bilateral]

Parties have agreed to relaunch bilateral negotiations on ____ [date] in _____ [place], with the goal of concluding negotiations within 24 months that will bring an end to the conflict.

[Regional track / Multilateral]

As soon as possible, a structured negotiation track with multilateral participation will begin on an ongoing basis in parallel with the bilateral negotiations to address issues of common interest such as [not a determined list; illustrative]: Energy, Refugees, Water, Health, Education, Interfaith dialogue, in order to create new realities in the region.

[Comprehensive peace]

We will also pursue peace between Israel and Lebanon, Israel and Syria, and broader peace between Israel and its many neighbours.

[Goals – provided separately in hard copy]

The goal is clear: bring an end to the Israeli- Palestinian conflict and to resolve the open disputes and claim between the parties, including the territorial and security issues addressed by UN Security Council Resolution 242 and 338, by reaching realistic, effective, and enduring agreements and arrangements which will enable two states to live side by side in peace and security—the state of Israel with secure and recognized borders and an independent and territorially and economically viable Palestinian state. [Without prejudice to the location of the borders, the land being discussed is the territory occupied in 1967.]

It is understood that this will be achieved through direct bilateral negotiations which will resolve previously identified issues such as security, borders, settlements, refugees, Jerusalem, relations and cooperation with other neighbors as well as other issues of common interest. The U.S. will play an active and sustained role in supporting the parties in this effort. The parties will need to: agree on the conduct of negotiations, reach the necessary agreements and arrangements, and ultimately attain their long awaited mutual reconciliation.

[Character]

Lasting peace can only come through the re-energized efforts of all concerned and can only be based on an enduring commitment to mutual recognition, freedom from violence, incitement and terror, including socialization for peace, and the two state solution, building on previous agreements and obligations.

Consistent with this principle, neither side should take any actions that could prejudge the very issues under negotiation. Unilateral actions will not prejudge the outcome of these negotiations.

[Gaza]

Conditions in Gaza present a tremendous challenge. It is in the interest of the parties and the international community, including the United States, to overcome this challenge in a manner that facilitates the flow of aid and commerce to meet the legitimate needs of Palestinians in Gaza, while addressing Israel's legitimate security concerns.

Palestinian Authority (PA) Steps

- The Palestinian Authority (PA) has committed to continue its efforts on security reform and to undertaking operations aimed at confronting all those engaged in terrorism, including the confiscation of illegal weapons.
- The PA will finalize the Interior Ministry's "Plan for Re-organization, Restructuring, and Development of the Palestinian Security Establishment" and begin implementation, including the following priorities:
  - o Reduce where possible the number of security services through combining them.
  - o Rename some of the security services to be consistent with higher national strategy of promoting law and order and preventing terrorism.
- The PA will continue over the next 12 months its security initiative in Jenin.
- The PA will enhance specialized training courses for security services focused on law enforcement and counter-terror operations.
- The PA will enhance efforts to combat terrorist-financing, through the Palestinian Monetary Authority (PMA) Financial Follow-Up Unit (FFU) and by continuing to develop capacity to track and deter financial transactions used to fund terrorist activity.
- The PA will intensify efforts to develop judicial, administrative, and economic institution, consistent with the Program for the Thirteenth Government, to ensure that the Palestinian state is viable, provides safety to its citizens, and is a good neighbor. The PA will continue with criminal justice sector , including training of criminal investigators, prosecutors and judges, and infrastructure projects such as police stations, jails courthouses and prisons. In Particular, the PA will resolve ongoing jurisdictional conflicts among officials in the justice sector that have hindered reforms to date and facilitate the timely and effective prosecution following arrests.
- The PA will continue to improve its public sector to ensure effective service delivery and revenue collection, and strengthen its fiscal position through structural reforms to the public pension system and the electricity sector. The PA will continue efforts to create a regulatory and judicial environment favorable to private investment.
- All official Palestinian institutions end incitement against Israel.
- The PA will help to promote a positive atmosphere conducive to negotiations; in particular during negotiations it will refrain from pursuing or supporting any initiative directly or indirectly in international legal forums that would undermine that atmosphere.

MEETING MINUTES

Attendees:	**Marc Otte, Thierry, Nadia**
	Dr. Saeb Erakat, Issa Kassassieh, Rami Dajani, Hala Rashed
Subject:	**General briefing**
Date:	**Monday, Oct. 12, 2009, 2:20pm**
Location:	**NAD**

MO

- Visited Sheikh Jarrah families and promised to *do* something.
- Saw Israelis. Told them that we've seen some ground improvements, but more is needed. Gaza is unacceptable, and your reasons for Gaza are unacceptable. *E.g.*, cement – I saw cement in Gaza, so you're not denying Hamas cement.
- Spoke to GM: told him it's not good to weaken a negotiating party that is already weak. Also told him we can't keep supporting the US without knowing what it is we support.

SE

Sett freeze:
- US has reached a package with the Israelis that they say is the best we that they can get from the Israelis. It would exclude (i) EJ, (ii) 2,500 units under active construction, (iii) 492 units approved by Barak [*Hala: Not sure this is accurate. Will get clarity from SE]*, and (iv) public buildings.
- I told Obama there'll be more setts in 2010-11 than 2008-09.
- We were told that we've never had such a committed US president, etc.
- Israel is basically erasing Phase I of the RM.
  TOR:
- US inserted language: "Without prejudice to the location of the final border, the land to be discussed is the territory occupied in 1967." Yet, during Annapolis, Rice set the baseline as the 1967 border, including EJ and the Dead Sea.
- We also talked about "nothing is agreed until everything is agreed."
- So there goes the 3rd phase of the RM.
- So what is left is the 2nd phase of the RM.
- Then there is all the Goldstone business. Help us by voting in favour of it, and let it take its course. Support us in Geneva and in the UNSC.

- BN has started again his "no partner" strategy. AM is convinced of this. Israel leaked the deferral of the Goldstone report. Israel linked AM's son to Wataniya. Israel caused the recent events at Al-Aqsa. This is what AM told GM. AM will not go the way of Arafat.
- We will not stop security coordination. But we have a BATNA: one-state solution. IF BN can't live without Hebron, without Nablus, etc., let AM declare the end of the 2SS. This was also related to GM.
- So if this is all the US can get from the Israelis, something else that may happen (we did not tell this to GM, but I told the Americans today) is that AM may resign in one month.
- On 1 April, I called Uzi Arad. He invited me for dinner in TA, but then he cancelled just before I left Ramallah. So it wasn't us who refused to talk to the Israelis.
- I don't need the IC to get an SPB. I didn't engage in 16 years of PSN for an SPB.
- We have a fantastic PM who has done a great job with security, reform, rule of law, etc.
- It's time for you to recognize the Pal state on the 1967 border.

MO

- What was GM's reaction?

SE

- He was shocked. He said, "No, Israel is your partner."

MO

- What is your reaction to Meshal's speech?

SE

- It was to be expected.
- GM wants me back in DC on the 20th.

MO

- What can be expected in this round?
- By the way, I told GM he has to see what is happening on the ground, not just in EJ but also in the outposts, which are creating corridors between the settlements.

SE

- By the way, outposts are no longer those created since March 2001. They are now the 23 so-called "illegal" outposts.
- What does GM say to you about the package?

MO

- Same thing he says to you.

- About your alternative (*i.e.*, BATNA), can it happen without bloodshed?

SE

- We will do our best to avoid bloodshed.
- If Israel does not reaffirm the TOR, then I need to apologize to Hamas for telling them to accept previous agreements.
- I got a unanimous decision from the PLO Executive Committee and from the Fatah Central Committee that decisions have to be made by the leadership from now on, not by any one individual (not even AM).
- Egyptian want Hamas and Fatah not to sign the unity deal, so that they can be off the hook. But we will sign it on the 14th. When you impose sanctions on us, I want to address the EU foreign ministers, as well as the US Congress.
- AM told me yesterday that he pledged to send me to DC on the 20th, but he's not sure he'll send me. If I go to DC, we'll see what they have to say and bring it back to the leadership.

IK

- There was another house demo today in EJ. There are more scheduled for tomorrow. It's time for the EU to endorse its recommendations in its Jlem Report.

MO

- We can't endorse our own work. Actions are required.

Meeting Minutes
Saeb Erekat (SE) – Robert Serry (RS)
NAD Ramallah
October 13 2009

RS: I met Daniel Rubenstein for the first time. We are seeking an envoys' meeting. Frankly I am pissed off that the US is not involving any of us – also Marc Otte – in the Quartet. Since it was my first meeting I didn't want to be angry, but the Quartet needs to take responsibility per the Trieste Declaration – the 4 principals … The last thing, however, that we want to see is a complete impasse leading to US disengagement. What we are hoping for, rather, is a US re-engagement. The Israelis want to finish it off. I saw Mike Herzog…

SE: Of course that's what the Israelis want. They've been given the biggest ladder. The question you should be asking the US is: "What is it that you want us to support?" They want your support but they won't tell you what for. Now we know they have concluded a "package" [discusses details]. Politically, under no circumstance can we accept the exclusion of East Jerusalem. We told them it is a non-starter. Essentially they are downgrading Israel's Phase I obligations and upgrading ours. They've cancelled Phase I. On the ToR they won't even mention the 67 border, after all we have been through with Rice, and all the far-reaching discussions with Olmert. There are limits on what we can tolerate. All this means that Bibi has succeeded in canceling Phase I and Phase III. He's brought the Americans to the Likud position that even Sharon didn't accept. Now it's only Phase II left.

RS: Are the Americans pushing a state with provisional borders?

SE: They are only saying "go with this process". Barack Obama is your best chance. I don't have any disagreement with the US. They are our friends and allies. My problem is not with Barack Obama, it is with Bibi Netanyahu and the occupation. It is time for the Quartet to say "two states on the 67 border" – and I am willing to accept "with agreed modifications".

RS: That was my statement in the Quartet…

SE: Yes and I thank you for it. Europe is ready. The Russians are ready … [side discussion on UN Rapporteur Falk's statements on Al-jazeera regarding the PA position on the Goldstone report and his subsequent apology].

I told the Americans, if you take me down this process, you will do the following: you will crown Netanyahu king for years; you will doom even Sharon's line; you will kill Livni; we enter negotiations, then Bibi announces building in Jerusalem, and the negotiations collapse. I asked them for a change of approach. This time there is absolutely no force on Earth that will push us down this path. I told them we have our BATNA. We will not

1

repeat what Arafat did. We will continue to maintain security, one authority one gun, the rule of law, but we will demand equal rights in one state…

RS: I understand it was a frank discussion …

SE: He [AM] told Mitchell the alternative is the one state. And I told the Americans he will call for elections and resign.

RS: I warned Daniel Rubenstein and David Hale: Don't push your only reasonable partner into the abyss. In our report …

SE: I appreciate what you did …on Goldstone … security council tomorrow.

RS: The SC will be just a talk. Geneva is the important forum now. The majority in the SC want to follow the procedure to go through the HRC before the SC. Did you talk with Marc Otte?

SE: Yesterday – after his communiqué. I told him don't talk about rapprochement without the 67 border. The Quartet needs to spell that out: 67 border with minor agreed modifications.

RS: Have you changed position on settlement freeze if you get that?

SE: No. There is no quid pro quo. We explained to the Americans how there will be more settlements and more settlers in 2010 and 2011 than in 2008 and 2009. We gave them charts and figures, which we will pass on to you. So it's both: Settlement freeze and the ToRs.

RS: We have a setback. The challenge is we don't want US disengagement, but we need US re-engagement.

SE: It's important that you go to them with substance …

RS: I will get to substance, but here are my thoughts: it is time for the international community to put the cards on the table. So the US should drop the pressure, win some time without losing engagement. Maybe Mitchell should start discussing with each side on substance.

SE: This is what we said at the beginning. Instead the US opted for the matrix of responsibilities – fine but they did not get the settlement freeze. We told them we had far-reaching discussions with the Israelis on the swaps, the numbers of refugees, we agreed security for the day after with Jones …

RS: So we have to come forward with a framework …

SE: Yes. The End Game. Quartet Parameters.

2

RS: It has to be US led, but with a greater role, and endorsement by the Quartet. A clear End Game proposal. Even if Bibi balks, it will be very difficult for any Israeli government to simply reject this for long. Maybe we need the dip we are in to get the US to refocus. We don't however want them to disengage and blame you.

SE: I agree. This is the best course of action.

RS: We need to go public with this, but it is a matter of timing.

SE: We should issue a statement after every meeting …

RS: Put the cards on the table. If the US doesn't it means they are not showing leadership.

SE: I told the US: I count on you. You are not my problem. The problem is Netanyahu. I told this to Hillary, to Jones, to Mitchell.

RS: This is a dip, but let us not be apocalyptic.

SE: Let's not. I want to convey our thanks to Ban Ki-Moon for supporting AM when every one abandoned him. Eventually Hillary and Mitchell said the right thing.

RS: I've been seeing Salam Fayyad on Jerusalem. One thing is we need to find a dignified solution for the Sheikh Jarrah families – give them a package to rent something in the area, in Jerusalem. We have also been talking to the Jordanians.

SE: It has to be Salam -- not you or the Jordanians to pay them.

RS: Of course.

3

Meeting Minutes
Dr Saeb Erekat – Sen. George Mitchell
State Department
October 20 2009

Attendance:

Palestinian: Dr Saeb Erekat (SE)
                      Amb. Maen Areikat (MA)
                      Rami Dajani (RD)
                      Khaled El-Gindy (KE)

US: Sen. George Mitchell (GM)
                      Amb. David Hale (DH)
                      Jonathan Schwartz (JS)
                      Mara Rudman (MR)

GM: Give us your account on where things stand.

SE: The president sends his best wishes. In the meeting with Hosni Mubarak three points were discussed:

1. Reconciliation – since Hamas did not respond they won't follow up so much
2. AM asked Mubarak: next time before sending us a paper make sure the US has seen it and it will not cause another siege
3. Discussed your efforts and the peace process

GM: We spent a lot of time on reconciliation discussions with the Egyptians.

SE: I told Daniel we can't deal with this kind of pressure. This time, let them sweat. So you said they told you it was OK. Then they sent us the document – take it or leave it. So AM signed it. Following Goldstone we could not say no. So Azzam went to Cairo and signed. We know you are having talks with the Egyptians, at your level, and maybe higher …

GM: At all levels.

SE: We knew Hamas would not come. So we said whatever is in the paper, here it is. Past midnight, it is off the table. In real life, you know, it cannot be accepted – contradicts the basic law and re-imposes the siege. This is a joke – taking us for granted. So we need to stop this behaviour with us. We have the previous example of Saudi Arabia and Mecca. They force us in that positions and we get punished.

GM: I assure you our effort was intended to prevent anything bad…

1

SE: I know. Egypt did not want your efforts. They wanted to put a paper that both us and Hamas reject. So they avoid any responsibility. So we have come out … they need to be aware of their responsibility.

GM: AM said in a press conference – was it with Amr …

SE: Amr was not there. You should understand the power of the Moslem Brotherhood and Hamas, with all the satellite channels directed at us – it's a parallel government in Egypt. You need to sort this out with the Arabs. We started with Egypt and told them we know what happened with you and the US. Things need to be said to AM…

GM: We know how they treated you.

SE: Abul-Gheit was candid. He said in public "Goldstone finished you. You're finished". Then he goes to Jordan on the 5th with Nasser Joudeh, and dares to say Egypt had no knowledge. Then hell broke loose – because this was Egypt …

GM: It's not true?

SE: Of course not. Hisham Bader was in the meeting. They were consulted. We are not even a member. It was the Pakistani who read the resolution on behalf of the three groups. Instead they said AM sold out – and the story about Wataniya. I know life's not fair – but this was despicable. The Emir of Qatar going on the phone personally, calling intellectuals telling them to attack AM – calling Azmi Bishara and Abdul-Bari Atwan. This is because AM wouldn't go and do reconciliation in Qatar like the Lebanese. But there is nothing you can do with Qatar …

GM: We do talk to them.

SE: I know it's about interests and your base. They do the opposite of what you tell them. On Goldstone, we have an internal investigation. It's not about individuals. We could resign if needed. AM said the decision was with consultation of all who were there. No one objected. Now they even deny the mere fact they were there. Joudeh goes like a lion in front of the Muslim Brotherhood – verbatim – he says it's not true Jordan said resume negotiations without settlement freeze… The Egyptians today told AM their position is no negotiations without full settlement freeze – unlike the paper I saw here. On the first point they agreed not to court Hamas on this. Second, in the future, if there is a paper, instead of putting us in this situation, share with the US – because if the siege is re-imposed, we will be punished, not Egypt. Third, they agreed that negotiations cannot resume without a full settlement freeze including East Jerusalem – not that I care about their position.

Now, we don't want to surprise you. I saw the Israelis, Shimon Peres, on the 4th. Two days ago I met with Amos Gilad and Etan Dangot -- delivered a strong message. I told them the hell with you. After 19 years we are still being taken on a ride. Now you insinuate about Goldstone. You think you can punish AM! In no time you will have Aziz Dweik as your partner. 19 years of promises and you haven't made up your minds what you want to do with

2

us. Lieberman is too precious - while you have Livni there, the head of the largest Zionist party. Instead you will get Qatar and Iran. Maybe Abdallah can drive Meshal and bring him to you. That's it. 19 years. We delivered on our Road Map obligations. Even Yuval Diskin raises his hat on security. But no, they can't even give a 6 month freeze to give me a fig leaf to see, to find out, what we can do … on swaps, but no. You don't see me on the same ship. Your focus is on PR, quick news, and we're cost free. You know my word is nothing compared to you, in congress. What good am I if I'm the joke of my wife, if I'm so weak.

Tony Blair goes and says he got Israel to remove a roadblock in Jericho. It was Dangot who removed it because I asked him. It was not Blair or Selva. What has Netanyahu done since he became PM? One thing? Jericho? Extending hours at the bridge? It was Etan and me. We have the Russian guns still in Jordan. BN has done nothing. I asked AG: what is it you have done? Show me something in the last 6 months. Nothing. Not a single step.

This is my situation with Israel, with Egypt, with Jordan, and with the US. What do you expect me to do? You are nations with power, with interests. We are the only ones that are cost free. If you want to look back to the past, you will not get what happened with Arafat – make him "no partner". We will not stop the rule of law – no intifada. That's what Lieberman began, the smear campaign – saying there were tapes about us organizing the Gaza war. Lies. Wataniya – it started with the Israeli government – Barak Ravid who works for the Israeli government.

All this I said openly to Shimon Peres. As a friend I told him that after 19 years we are in the same situation. I can't leave Jericho without an 18 year old boy's permission. And there is no light at the end of the tunnel. If you think this is what the peace process is about you are wrong. I told him to convey that to the PM. Maybe you don't need a partner. We don't want to go to another round of bloodshed. Livni gave him two conditions to join coalition: genuine two state solution, and resuming negotiations where they left off on all issues…

GM: Not rotating prime ministers …

SE: To her credit, no. That was not on the table. She was decent and would not join coalition with Shas conditions on Jerusalem. I've been requesting to see the PM's people since April. They said no – they are still deciding if we're a partner or not. Let's see till later – how much they will be pressured into by the US, so we can come and dictate. I told them this will not work. I told Amos Gilad and Yuval Diskin the president will see them at any time as envoys. This is straight-shooting. No games. Officially, on behalf of AM. We are maintaining communication but with AG and YD – any time.

GM: Are you concerned about dictating who …

SE: Not dictating. The PM's people chose to go to war against us. They won't talk to us! Imagine if I said such things about Netanyahu …

GM: Aren't you concerned they would do the same in return?

3

SE: I don't care. These people have been coming to see him. Only recently Netanyahu is sending Molho. So AM is sending a message. He won't terminate contact. Any time they want to see him it's AG and YD. My quarrel is not with you and the US administration. Our quarrel is with Netanyahu. We know each other. They were honest with us. It's state with provisional borders – in area A and B – to put it bluntly. I could have done this without a peace process! It was better before Madrid. As a citizen of Jericho I could go to Gaza, to Jerusalem, even if we were confined to municipal borders. So we're back to the same arrangement of 89, 90. After 19 years. So if two states is no longer an option on 67 – we will talk about one state.

GM: We think it is an option …

SE: Senator. I am just briefing you on my meetings with the Israelis. I am not giving you a message. They were good meetings. I told AG: you are Egypt's man. You know the Egyptians. 11 kms! What's going on with you and the US, the $23 million and ditches – it's business as usual in the tunnels – the Hamas economy … AG started laughing!

GM: What did he say?

SE: They don't want to say anything negative about Egypt. It's their strategic relation with them. But they make me pay the price. I am no longer there. I am not alone responsible for the coup d'etat in Gaza. Now what do you want? I asked AG – you are coming to me – you are angry that we accepted Egypt's paper! I was about to leave the meeting. Egypt is Egypt, and you are going to punish me. AG acknowledged the righteousness of what I said, and the honesty. He said we can't do anything with Egypt, so we are pressuring you. So Isaid let's not repeat the mistake of what you did to Arafat. I saw it happen. They even sent Palestinians to DC … it's not going to happen to AM. Either they are partners – 67 border, swaps – anything short of that, that's it. This is a defining moment for the government. Don't listen to him [BN]. He's dead, if he has no engagement with us.

GM: You mean politically…

SE: Yes. We engage on security with you [AG]. He [BN] could not give us a moratorium, even if only a fig leaf to engage for a few months. So come on Amos – he needs us! Dan Meridor is saying we are close to resuming PS negotiations. I had to respond on the radio – Galei Tsahal   from the Tel Aviv airport. I told Dan, you are a friend, but what is it that you see that I don't see. And Barak, we're in touch with all his people. Now David Ben Simon resigned – his resignation is related to Barak's authorization of settlement activity. Barak has 13 members. He can end up with 5. I'm in touch with all of them. He killed Herzog.

I need to discuss with Egypt. They were there for all the dialogue. And not one Egyptian can say that Hamas sabotaged the talks? They don't want to anger the Moslem Brotherhood. I asked: is there a parallel government in Egypt? It's similar in Jordan – the foreign minister attacking in New York – and in the media and the parliament. Then there's Syria. All the steps we took and the discussions with you… then Meshal delivers the speech under Bashar's picture.

4

Internal situation: we have elected the Fatah revolutionary council. PLO executive committee had its meeting… AM will call for elections on the 25th.

GM: For January 25th?

SE: Yes.

GM: I recognize and understand the concerns you expressed and the feelings you have with what you have experienced. I want to help, to find ways to move forward, to help you and your colleagues and President Abbas – for the creation of a Palestinian state. I can't put myself in your shoes entirely, but as someone who served a long time in public office I can understand. It is important to try to move together toward the objective we want and that we believe is the right one. You repeated president Abbas said about moving to another alternative – one state. We have expressed our view before. You said we tried and failed, you said there is no light at the end of the tunnel. We are saying negotiations with an objective and time limits. We recognize and are humbled by the complexity you face and the difficulties you describe. We have exerted so much effort on this reconciliation thing, and ended up with the Arab effort you commented on. But we do want to be helpful. We want to continue efforts on the language for recognition of 67 which you asked for. It is a difficult effort – so far we have not found language agreeable to all. So I would like to spend some time on the document you submitted to us [the draft ToR]. The goal remains the resumption of negotiations. I don't know the basis of Meridor's statement …

SE: Internal consumption. They are under pressure. Livni told them in the Knesset – we are with you on opposing Goldstone, but what have you done for peace? You have done zero – other than eliminating everything we've done with them.

GM: And there is another report I read this morning. Netanyahu announced we have an agreement.

SE: With Zapatero – I have the article here – Barak Ravid, he works for the PM office.

GM: I've seen it. The situation remains as it was – as I reported it to you. There remain issues of disagreement – primarily about the length of the moratorium.

SE: So there's no truth to a joint plan?

GM: We've agreed on a number of issues, but some areas are not resolved: length; when it begins; circumstances under which it begins – but we have agreement on other aspects over which you have expressed disapproval.

SE: President Abbas is being asked about this report. He said SE is in DC and we will find out.

GM: As I said, there is tentative agreement on many issues …

5

SE: I won't repeat our position. You know it.

GM: Yes. We have your point of view on that and have expressed our view. To be clear: there is no formal agreement on a total package. There is agreement on substantial parts, which I have informed you. I am well aware of your objections, but continue to believe that the package would be helpful if it is in effect for a period of time. It will lead to substantially less construction in the West Bank, even though it will not halt all. I appreciate the concern it does not cover East Jerusalem …

SE: Take note of Ben Simon's resignation. He said it's over the 24 settlement expansions ordered by Barak …

GM: On East Jerusalem we will issue a statement that disagrees with Israel's policy in East Jerusalem. I recognize it is not sufficient for you … so to resume our efforts in the current situation, continue our efforts on agreeing ToRs. We propose the possibility of side letters, for you and for the Israelis on issues that you don't agree and don't want to be seen agreeing. So for you that would be on Jerusalem and for them reaffirming our commitment to security. So these would be 'independent' issues in each side letter.

Another point: after the meeting with President Abbas, I left to Egypt, then I came back and saw prime minister Netanyahu on Sunday. David followed up on elements of that discussion. I expressed President Abbas's concerns to BN, regarding some Israelis actions aimed at undermining him. I told BN that if he genuinely believes that AM is a partner, then he needs to take actions on current difficulties. In the discussion, AM said he believes Israel may be going to make a deal with Hamas because they will accept a state with provisional borders…

SE: The Israelis told me these are conspiracy theories, hallucinations, to use polite language …

GM: I will use polite language as well – so I said you must do something to be of assistance. He agreed to discuss some steps. I specifically asked about a prisoner release; also, as I was aware from previous meetings with Palestinians, there is the issue of incursions – and I requested that they halt incursions into areas A and B. And I asked him to consider the redesignation of some of area C to B or A, to enlarge the PA jurisdiction. All these are consistent with improved security performance, so it's only logical to turn over more area. They agreed to discuss, not to do. Other ideas were conveyed to you by Daniel …

SE: AM said he did not want to listen … he was really angry. But I want to hear. I am a curious man…

GM: There is a checkpoint around Nablus, not sure which one … [asks DH and MR for name of checkpoint, consults notes]. Can't find out which one…

SE: It's Beit Furik. [Discussion on various checkpoints around Nablus].

GM: Then there's 20,000 Gazans in the West Bank whose status is not approved.

6

RD: The issue is much broader than that. Israel is illegally using the residency in the population registry to prevent Palestinians moving to the West Bank from Gaza. We can brief your staff in detail on this issue.

GM: Then there are some people to get ID cards; and increase of some cards ...

RD: BMC cards.

MR: Increase from 1200 to 2000.

GM: We did not include the economic matters because President Abbas would not hear them – for example on Watainya or Rawabi. There is one more significant item, but I cannot discuss it yet. Regarding incursions, you have security people that discuss this regularly. Is there a way you can get them to, to encourage them to, get to an arrangement on areas A and B, and a redesignation ...

SE: On the first point, all that is needed is an Israeli decision. It's in the agreement. On the second ...

GM: But a discussion is the way to get to a decision.

SE: I will convey this to President Abbas. They meet everyday ...

GM: Should we elevate?

SE: I will convey to President Abbas. It's not for politicians to discuss security.

GM: What about a meeting with Molcho? Are you disposed to meet him?

SE: The question is: are they willing to touch me? They attacked me and the president. My message back to them is clear. We are not terminating contact, but the same way you chose not to touch us, our channels are AG and YD. They've been doing this to us for 19 years. This time we will do it – for a month or two. They rejected us, so for this time, the president will see YD and AG.

GM: But I'm saying *you* [SE]

SE: You went to them and they rejected!

DH: He said he is not "ready yet" – yet.

SE: He's a friend. He told me it's not personal – it's Netanyahu.

DH: I don't want to have him say yes and you are not willing.

7

SE: I will convey to the president. When AG called me, I had to consult with the president and call back. I told him if it's in his security role it's OK but not people from the PM office. So I have to go back. I work for the president. I don't say a word without his approval.

GM: I'm in the same boat. I want the process moving – you say a month or two …

SE: We're saying for the time being – not terminating contact – but will only meeting with designated people.

[Break – Senator Mitchell leaves to take phone call. Discussion with JS on developments on the Iran nuclear file]

GM: Do you think it's worthwhile to continue on the course I suggested – agreement on ToRs with side letters, to enable the relaunch of negotiations?

SE: That's why I'm here. I want us to succeed. I want to negotiate starting yesterday but need two things for success: Netanyahu must come down to earth – moratorium on everything for 6 months – even less, 5. During that time, we discuss the issue of swaps based on the 67 border. We will be able to find out if we can come up with and understanding. Our advice: it's not the duration, it's his ability to invest in us. So a total moratorium, including East Jerusalem. He can do it – legally…

GM: OK. You answered my question. So, in the absence of a complete halt, there can be no negotiations?

SE: Yes.

GM: So you would no longer be satisfied with language on 67?

SE: We told you from the beginning – a full settlement freeze.

GM: I have a big folder of clippings of you taking this position for years, at least since 2006, you, President Abbas, Yasser Abed Rabbo and others – yet you were negotiating regularly. So it's true you've been clear – but that did not deter you for years.

SE: Senator, I am going to be as honest as can be. I appreciate what you did and what you will do. But, the PLO executive committee has taken a decision – so did the Fatah central committee. It is the President's decision. So it's clear. This is not the end however.

[Meeting breaks. GM and SE proceed to closed meeting]

SE to GM:

1. President Abbas will announce presidential and legislative elections by decree on Oct 25. The elections will be scheduled to take place on January 25 2010.

8

2. He will inform the Fatah Central Committee on the 26th to choose another candidate to run in the elections.

3. If Fatah refuses, he has no alternative but to resign.

GM asked if this was serious. SE replied yes, noting the problem of the Americans thinking he is the black sheep. GM said this was not far from truth – that SE was the wise guy, but the one who knows his file most. He said he asked if SE was serious because he knew he did not play games. SE replied this was the message from the president – not SE's opinion. He said he personally did not agree with it, noting that AM is not doing the US a favour by staying in his position – he is doing it for the benefit of his people. Without AM, neither SF or SE would last. Without him only Hamas remains.

GM: So what can we do?

SE: It's your problem. You sat with the president many times. You know he is not a bargainer.

GM: OK. Let's go upstairs.

2. Meeting Summary
Sec. Hillary Clinton, Sen. George Mitchell, Dr. Saeb Erekat
US State Department
October 20 2009

[GM spoke to HC for 10 minutes before they came in together.]

HC: What is this? What's GM telling me?

[SE repeated the three points noted above, noting that President Abbas is not bargaining]\

HC said she would go to the White House to see the president. She said she knew AM and that he is not bluffing. She said that President Obama and she would call him – wont involve the Arabs. With this she said BN will be the heaviest person. The Arabs, his brothers, will rejoice – they don't want him, they don't want a Palestinian state, or democracy. She asked why Palestinians are always in a chapter of a Greek tragedy? She said you will harm yourselves and asked what led AM to think this way.

SE explained:

- Israel – after 7 months with BN we have nothing.

9

- He continues with settlements and fait accompli; provocations at Al Aqsa, home demolitions etc.

- Had BN wanted AM to be a partner he would have invested in him; he would have offered a moratorium for a few months to solve the swaps.

- With Goldstone, Lieberman announced the story of tapes and attacked AM

- BN's office leaked the story on Wataniya – AM got screwed by BN

- Egypt, Jordan, Saudi Arabia denied any knowledge of Goldstone – they threw the towel in AM's face, blaming him alone. Abul-Gheit said "you're finished". Nasser Joudeh blamed him in the Parliament. The Saudis sent a message through Abul Gheit. Syria cancelled the meeting, Meshal gave the speech. Qatar's prince, your ally, is conducting a personal campaign against AM.

- The Egyptian paper – the way it was handled by Mubarak. They wanted both AM and Hamas to reject so they are off the hook, and we get punished.

- You go from no full settlement freeze to non-freeze with 3000 units. You know Ben Simon resigned over this. 9 Jewish organizations in the US are against Netanyahu. Why not get rid of Lieberman and bring in Livni. You are giving him the crown over the Middle East. Who will believe you in the region. It's too bad it's over for you so soon in the Middle East. AM wants your help – Clinton Parameters…

HC said she will go to the White House the next day. She and President Obama will talk to AM. The US is determined to get a Palestinian state. She asked 2 questions:

If no settlement freeze, no negotiations?

SE: Yes. Cut the story short. It is a non-starter. AM won't crown BN.

HC asked about prisoner release, incursions into areas A and B, redesignation of area C.

SE: These are security issues - let the security officials meet. GM is asking me to meet Molcho. Let the security people handle it – including the release of prisoners.

HC: If we were to move and develop our own map.

SE: 67 with swaps?

HC: Yes.

SE: The leadership would welcome this. This is the approach we encouraged in NY. Your approach in Northern Ireland – no trilateral there till 8 months. So if you develop the end

10

game, with 67 baseline map that would be welcome. Don't trust BN. He wants a state with provisional borders.

HC: Will speak to President Obama and we will call AM. AM not running in the election is not an option – there is no alternative to him.

Parties agreed to a meeting between GM and SE the following morning at 9am.

11

Meeting Minutes
Dr Saeb Erekat – Sen George Mitchell
October 21 2009

Attendance:

Palestinian: Dr Saeb Erekat (SE)
                          Rami Dajani (RD)
                          Khaled El-Gindy (KE)

US: Sen. George Mitchell (GM)
                          Amb. David Hale (DH)
                          Jonathan Schwartz (JS)
                          Mara Rudman (MR)

GM: Good meeting with HC yesterday. Can I discuss what we talked about in private?

SE: Go ahead.

GM: I will talk again to HC, to firm it up, and then we will go to the White House.

SE: I spoke to him. I told him the message was delivered. I did not tell him the reaction, other than surprise and shock. I said you will hear from the US. He said not to put it to them like that.

GM: I appreciate the spirit he authorized you to tell us, but he must have anticipated our reaction. This morning, however, we want to have a specific discussion on the ToRs and side letters. We are making efforts to find language that is satisfactory to you. Then we will make an effort to get Israeli agreement. I had said we would have preferred if you came before the Israelis but your schedule did not permit. So our discussion with them earlier was general and did not get into the precise language as we intend to do with you today. From our prior discussion the key issue for you is the territory issue. We've listened to the concerns of both sides, and we appreciate your concerns – that negotiations are not about dividing the West Bank. We understand your preference for the 67 and swaps language. Because you told us you accept there will be adjustments – with the so called blocs – that will be offset by benefits to you. We need as straightforward a formulation of that concept as possible:

An independent and viable state encompassing all of the territory that was occupied in 1967 or its equivalent in value.

SE: What is this? What is it part of?

GM: ToR or side letters. This is better than swaps for you, and I will ask JS to comment on the language.

1

JS: Your ToR language didn't say equal.

SE: We said agreed.

JS: We did not want a mathematical formula, so we used "equivalent". I know you have a specific area …

SE: 6258 squared kilometers.

JS: But you had a more complicated position …

GM: Note we do not have Israeli approval of this.

SE: So do you plan to give me something in writing.

GM: I will read it all out loud and RD can write it down. I recall our discussion on territory and your concern on the previous language, that it would preclude swaps from their territory. I raised it with them – that it meant they would get the blocs and you would get nothing – and they said that was not the intent and it did not occur to them. Now we need to think of the context in which this language can occur. Only way is to set the US belief – I emphasize this is not a done deal –

[Missing text and minutes because GM insisted at a later point in the meeting to get back all language dictated on the ToR text from RD and KE. It was later read to RD on the phone by GM's staff, as follows:

The issue of territory has figured prominently in our discussions.

The US believes that through good faith negotiations the parties can mutually agree on an outcome that achieves both the Palestinian goal of an independent and viable state encompassing all the territory occupied in 1967 or its equivalent in value, and the Israeli goal of secure and recognized borders that reflect subsequent developments and meets Israeli security requirements.]

GM: Obviously "subsequent developments" refers to the settlement blocs. We would also stress "mutually agreed." This is as direct and straightforward as we can get. Just so you're clear.

JS: There will still be language on goals other than this.

SE: So no Road Map?

GM: We have the paper you submitted on ToRs.

SE: We only read it, we didn't submit anything.

2

GM: Instead of "treaty" we have "outcome"; "within 24 months" will be somewhere in the document; "with an active American role" is in; all core issues, we prefer the language used by President Obama in his speech – he named four issues: Jerusalem, borders, security and refugees. Water and prisoners is not essential. If you want to add settlements, that's fine.

SE: Release of prisoners is essential – it is essential to 11,000 families.

GM: You liked Obama's speech …

SE: We liked parts.
GM: We also have "other issues of common interest" which should cover the rest of the issues; "based on the agreed ToR … including the Road Map" this will be referenced in another part of the document …

SE: Is this one paper, or will there be many papers?

GM: One.

JS: We need to keep options open, and don't want to rule out the possibility of separate side letters.

GM: So on Jerusalem we will make an independent statement – they will not agree to it in the ToR.

SE: You tell me what will be in the joint ToR.

[GM reads draft text, having requested that no notes are taken. Text is based on what DH read out on Oct 2 with notable additions and subtractions].

GM: The steps may be in the document or a different document. Side letters are possible. And a US statement on its position on Israeli policy on settlements.

SE: When can you give me something – a document or a package, so I can take it to AM, so we can study it in good faith? Now I can give AM the minutes, but it's better if you can submit the whole thing to AM.

GM: Much of what I read is not controversial…

SE: I disagree for example on the PA steps and not going to international bodies.

GM: This is only during negotiations.

SE: They won't refrain from doing the illegal things that they do. If they refrain OK but they wont. This is my only weapon. We have actions by settlers, attacks, provocations, Al Aqsa, home demolitions, families thrown out of their homes. Either we retaliate in a civilized

3

manner or through violence. Which one should we choose? On going to the UN we always coordinate with you. It's our only weapon. Don't take it away from us.

GM: But if you have good faith negotiations …

SE: They have a different interpretation of good faith, if you ever dealt with the Israelis.

GM: I would agree with Israel if you were negotiating and bringing actions against them it would be in bad faith.

SE: If they don't take illegal measures, I would have no complaint. You think I complain for nothing! You know even rabbits have defence mechanisms. Let say they throw more families out of their homes. They defied you on this, and the UN.

GM: You can go for a public statement. The ICC is a different thing.

SE: I might go to the General Assembly.

GM: You would go to the GA if two families are thrown out?

SE: Maybe if it's 50 families.

GM: Let's not get diverted. You said 67 is a key issue… [GM has to leave to see HC] Why don't you discuss?

SE: We will talk. It's OK for DH to stay. We will talk with them. [To DH] Are you clear on the settlement freeze? Do you understand the message?

DH: It's clear: regardless of the ToR language?

SE: Yes. Just get me 4 or 5 months of a full moratorium so we can talk. BN needs to budge.

JS: Does your position include 'proximity' talks?

SE: We cannot have resumption of negotiations with this government. We will punish Netanyahu. He can't survive without a process with us. We won't give him leverage of taking us for a ride and continuing settlements while we negotiate. Am I clear, David? This is the decision of the leadership – the PLO executive committee and the Fatah central committee. They won't allow it. Period. Finito.

DH: Your staying in this position means no direct negotiations.

SE: No direct negotiations if there is no freeze and an exclusion of Jerusalem.

DH: So what do you propose?

4

SE: I know what I'm talking about and I see where things are heading. I am bothered by my message to Sec. Clinton yesterday. Netanyahu will celebrate with a 100 champagne bottles, and the Arabs will celebrate. Number one, On the 25th – next Sunday or the 26th AM will make the request. That's it. He won't bargain. I can see the collapse unless something happens, unless someone convinces him. Number two, you have the decision of the PLO executive committee and the Fatah central committee. Then you have what AM and Mubarak discussed: on the dialogue; next time they have a paper it should be reviewed by the US legal experts; and that Egypt cannot support negotiations that exclude Jerusalem from the freeze. This was echoed by Nasser Joudeh, after he presented his credentials to you in NY. Then he went to Amman and the Moslem Brotherhood. [SE reiterates the actions of Saudi Arabia, Qatar, Syria]. So no Palestinian decision-making body will change this position on the freeze. Not after Goldstone.

DH: You're establishing a standard, as we said yesterday, that you yourself did not follow.

SE: I know. You don't have to tell me. We had Baker who said the US will stand shoulder to shoulder with us, that we shouldn't miss the bus. Then we had Clinton – Camp David did not fail – it was the petty politics – it made Clinton look like a chapter in a Greek tragedy. Then with the Bush administration we had promises to be the judge of phase I of the Road Map. We got Frasier and Selva who did nothing. They lied to us. I know we can't say it but this has been the behaviour of previous administrations. You expect to fool us like the others?

DH: So if no direct negotiations, then what?

SE: We are on the record. I am personally on the record that GM should use the approach he took in Northern Ireland. It was brilliant. He did not bring the parties together until asking all the right questions. So he should ask: 67? Swaps? what will be percentage? You have the different offers. Can your experts define a number? The same applies to Jerusalem. Even Lieberman and Yishai don't want to keep the 300,000 Palestinians of Jerusalem. Even the Old City can be worked out [discusses breakdown of sovereignty over Old City] except for the Haram and what they call Temple Mount. There you need the creativity of people like me …

[GM rejoins the meeting]

SE: I want to point out I am answering in my personal capacity on these questions. 19 years after the start of the process, it is time for decisions. Negotiations have been exhausted. We have thousands of pages of minutes on each issue. The Palestinians know they will be a country with limitations. They won't be like Egypt or Jordan. They won't have an army, air force or navy, and will have a third party to monitor … Palestinian will need to know that 5 million refugees will not go back. The number will be agreed as one of the options. Also the number returning to their own state will depend on annual absorption capacity. There will be an international mechanism for resettling in other countries or in host states, and international mechanism for compensation. All these issues I've negotiated. They need decisions. The

5

same applies to the percentage. A decision on what percentage. We offered 2%. They said no. So what's the percentage. You can go back to the document we gave president Obama in May.

GM: You're saying no direct negotiations at all?

SE: Once you've established parameters of the end game, with a timeframe with incremental steps, every single thing will have to be negotiated for implementation. So either you put me in a position to eat the apple from the start – and BN tells me we have a new era and takes me on a ride – or the other way I just described – I already ate the apple. Once you have one or two pages, once you accomplish this, you will be in a position of peacemaking, not a peace process. This will be your hallmark. It has been 19 years and I've been in all the meetings.

GM: Are you suggesting, then, no direct meetings until the borders are determined?

SE: No. I was answering DH's question when you came in.

MR: But how do you get discussions started?

GM: How would the process begin?

SE: It's been happening. Netanyahu tested you – what can be done. He's getting the message. You should tell him you're not going to have the cake and it too, if you want Lieberman and the settlements. And you're not going to get me to sit with him under these circumstances. We know Bibi. He's nervous. That's why he is making a campaign now 'asking' AM to be a leader.

GM: So no talks with him while settlement activity continues.

SE: Yes. You asked me yesterday and I said that.

GM: So why are we having a discussion over the language?

SE: That's a good question.

GM: So even if we give you the your ToR language, there will be no negotiations without the freeze?

SE: Yes.

GM: Then please rip out and the text I read out. [RD and KE hand GM papers] So you want us to give you the outcome. You're saying there won't even be negotiations. That's your position.

SE: As long as BN continues as I said. They can send YD and AG to talk to us.

6

GM: So we reconsider the whole approach – why talk to both sides?

SE: It's important. To get them to make decisions.

GM: But they need to make decisions with you, not us. And you're not taking the same position as before. You negotiated without a freeze all the time.

SE: I told DH while you were out: don't fool us. All the promises over the years – not delivered. The last time it was Bush, with Frasier and Selva. They did not deliver Before that Clinton and before that Baker.

GM: It was never promised. They said they would make an effort.

SE: They promised us last time they will be the judge.

JS: Yes: judge.

GM: What will you gain by not having negotiations. You think the US will just give you ..

SE: It's a moment of truth in the Middle East. Ahmadinejad is in Gaza and Lebanon. Pakistan is going failed. And you have Sudan and Somalia. The Arab states are doing nothing. You know AM had to convince a businessman to pay for Moussawi to have a radio station.

GM: AM does not represent all Arabs. He represents Palestinians.

SE: But they will ride on the Palestinians, and use them.

GM: Even if I were to accept that, he has to do what's best for Palestinians.

SE: Yes. They turned us down. We need to have weight with our own people, our constituency. Netanyahu has to implement what you (not us) wrote in the Road Map. And remember he needs us.

GM: In all candour, your assessment of the political situation in Israel is totally wrong.

SE: I know the Israelis. If someone sneezes in Tel Aviv, I get the flu in Jericho. We know what it take, after 19 years. They cannot decide if they want two states. They want to keep settling in the areas of my state.

GM: But they will settle more if you continue this way.

SE: Then we announce the one state and the struggle for equality in the state of Israel. If our state will not be viable and will have the wall we will fight against apartheid. You either have a decision for peace or a decision for settlements. You cannot have both. Maybe as

7

people keep saying that we never miss an opportunity to miss an opportunity, but we were never given an opportunity, not my grandparents or my parents, like I am not being given an opportunity.

GM: You've expressed your frustration over the last 19 years. But I tell you there has never been a president on this issue like this one. You are denying him the opportunity to create the state that you want. By saying one state you are telling him to get out, even though you negotiated with every Israeli government before under different administrations.

SE: We're beat. We're like a horse without rations who can't walk.

GM: So then summon all your energy.

SE: To focus on …

GM: Apartheid?

SE: I am a founder of the peace camp. Do you think it's easy for me to tell my own daughters I made this mistake.

GM: So give Obama the chance to help.

SE: How can I convince anyone if he could not even deliver a temporary settlement freeze? It's not up to me to decide your credibility in the Middle East. He has lost it throughout the region. When he got the Nobel peace prize I was asked about it in the media and publicly congratulated him. I was attacked for it in the Arab media – just for congratulating, like I would congratulate anyone who wins a prize.. Believe me there is no president in the Middle East who wants to help Obama as much as AM…

GM: I have a 6 inch folder on my desk containing all your statements on the settlement freeze, and despite that you negotiated. Now with the first president who wants to make an effort – he's being penalized by you.

SE: Not me. He has Netanyahu. He came to Cairo and said full freeze. We will not convert to Judaism, so if Netanyahu charade of two state is followed, it's going to be one state.

GM: So another 60 years like the previous …

SE: It will be with what you are proposing.

GM: Does the language we read to you not mean anything?

SE: Distinguish between me and the message and instructions I am carrying. Maybe you won't have to worry about this because you may not have this president by the end of the month. You may have to deal with Aziz Dweik.

8

GM: We are trying very hard, desperately, to satisfy on 67 language. You're saying not enough ...

SE: Settlement freeze is Israel's obligation. The ToRs are for all parties.

GM: So how do you justify that you had all previous negotiations without the freeze?

SE: AM will tell you it was a mistake. Now it's a moment of truth. It's about our future. Watch what's happening around us. We don't want to be finished. AM cannot go back to negotiations with settlements and business as usual.

GM: Then there will never be negotiations. You are the party of negotiations and Hamas is the party of armed resistance.

SE: The way it's going with you and your Arab allies, Iran is winning. No wonder with Qatar ... and with Petraeus there in Central Command. What is the strategy? Where do we fit? What about Turkey? Saudi? Why does it take the US to get them to pay us? What's going on? Did you ever sit with us and discuss strategy – like you do with Israel and with Qatar?

GM: There are a lot of unpleasant facts in the Middle East but they did not begin last month.

SE: I know. I told you before. You are what's in it for us. We have nobody but Mitchell and Obama. So my personal conclusion is to shoot for the end game. This is your ladder. Salam Fayyad spoke to me last night for 27 minutes. He never did that before. He wanted to make sure I was honest with you on settlements and Jerusalem. This decent man, he knows the heat and he knows the risks, You should sit with SF next time and tell him what you tell me. Tell him SE said no, and ask him why.

GM: I will. So what's the way forward?

SE: The decision-making approach. On borders, once you define the borders and percentage of swaps then I can negotiate the rest. You are going to have to talk between us. You have to go the extra mile. I say this in my personal capacity – even though not mandated – so I am not saying any of this.

GM: I am willing to go ten extra miles. If we start with separate proximity talks, can they be accompanied by private discussions?

SE: At this stage AM cannot touch them. After Lieberman came up with the tapes smear... We have channels: YD and AG.

GM: That's AM. But how about you and Molcho?

SE: Now it is difficult, but in the days to come I may be able to find a way.

9

GM: Days, what does that mean?

SE: Not months, not weeks. We need you to succeed. We want to help you.

GM: Our objective is a comprehensive peace. A Palestinian state. Peace between Israelis and Palestinians. We don't have ulterior motives.

SE: Regarding Molcho – is he willing to sit? Not permanent status negotiations – just to sit.

GM: Yes. But what approach do we take? What do I tell President Obama? Talk separately – what would that lead to?

SE: Borders. Percentage …

GM: I can't get an agreement on that from them. You need to talk …

SE: About what?

GM: Talk about the issues and maps …

SE: Do they have a map? Can you get a map from them? I showed you our maps.

GM: I will ask – but they will want to couple that discussion with security discussion.

SE: I said security talks will always continue and you have our word on that.

GM: I have to go. I will tell Jones that there will be no negotiations without a complete freeze that includes Jerusalem.

SE: Yes, and I will tell him the other thing.

GM: I will tell him you are suggesting an alternative – separate meetings.

SE: My personal opinion – not an official position. That is what I would do if I were in your shoes.

GM: The best way is to have direct meetings. I've been through proximity talks and they take 10 times as long.

SE: Did ask them about the end game? Ask them. And ask them: do you have a map?

GM: I will ask. They will also want to discuss security.

10

SE: Let them talk to the security commanders. General Hazem Atallah is mandated to talk also about permanent status. They can talk on all security issues.

[GM leaves the meeting]

DH: Let's continue the discussion on proximity talks.

SE: People in the Middle East are not taking Barack Obama seriously. They feared Bush, despite everything. This is important. BO has lost it with the decision-makers, although not the street. Look at what's happening in the Arab world. Did you see the cartoon in the Jordanian papers – you know Jordan, David – so tell me what's going on? In Al-Dustoor! Why is Joudeh saying this?

DH: They have political needs – the king's position within the country. They anticipated the criticism … I'm not justifying what they did. Let's get back to the discussion. So two tracks …

SE: First, on redeployment, incursions: don't politicize. Leave it with security commanders. They know how to deal with it. Life goes on. I want to reiterate on that that we are committed to working with USSC and EU COPPS, to rule of law, one authority, one gun. We give you our word on this.

Second, the channel of communication with the Israelis will continue through YD and AG. They can convey what the Israeli government is doing. Our trust with the government is zero. AG spoke to Lieberman – told them about the claim that AM was colluding with them in the Gaza war. He went to AM before the attack and asked him. AM replied that he will not go to Gaza on an Israeli tank. AG testified about that. He was honest. So we can maintain the channel.

Third, if the PM people want to deal with the day to day issues, we may find a way. That's why I asked you to speak to Molcho. I'm not excluding the possibility but have to speak to my boss.

Fourth, your role: The Arab scene with your allies is bad. You need to revisit Egypt. They should not submit a paper without you [to JS] seeing it. Can we get guarantees from you? Because otherwise we will be punished. The same with Nasser Joudeh. He is your friend in NY – Why did he go to the Parliament? Is he copying Abul-Gheit? Tomorrow when I need to make decisions on refugees – it's the survival of your nations…

DH: Did you speak to him?

SE: No. My counterpart from the Royal Court is Naser Jozi. He is honest and said the right thing – that mistakes were made. There was no statement from the Royal Court, but he almost apologized and said the King was with him.

DH: So you're saying we need to shore up our position with the Arabs.

11

SE: And the Saudis… to say they had no knowledge! Throwing us in the fire. And Qatar, their emir personally calling intellectuals telling them to attack AM. I saw him in NY and he told he had an excellent meeting with HC and everything is OK. And the Syrians – Meshal's speech under Asad's picture. Distasteful. The Israelis: we're also in touch with Israelis and Jewish groups – not J street or just the Labour party. We don't see Netanyahu as the end of the world – the Lieberman – Netanyahu cabinet. If we go for negotiations with them we will kill the others. We're not going to do that. He has not taken a single step … and his PR abilities: he can blue to red and red to yellow. It's fantastic. He is the one who attacked us – we did not hit him below the belt - yet. He did that to us. Statement by Netanyahu that AM is not a partner – OK if he wants to destroy the 2 state solution. Ask your people at the embassy and the consulate what it means if Bibi has no partner…

DH: The senator covered this ground … you are abandoning a long-held Palestinian position.

SE: I'm not. Bibi is canceling phase I and phase III. Just a state with provisional borders. Why deal with our obligations, he is saying, or make the stupid concessions of Olmert and Livni sell outs. So he will not get this. I am planning to appear on Israeli TV, the main channels, but delaying it.

DH: But you're giving him what he wants. First thing he will say is "no partner". He's set you up. You're in a trap.

SE: No, I will tell them [Israeli public]

DH: They won't listen to you.

SE: If AM abdicates – you get Dweik. Netanyahu is great. He defeated Barack Obama and brought you Ahmedinejad and Hamas.

DH: Why are you playing along with this?

SE: I'm not. They're the ones saying "no partner". They wouldn't even meet with me. You know what this will do in Israel, if I reveal my meetings to the Israeli public. What we've said – on security and zero tolerance for terror – but your PM's choice is Ahmedinejad. He twisted Obama's arm and has ended up with Aziz Dweik as his partner.

DH: But the context they will use is that you rejected the US effort.

DE: No. There's an easy answer to that. We didn't say matrix of responsibilities. We argued to shoot for the end game. Who cares about settlement freeze if you have an end game? You chose the matrix, and the freeze, and the words of Cairo. Then Bibi didn't comply. Now I'm the one who's cost free. My word is nothing compared to his in the congress. But I can explain to the Israelis – I can get more support in the Israeli Knesset than in the Jordanian Parliament!

12

DH: You work that out.

SE: I am going on the Kirschenbaum show on Monday.

JS: While you're pursuing the IDF at the ICC …

SE: It's not going to happen. Ocampo is using it against Bashir and Darfur. In any case it will take years. Did you see the piece by Yossi Sarid congratulating Netanyahu for killing AM?

JS: Israel is really concerned about the prosecution of its officers.

SE: Look at the Israeli reaction after the postponement of Goldstone. There was more sympathy for the PA's action because they saw what happened. The Israeli public is not Netanyahu.

DH: The senator had a question. It seems you don't have an answer.

SE: I do. You go to each side. You have a map. Close the deal on borders with swaps.

JS: Would this be a known or private process?

SE: Dead private. If it becomes public it will be killed.

JS: If it succeeds …

SE: For borders it is 67 with a percentage for swaps. 24 months while the parties negotiate.

JS: So it's the border itself that is decided, not just the percentage.

SE: The percentage. Then the parties negotiate the exact border.

JS: So it's like the Clinton Parameters but with a specific percentage, not a range.

JS: What if Israel says territorial link.

SE: 0.07%. It is part of the swap if we get sovereignty. Otherwise no.

JS: So your suggestion on private talks would have to solve this.

SE: Yes.

JS: So swaps, percentage does not preclude different numbers …

13

RD: No. Equal on each side.

SE: 1 to 1.

JS: And value?

RD: Value can be negotiated in the bilateral.

KE: It is not an exact determination of value, so it can be negotiated.

JS: So the transfer is part of implementation. With timelines – many "provisional borders" …

SE: Until completion of withdrawal according to the timeline, incremental steps – until all that is completed we do not declare a state. Until then it is only a transfer of jurisdiction. No state until we reach 67. This way I accommodate Israeli security and settlement concerns. And I get functional jurisdiction in these areas pending full withdrawal.

JS: How do you see the steps?

SE: Phased withdrawal by area. For example, in three months withdrawal for a given city or area etc. Same as in Sinai.

JS: What if the Israeli position is the percentage depends on security positions?

SE: The security commanders can discuss security. We also have Jones' paper on the day after.

JS: Security commanders can discuss PS?

SE: Yes. Hazem Atallah is there, and he is authorized by the president.

JS: Discuss Jerusalem with the borders or separate?

SE: It's solved. You have the Clinton Parameters formula. For the Old City sovereignty for Palestine, except the Jewish quarter and part of the Armenian quarter … the Haram can be left to be discussed – there are creative ways, having a body or a committee, having undertakings for example not to dig. The only thing I cannot do is convert to Zionism.

JS: To confirm to Sen. Mitchell, your private idea …

SE: This conversation is in my private capacity.

JS: We've heard the idea from others. So you're not the first to raise it.

SE: Others are not the chief negotiator of the PLO.

14

JS: I meant this gives you cover – that it's not you who raised it. So you would separate Jerusalem from the border?

SE: No. But we use Clinton Parameters – except for the Haram [separate from border]

DH: So you're not talking about the border only. You're talking about Jerusalem, security …

SE: Yes. Once we define these, we can move to bilaterals.

DH: So this is a way of moving from proximity talks to bilaterals …

SE: I repeat my message: no bilateral negotiations without a settlement freeze.

DH: You succeeded in making the point.

JS: Do you have a timeline?

SE: I can give you 36 months for negotiation and implementation.

JS: I mean how does this fit in with other events – reconciliation, elections …

[Repeat discussion on the Egyptian role in reconciliation and Egyptian paper]

SE: In two months, we'll have another Egyptian effort. They don't want to appear like they failed where Qatar succeeded in Lebanon. This time you should tell Egypt about your congress and laws and tell them to make sure they don't cause sanctions to be imposed on these poor people.

DH: We told them. Senator Mitchell told them.

SE: We are transparent with you and tell you everything. Sometimes this is not appreciated in this town.

DH: We value that.

SE: So if you have anything to share with us we'd appreciate that.

END

15

Meeting Minutes
Gen. James Jones – Dr. Saeb Erekat
White House, October 21, 2009

SE: Thanks for meeting us today. I am here to deliver a message from the president. He will issue the decree for presidential and legislative elections next week. On the 26th or 27th he will ask the Fatah Central Committee to choose a candidate. If they refuse, he will have to submit his resignation. I want to make it clear, he is not bargaining. He just wants to make sure you're not surprised. He values your relationship. He trusts you. You, Barack Obama is what's in it for us. The last few weeks have been troubling. He haven't sat with you to strategize. And we know how much you need all these states.

What's been happening is that Israel, since Netanyahu, they don't want to touch us. I had arranged to meet with Uzi Arad, and two hours before we were supposed to meet he cancelled. He cancelled 3 times – they are sorting things out, "need time". I asked David Hale to arrange a meeting with Molcho. They haven't taken a single step. I wanted to cut the story short: what are you willing to do? We meet with Israelis regularly – on security, irrespective of politics we will continue to uphold the rule of law, one authority one gun. No games like 2000. This is a commitment I delivered to Etan Dangot, Amos Gilad and to Uzi Arad by phone.

Since April we've had nothing from them. Then came Goldstone and all hell broke loose. You know the first public response to the Goldstone thing came from Lieberman, who said Abu Mazen agreed to postpone the vote because the Israelis threatened to release the "tapes" showing him coordinating the attack on Gaza with Israel. Then there was the report that he did it for Wataniya, which they said is owned by his two sons.

I told Etan Dangot and Amos Gilad: we are 19 years into this peace process, and we don't know anymore where we are going. This is a defining moment. We started by talking about how we're going to share [the land of historic Palestine], and are ending up talking about how we're going to share the West Bank with you. If he [Netanyahu] wants to keep Lieberman and settlement construction, then we will say to him, fine. But all you are doing is giving the region to Ahmedinejad, and to Aziz Dweik (to Hamas), and to Hezbollah. You will have Ahmedinejad in Gaza, in Yemen … Pakistan failed, Somalia … the Palestinian question is everywhere. Maybe Israel wants to repeat the chapter with Arafat. My message to them is: we will not allow Abu Mazen to go the way of Arafat, to be accused of being a "non-partner". This will not happen. Nations can choose between the comfortable position and the right position. If he is going to choose Lieberman and Yishai, and another 3000 units in the West Bank and settlement construction in East Jerusalem, we are not going to touch him, and crown him "King of Israel". Maybe that makes George Mitchell angry, or makes you angry. But, this is the message. By the way, Netanyahu cannot survive without us. Most Israelis want peace and a two state solution; it's their survival. So if he wants a smear campaign, I will respond.

I am planning to go on Israeli Channel 10 to say one thing: congratulations Mr. Netanyahu. You defeated President Obama. You defeated Abu Mazen. Now you have Aziz Dweik as your partner. And I will end with a nice little bit about the one person who knows this better than anyone is Sara Netanyahu, who took Molkho as a lawyer to make him sign a paper that he will not do so and so. That's the kind of trust people have in this man. We did not play in their court, but they played in ours. I know am cost-free. If it's my word against theirs in your Congress and your Senate, I know I do not stand a chance. But now it is a defining moment.

Number 2 is Egypt. It has been our ally, our backbone. We always consulted them. And then their Foreign Minister Abul-Gheith comes to us and says—verbatim—'You're finished!' Then he attends a press conference in Amman to say he did not know about it in advance. Then, they say to us, 'Come to Cairo on Oct. 25 so you can sign this document." When we ask if we can see the document or know what's in it, they say, 'No. Come on the 25th and we will send it to you on the 10th.' I was here in Washington at the time, and I told Mitchell and the Secretary, you have to ask the Egyptians to see what they have. Then when they said 'take it or leave it', we said OK but whoever does not sign you have to say it publicly. They call us to denounce Hamas and then call Hamas to denounce us, so they can get off the hook. We said let them all sweat: We will sign, and we sent Azzam Ahmed to Cairo. When Hamas didn't show up, we said it's off the table. (This is the worst document -- I would not sign in a million years, but we had no choice: this is the behaviour of nations in 2009.)

Number 3, Jordan, we have shared and consulted on everything. Then the Jordanian Foreign Minister says the Hashemite Kingdom of Jordan 'will not tolerate negotiations that do not include moratorium on Jerusalem' –and that Abu Mazen is accountable. And he says he had no knowledge of postponement. Maybe there are parallel governments in Jordan and Egypt.

Then there's the Saudis—and thank you for helping us to get the $200 million. We could not have done that without you. They accused us of being "smugglers".

DR: That's true [re the $200M].

SE: The Saudis are too busy equating us with Hamas…

Five, Qatar. When you have the Emir of Qatar personally calling Arab and Palestinian intellectuals to talk about us… We know you have Central Command and Petreaus, and your interests …And Turkey… So where do we fit in all of this – in the bigger picture – AlQaeda and Ahmedinejad … Where are we? … Ten days ago, we had to convince a Palestinian businessman to pay $50 million for Mussawi to have a radio station [???]. In the past we went into negotiations and we trusted people and they failed us. We want to help you. But, why have negotiations anymore? On security, Gen. Jones, you have the paper we did. On borders, there are maps: we said 2% and they said 6%. We're not going to reinvent the wheel or eat the apple from the start.

If people are going to say, 'If you don't go along with this then you'll get more settlements etc.,' then we'll have to go back to our people and say, 'We were wrong about the two states,' and go for a one state! One state, from the river to the sea, and call it 'Israel'. I don't want to weigh two kilos in Jericho and 100 in Washington.

This is a defining moment. So please don't put me in a position where I say no to negotiations. We just don't want to surprise you with anything. I did not create the language that says "freeze all settlement activity (including natural growth)". I did not go to Cairo University and say "real freeze". You did. I presented you with a paper on the end game. Instead you went for the matrix of responsibilities.

If you can't convince Netanyahu to invest in a four-month moratorium on settlements, will anyone believe you're going to have him agree to discuss Jerusalem, or 1967?

The region is slipping out of your hands like sand. Look at the bigger picture – there have been 699 movements in political Islam – that used God rather than worship him. You don't fight them with military force. You fight them with ideas. The only force you have is the Palestinian national movement and it is being killed by Moslem Brotherhood and the Arab states. Netanyahu and the Arabs will be celebrating if this happens, so I know what the message may be self-defeating …

JJ: Thank you… This fits in well with the rest of my day, Afghanistan, Pakistan … A couple weeks ago my phone rang at 3:00 AM—I've gotten lots of phone calls at 3:00 AM and it's never good news. So, as I was waiting for the bad news, I was told the President has been awarded the Nobel Peace Prize. And I responded, 'And what's the problem with that?' [laughter] I said, 'You called me at 3:00 AM to tell me something you could have told me at 7:00AM? Don't ever do that again.' [laughter]

SE: When President Obama won the prize, I was contacted by an Arab reporter. I hadn't heard the news yet. I don't know why they called me… When anyone wins something, what do you do? You say 'congratulations'. That's what you do—even if it's Binyamin Netanyahu. There very next day, I was attacked all over the Arabic press.

JJ: Seriously, now. I know this is a very serious message, and a very troubling message. Speaking for President Obama, he really thinks that Abu Mazen is the leader of the moment and that he can make the difference despite all the challenges and the problems we've seen lately. It's hard to imagine anything other than chaos without him… undermining what we've discussed over 2 years and what have spent their lives trying to achieve. I know that the President—he has been informed of this by the Secretary of State and I'm sure he will be trying to reach Abu Mazen to see whether there's some way to correct this situation and get things back on track. I don't know if he'll be successful, but he will try. He is extremely concerned and will voice it directly. And I know that you and PM Fayyad and others are equally important.

President Obama has signaled by word and deed from Day 1 his commitment and genuine support for a just peace and the goal we all share of a Palestinian state. This is a deeply held belief of our government. He understands that that a two-state solution is the only solution, which has not just regional implications but also global implications. I know I've told you before that if President Obama could solve only one thing in the world, I'm sure he would choose the Middle East—not Afghanistan, not Iraq—but this. The two state solution will be the one thing he invests the most in to bring about justice and equality, not just for Palestinians, but this is in Israel's strategic interests as well. They must recognize that the 2 state solution enhances their long-term ability to co-exist and thrive as a viable state.

Everyone knows what an end state is, but the real problem is finding the path to get us there. I think in the immediate term, you've raised the alarm. We need to get one of the key leaders of the Middle East to walk back from his decision. I don't know if that's possible… but our commitment is unshaken - if it's a matter of redoubling our efforts, we will redouble them. If there's something we haven't done that we need to do, we want to hear that…. We've said some tough things to the Israelis—Dennis was part of many of those discussions… But I can assure you the President is absolutely committed not just to having negotiations, but to seeing a state within two years.

Dennis, do you have anything you want to add to that?

DR: Yes, actually. And I will speak from the heart because we've been through a lot together. One thing we've always been is honest with each other.

SE: We've have fought and hated each other – but we respect each other and tell the truth.

DR: We always told the truth. I would just say the following: you said Obama is what's in it for you...

SE: I shouldn't say this, but my view is it would be a mistake... I told Abu Mazen he should stay the course. He's not bargaining. You don't need to convince him about Obama, but the problem is how you convince him. President Obama should speak to him.

DR: Because we're what it's in it for you... and keep in mind the President is still only in his first year, and has many different challenges to deal with. You know, without the American president playing the role, it just can't be done. I would appeal to Abu Mazen to see that he really needs to give Obama a chance to work with him... You mentioned, let's just cut through all this [current process]... As your friend, I would say ... creative ways to solve problems. I appeal to him to give Barack Obama a chance to work with him in a way to benefit Palestinians.

One thing I am convinced of, based on the discussions we've had, we actually think the two sides are much closer together on substance than people think—there's much more potential there than meets the eye. The process so far has not focused on that. You haven't heard from each other what's important. I'm not saying it'll be easy, but there are possible points of convergence – what you can or cannot do, develop the right corridor, how to create space. You just haven't been given a chance to explore that together. What we're asking is that now is not the time to give up. You said you know this could be self-defeating, like so many other self-defeating choices in the past. You have to give him a chance to do it. Maybe he can't start exactly where you want, but we have a lot of other ideas.

SE: I'm glad to hear you say that. As I told George Mitchell and his staff: you don't need to put on blinders ...

DR: We're looking at a variety of options, but don't want to be on a path that's a dead end. At the end of the day, both of you have to be able to agree. So we need Abu Mazen there.

SE: I appealed to Abu Mazen. Really, I did. But that's it for him: he's not bargaining here. He's really the most decent man. So what he needs to hear is what Gen. Jones said, that this is the most important issue [for Obama].

DR: There's a chance to write a legacy now...

SE: When we speak of options, without Abu Mazen, no one else would last 15 minutes.

JJ: We got the message and we will act on it with urgency. And thank you for what you did a couple weeks ago; it was very courageous.

DR: Just one question. Regarding this whole approach to the Arabs… what's driving it? – we're going to deal with them.

SE: Let me just say, if they know I'm here complaining about them we stand to lose a lot. But with Egypt, you should tell them, next time they need to share things with you. The next time there's a paper your legal adviser has to review it.

DR: I can tell you we did put pressure on the Egyptians. I read the document [on reconciliation]—it's a disaster. We were blunt …

SE: The Saudis are also crucial … With Iran, Hizbullah, Syria – jumping around the region. They are doing nothing. Abu Mazen is doing Saudi Arabia's job. Instead they equate him with Hamas. The region is slipping away like sand through our hands.

JJ: I agree with that.

SE: You have to put together a matrix of interests to see where we stand. There's this pattern of Arab reconciliation - and we pay the price. This pattern must stop. I hope the Egyptians see us now in action. We didn't want to let them off the hook. I said to Omar Suleiman, 'How can we sign a document without seeing it?' And then you say, 'You're finished.'!

JJ: It's insulting. We'll take care of this.

-END-

Meeting Minutes
Dr Saeb Erekat – Amb. David Hale
Friday 15 January 2010
NAD Jericho

Attendance:

Palestinians: Dr Saeb Erekat (SE)
                Rami Dajani

US: David Hale (DH)
                Daniel Rubenstein (DR)
                Rick Waters

DH: Got back yesterday from Brussels. Senator Mitchell will be coming next week …

SE: When will he be here?

DH: He's going to Beirut and Damascus Tuesday and Wednesday, so he will be here at the end of the week – Thursday or Friday.

SE: We have Thursday open to meet AM. On Friday he is seeing the leader of Kadima.

DH: Has anything developed with Molcho?

SE: No.

DH: We have a lot to talk about. We've met with the Jordanians and Egyptians, Omar Suleiman, Nasser Joudeh in DC. In Paris we met Kouchner and [unclear]. In Brussels we met with the new European leadership – lady Ashton. We had a bilateral with Russia-Sultanov. And of course the Quartet meeting.

SE: I've been briefed by all the parties but want to hear from you.

DH: Yes. We wanted to get a sense of what is possible. Our desire is to get into talks right away, but want to do that in a way that honours your positions, and your dignity. We realize that the outcome may not resolve all issues. We now have 67 lines and swaps on the table, which wasn't there before. The Egyptians brought ideas similar to our thinking.

SE: Did they give you a paper?

DH: Yes. The same in substance to what you have.

SE: The Jordanians and Saudis too.

DH: Nasser Joudeh did not give us a paper.

SE: No – but we coordinated the position.

DH: So you're approach is either an un-announced freeze in Jerusalem, or adoption of the principles. Neither of these is feasible. They won't happen. You know about Netanyahu's position on the freeze. And the paper describes the end of the negotiations not the start. But there are ideas, as we discussed with the Egyptians, that we can build on. They've talked with Netanyahu and think he is serious. We should look at what more will Israel do beyond what it has done already. However a freeze in Jerusalem is beyond reach. We are thinking of building a conditional ladder: talks with us present over measures to build confidence. And there is the 'American letter' – Sen. Mitchell calls it a 'set of notes'. The origin is a request from Saudi Arabia to put down on paper what Mitchell said to Saud Al-Faisal. It's nothing you haven't heard before – ToRs, the US position on key issues – position on Jerusalem and settlements in a way that's helpful. Such a letter can help provide cover for AM, but it will only be there if we are convinced we're entering a negotiation process.

In the Quartet meeting in Brussels there was unanimity that we need to get into talks soon. It's not about pressure or coercion …

SE: Did they raise the freeze in East Jerusalem and the end game?

DH: There is unanimity that it's not feasible [the freeze]. We also discussed assistance and the need to support Fayyad, to front load assistance and get the Arabs to contribute. For the creation of the Palestinian state there is the diplomatic front, and also the resource front. There is a strong commitment for both, but frankly if one isn't working it is hard to keep the other on track.
\
SE: Yes they are integrated.

DH: We want to use Sen. Mitchell's time efficiently in his next visit. We'd like to look at it as a deadline. We are fearful that [example of recent events in Nablus] that in a vacuum of diplomatic efforts things can unravel on the ground.

SE: Thanks for the briefing. I got a briefing from Muhammad bin Jasem – he wants me to put down a new road map. I've also been briefed by Egypt, Jordan, France, Marc Otte, Robert Serry – so I'm moving two steps ahead of you.

First, you don't need to convince us of the need for negotiations. We know the devastating impact of a stalemate – vis a vis Hamas, Iran, relation with Israel on the ground. Keep this in mind: our cardinal interest is to resume negotiations. But (and I'm telling you the truth as AM sees it – he is not a tactician) AM has assessed the impact of Netanyahu's conditions. If he goes into negotiations with these conditions, it will destroy him.

DH: Conditions?

2

SE: Netanyahu says East Jerusalem is just a neighbourhood, like Tel Aviv, so it's building as usual, tenders … it will finish AM off. The problem with all US administrations is they underestimated the significance of Jerusalem to the Palestinians – for internal Palestinian politics. This was the failure of Camp David. AM is not planning to run in elections. He is ready to resign – but he will not be thrown out of office. Our credibility on the ground has never been so low. Now it's about survival. There is Hamas and the bigger picture in the region. I told the Israelis from the beginning: let's not waste time, let's not wait. Let's see what you have to offer and see what we can work with. I called Uzi Arad before Passover and arranged a call from AM to Netanyahu – to congratulate him. I got nothing – come Ramadan, the feast, nothing. I called them to meet from the beginning, they kept canceling. This is Netanyahu: Recently six presidential guards in civilian clothes on their way from Bethlehem to Ramallah were stopped by Israeli soldiers and stripped to humiliate them in front of their people. Nablus was to humiliate Fayyad and AM. This is Netanyahu,. I can't compete with him – ask President Clinton! I was there at Wye River. Note what Shimon Peres relayed from him, or what Netanyahu told the Egyptians – he said "when peace comes" it will be … He didn't commit to it. He didn't say I am committed. He wants to begin with whatever he can. Molcho has the talking point: "Jerusalem is a neighbourhood – you know it's excluded". Come on!

You give me goals. You got the Israeli goal right: Jewish state, secure borders, security arrangements, and subsequent developments. You said my goal is a viable and independent state based on the 67 border with agreed swaps. That is not my goal. Swaps are a Palestinian concession in the interest of peace and reaching an agreement. My goal is a sovereign state on the 67 border.

DH: Noted.

SE: So we look at what's doable. The Jordanians will support whatever AM decides. Egypt, I don't know – they want to bring Netanyahu in. The Russians want a meeting in Sochi … The French – I told them stop this, don't try to bypass the US. You are what's in it for us. There is no other way. We have to avoid fragmentation. We asked you to give us your position on the end game, not a treaty- give us your position. Countries have positions. Your position is two state solution, Palestinian state, ending the occupation. So we said 67 borders with agreed swaps. That's your position, so say it! If you put down such a paper we will call an emergency Arab summit and get it accepted. Netanyahu will reject. Either he will change his coalition or there will be elections. Israelis want the two state solution but they don't trust. They want it more than you think, sometimes more than Palestinians. What is in that paper gives them the biggest Yerushalaim in Jewish history, symbolic number of refugees return, demilitarized state… What more can I give?

DH: Can we be more specific …

SE: On process … will meet with Uzi Arad. You know the paper – the paper I gave to Daniel, AM wrote it himself. We translated it. AM knows the Israelis well. He understands Netanyahu. He saw the minutes of his cabinet meeting where he talked about his book "Under the Sun" and called AM an extremist and a terrorist. AM will not allow Netanyahu

3

to do to him what he did to Arafat. AM is the father of the peace camp, Oslo – and 18 years later Israel remains the source of authority. His heart aches when he sees families thrown into the streets of Jerusalem. And Fayyad as well –with the events in Nablus. So these are the choices. [SE prints copy of paper]. Why can't you adopt the paper?

On handling the meeting with the Israelis, AM wanted to choose who. His logic is that if it's Arad, then it's not negotiations. But we can't choose. We can't get into that.

DH: Then they'll do the same with you.

SE: The focus is not on negotiations. It's on the security situation and strategic relations. This is what Sen. Mitchell should assure AM. So first we need a channel so things don't collapse in the West Bank. We will use the channel also to see where we can go. This is the 64 million dollar question. Second, we need to restore confidence within our security people. We said to DR to arrange a meeting with the US and with Diskin, to ensure they will stop humiliating them. Third, on the steps that DR spoke about last time – incursions in area A, prisoner release, roadblocks, redeployments – C to B and A, reconstruction in Gaza (by the way I'm glad it was discussed by the Quartet – I sent a letter requesting this. It should be dealt with by the UN and Blair's office). Regarding the steps, Netanyahu should not expect anything in return. These are his obligations that he has already breached. We've already paid in advance. We've delivered on security.

DR: On the meeting with the security people, President Abbas said he understood the difficulty of setting it up and asked to follow up with ways to deal with it.

SE: AM said that to give you a chance to follow up,. You're our partner. Don't let it all go down. If they're humiliated further they will shoot. They have their dignity. They would rather die than be humiliated like this. This is what happened in the Intifada.

DH: I would still like to get back to the paper. If you still ask us to adopt this paper we might as well talk about something else entirely: This administration will not be in any way directive about the outcome of negotiations. Almost every line of the second section is a topic for negotiation.

SE: So can you get him to refrain from tendering in Jerusalem?

DH: We try. On the elements – the package – I know these are obligations. But is it enough, to maintain dignity, to get you back? Based on this meeting I don't know what I can tell the senator.

SE: Tell him what I said about AM's state of mind, about Netanyahu's conditions. Tell him AM will not negotiate under Netanyahu's conditions: Jerusalem excluded, no resumption from where we left off …

DH: These are your conditions, not the Israelis…

4

SE: Is the Roadmap his ToR? All agreements signed? Where is his position?

DH: Raise this with Molcho.

SE: I will. I've tried to meet him before.

DH: He's ready now.

SE: I want to construct a channel so it doesn't go down in one day. We can't say we're resuming negotiations. We keep the channel secret. Use it to discuss our strategic relations. The priority is not to have collapse on the ground. Let's meet again before Mitchell comes.

DH: OK. We need to make an assessment. I will inform Mitchell of what you said about AM's frame of mind regarding Netanyahu's conditions. There is a sense of urgency. Elements of what you said about a private dialogue may be helpful. Our ToR paper may also be helpful, with your remarks on the goals. The five issues we will continue to work on. You need to discuss them with the Israelis.

SE: The security people can discuss. Why political discussion? These are obligations they have to implement.

DH: Political discussions as well.

SE: They want to make us pay 16 times for the same thing. We already paid in Oslo for Area A and B. Finally I want to ask you about the paper you've been discussing. As we said in Washington we are your partner. Why do we have to hear about it from other parties? Why didn't you share it with us before you discussed it?

DH: We didn't share it with the Israelis either…

SE: Ask the Arabs next time you meet them about the November 12 statement they issued saying no resumption of negotiations before a settlement freeze including East Jerusalem.

END

5

ACKNOWLEDGMENTS

The adage "success has many parents" comes to mind as I write to thank all those who helped make this book possible. I must first acknowledge my very special wife, Wassila Oulmi. For the past nine months she carried our child with patience and steady demeanor while I carried on about diplomatic documents. No words can express the tremendous joy and excitement I feel on beginning our great project together as parents. God willing our little girl will experience the same love and sense of belonging that both our families gave us.

There were many at Al Jazeera who helped turn the Palestine Papers into television that I can't name here. Knowing they have my back is part of the reason I go to work each day, and I hope they trust that I'll always have theirs. Colleagues Laila Al-Arian, Mysa Khalaf, Sarah Nasr, Farhan Mustafa, and Gregg Carlstrom gave the Papers their undivided focus, reviewing my own drafts along the way.

Dr. Bashir Nafi brought penetrating critiques and insights. He had the wisdom and vision to see the forest beyond the trees, earnestly reviewing reams of documents to help me find the essence. Roane Carey, Editor of The Nation Magazine, lent his trusted eyes and editorial depth, as did the Guardian's Seumas Milne, another talented writer I'm proud to call a friend. Special thanks to Karl Sabbagh, Managing Director of Hesperus Press, for his own skillful edits and initiative to make this book happen. Unending gratitude goes to my best friends Marvin Ammori, MJ Rosenberg, and Dr. Tareq Abughazala, who unfailingly dropped what they were doing to sound out my ideas. As always, Donald MacKenzie offered his unyielding friendship and encouragement. While all of the above helped me write, I should mention that any mistakes and conclusions expressed are mine alone.

Thanks also for the support provided by my wonderful colleagues Dr. Salah Eddin Elzein, Asef Hamidi, William Thorne, Will Jordan, Mounir Daymi, Nessrien Rafaat, Mohammed Nanabhay, Jonathon Powell, Richard Santamaria, Iris Sabellano, and Abdulraoof Parambath.

Finally, I wish that others in this world, particularly those in Palestine denied the ability to live free, will take some comfort in knowing that a good number of others, including Americans, are increasingly unafraid to report their stories. In 1913, former Associate U.S. Supreme Court Justice Louis Brandeis opined that "sunlight is said to be the best of disinfectants." I could not more agree. Though he was an ardent Zionist, there is much to be admired by his advocacy for transparency. To that end, I hope that journalists will continue to bring more illumination through disclosures beyond the Palestine Papers.

When the masses are informed, we may find yet the greatest remedy to the common challenges and injustices of our times.